The Rise and Decline
of International Communism

This book is dedicated with love and gratitude to my mother.

The Rise and Decline of International Communism

Geoffrey Stern

Edward Elgar

Published by
Edward Elgar Publishing Limited
Gower House
Croft Road
Aldershot
Hants GU11 3HR
England

Gower Publishing Company
Old Post Road
Brookfield
Vermont 05036
USA

British Library Cataloguing in Publication Data
Stern, Geoffrey
   The rise and decline of international communism.
   1. Communism, history. Political aspects
   I. Title
   320.5'32'09

Library of Congress Cataloging-in-Publication Data
Stern, Geoffrey.
   The rise and decline of international communism / by Geoffrey
Stern.
      p. cm.
   ISBN 1–85278–042–8 — —ISBN 1–85278–045–2 (pbk.) :
   1. Communism— —History.   I. Title.
HX36.S84   1990
324.1'75— —dc20   89–26044
                                                                              CIP

ISBN 1–85278–042–8
ISBN 1–85278–045–2 (paperback)

Printed in Great Britain by
Billing & Sons Ltd, Worcester

Contents

Preface

As this book was completed in August 1989, Poland acquired its first non-Communist government in over 40 years. Since then, events in the Communist world have moved with bewildering rapidity. The ruling Communists in Hungary voted their Party out of existence, transforming it into a Western style Socialist organization. As such, they were hoping to give their revamped political movement some chance of success in a poll projected for early 1990 – Eastern Europe's first free elections for over 40 years. Meanwhile the dismantling of the 'iron curtain' of barbed wire, watchtowers and ploughed minefields between Hungary and Austria had led to the exodus of hundreds of thousands from East Germany, dislodging, in the process, the East German leader, Erich Honecker, and forcing the most momentous political and economic changes in what had been one of the bloc's least reformist administrations. As the bulldozers were puncturing holes in the Berlin Wall, enabling the peoples of the divided city to mix freely for the first time in 28 years, other bastions of Communist orthodoxy tottered. In Bulgaria, for example, Todor Zhivkov, Eastern Europe's longest-surviving leader, chose to retire before the 'wind of change' caught up with him too. In Czechoslovakia hard-line Communism was fatally undermined when the country's allies, including the USSR, repudiated the intervention which had ended the 'Prague Spring' of 1968. And in Romania, a long-suffering populace braved the bullets of Ceauşescu's *Securitate*, bringing down in the last week of 1989 the most feared 'Communist' regime in Europe.

As for the Soviet Union, its regional and communal tensions grew from bad to worse, with Armenia and Azerbaijan in a state of virtual civil war over Nagorno–Karabakh, and the Baltic states proclaiming themselves in favour of independence from the USSR. As the economic situation also worsened, the authorities had to call on the services of leading Western bankers and businessmen to advise on how to make the economy more efficient.

Outside the Soviet sphere, in Yugoslavia, a resurgent Serbia caused renewed ferment in Kosovo, as Albanian rights under the 1974 constitution were eroded, and led Slovenia to make constitutional provision for secession. Further afield, the completion of the Vietnamese troop withdrawal from Cambodia signalled an intensification of the Cambodian (and mainly inter-Communist) civil war.

Though Western alarmists who were speaking only recently of the 'Communist threat' were now forecasting 'Communism's demise', they ignored the fact that in countries such as Spain, the Philippines and Chile, the Communist party was growing in strength and that, contrary to expectations, the Mujaheddin had failed to dislodge the Marxist–Leninist regime in Afghanistan in the wake of the Soviet withdrawal.

None of these developments invalidate the general thrust of the argument in this volume. If anything, they underline the main thesis concerning the decline, though not necessarily the demise of Communism as an international movement. At the same time, however, they call in question many of the familiar 'cold war' assumptions made by East and West over the past four decades, and make it imperative for West as well as East to engage in 'new thinking'.

Acknowledgements

I should like to express my gratitude to Edward Elgar, who commissioned the volume; Prof. Fred Halliday, who persuaded me of the need to complete it in reasonable time; the London School of Economics, which gave me a year's paid leave to work on it; and Prof. David McLellan, Margot Light and Geoff Roberts, who all provided invaluable advice and assistance. I am also grateful to Hilary Parker, Yvette Brown, Rebecca D'Monte, and Elizabeth Ollard for their work on the typescript. For the book's failings, I alone am responsible. Finally, I should like to thank my children, Tiffany and Jonathon, for their understanding and fortitude in allowing me to monopolize the dining-room table for nearly two years.

Introduction

For the second time this century, Russia is in the throes of a 'socialist' revolution with global implications. The first, in 1917, which brought the Bolsheviks to power, held out to the world's urban workers an even more alluring prospect than the French Revolution had offered to the middle class – emancipation from all oppression, control of their own destiny, and a life of peace and abundance. Yet, though Bolshevism's triumph had been almost bloodless, many of its original objectives were to be sacrificed on the altar of political necessity in the bloody encounter between the forces of change and the upholders of the status quo in Russia and elsewhere.

The second, a 'revolution without shots', in the words of its chief architect, Mikhail Gorbachev, is pledged to remedy many of the 'mistakes' of the preceding years and to reinvigorate an economic, political and social system that has manifestly failed to live up to expectations. However, unlike the first revolution, of which the Soviet Union remained for long the only exemplar, the Gorbachev 'revolution' can claim no 'socialist' monopoly. Many rival 'socialist' models exist, and no matter how attractive the Gorbachev prospectus, it has many influential detractors, both within and beyond the Soviet state, whom the Kremlin is unwilling or unable to silence. Nor can Moscow's second 'socialist' revolution necessarily exert in the Communist universe the same gravitational pull as the first since several of its former 'satellites' seem to have spun into orbits of their own, and there is no longer any central guiding hand, visible or invisible, to map out a course or ensure there are no collisions.

For the many detractors of 'Communism', moreover, Gorbachev's 'revolution without shots' may have come too late to save either the Soviet Union or the wider Communist movement from political oblivion. For in their view 'Communism' has been tried and found wanting in almost every particular – as a system of rule, as an instrument of economic modernization and as a vision of the 'good life'. And even those traditionally sympathetic to the 'Communist' cause are having to admit that in 1989 the movement now faces its gravest crisis of credibility in the wake of the carnage in the Chinese capital, the communal violence in the Soviet Union and Yugoslavia, the war between Communists in Cambodia, the persecution of ethnic minorities in Romania and Bulgaria, the collapse of Party morale in Poland and Hungary, the high level drug-trafficking in Cuba, the stream of emigrés from East Germany and the flood of refugees from Vietnam. And, of course, when the 'immune system' that was supposed to protect the 'Communist' body politic from the 'capitalist diseases' of inflation, unemployment, labour unrest, indebtedness, organized crime and the like breaks down, it is difficult to sustain the notion of the superiority of the 'Communist' system over all others.

Yet even if 'Communism' finds itself on the defensive today and the once unified Communist movement is riven by factionalism and fissiparous tendencies, individual membership, which has often been subject to wide fluctuations in the past, remains largely undented. Latest available estimates[1] indicate that though there has been a fall of about a million worldwide in the course of a year, some parties are still gaining in membership; and with 88.6 million members (84.5 million in the Communist countries), international Communism remains a formidable political force. In postulating a three-and-a-half-decade decline in a movement which has continued to gain new members, this volume highlights a paradox which can only be resolved by a proper understanding of the distinction between 'Communism' – a twentieth century political movement – and 'communism' – a socio-political ideal – and of the use of the term 'international' in this context.

Strictly speaking, the title of this volume is a misnomer. For, whatever society Soviet Russia and its imitators may have evolved since 1917, it is certainly not communism as elaborated by the men who had inspired Lenin's seizure of power. For, by communism, Marx and Engels had meant a society of an entirely new type, created by proletarian power in the wake of the overthrow of capitalism in one country after another. In it, the state and its bureaucratic apparatus have 'withered away'; the 'class system', together with the 'exploitation' it engenders, has been abolished; the 'idiocy of rural life' has been eliminated; and the new order of things has become sufficiently agreeable to the masses to enable them to give up the 'opium' of religious belief. It is a state of affairs, moreover, in which the division of labour is no longer necessary, since people can realize their potential for versatility and turn their hands to whatever task the community requires of them. In consequence, they serve the community by giving 'according to their abilities' and are rewarded 'according to their needs' – though exactly how needs are determined and by whom, the founders of modern communism never make entirely clear.

Nonetheless, at no time would Marx or Engels have considered as deserving of the name 'socialist', let alone 'communist' or 'international communist', a bloc of states in which representative institutions are at best rudimentary; in which, as Mikhail Gorbachev constantly reminds us, bureaucracy thrives, privilege and patronage persist, and people continue to put self before society, while traditional myths, superstitions, aspirations, preferences and prejudices endure and exert influence at all levels. To be fair, neither the Soviet Union, nor Albania, nor any other country claims to have established a fully fledged communist order along Marxist lines. At most, they lay title to the achievement of 'socialism', but they present this as a transitional stage on the way to a communist society.

What, then, is the exact import of the term 'Communism', as on this book's title page? Here the term refers to a political movement created to promote the idea that through the seizure of state power by determined and disciplined revolutionaries organized into Communist parties, the Marxist millennium can be rapidly advanced. Its origin, therefore, lies not so much with Marx as with Lenin, who had concluded even before his success in 1917 that if Communists could capture one of the most backward countries in Europe they could succeed in the more advanced, and then, through concerted international action, propel Europe into the desired communist direction. Thus, the Communist Party -- a Leninist invention -- was deemed to hold the key to 'communism', and in popular parlance 'Communism' became a code word for the Communist movement organized world-wide. At the same time, the existence of what were once strong formal and informal ties between Communists of different countries seemed to confirm the suspicions of those regarding 'Communism' as inherently expansionist, and underscored the tendency of sympathizers and critics alike to append the adjective 'International' to 'Communism', in depicting the organization and aims of the movement as a whole.

Nonetheless, the vocabulary of politics is notoriously imprecise, and can be dangerously so when it fails to reflect the dynamics of a changing world. In relation to the subject under discussion, a couple of linguistic anomalies have arisen which can often confound attempts at objectivity. In the first place, people tend too readily to speak of a 'Communist state' wherever Communists rule, even though in strictly Marxist parlance this would be a contradiction in terms since only societies could be communistic, not states. Certainly within such countries the system is generally referred to as 'Socialist' rather than 'Communist', i.e. post-capitalist but pre-communist. At the same time, the expression 'international Communism' is still all too frequently used to convey the impression of a solid, monolithic, and relentlessly expansionistic force, even though what was once a cohesive world movement is now in disarray, while the various Communist parties which used to comprise it have become increasingly infused and permeated with nationalist sentiment. As E. H. Carr foresaw in a study of nationalism written at the end of the Second World War: 'The socialization of the nation has as its natural corollary the nationalization of socialism'.[2]

At the time, Prof. Carr had only the experience of the Soviet Union on which to draw, but the pattern of Communist rule in other countries – China, Vietnam, Albania, Romania, and the GDR, for example – would seem to provide ample evidence for his prescient observation. It is in consideration of what has come to be known as 'national Communism' that in this analysis we can speak of the decline of 'international Communism', even were the number of Communist parties and members to be on the rise. There is surely an analogy here with the history of Christendom, as the churches have proliferated along with the divisions, the doubts, the disillusionment, and, for some, the despair.

Meanwhile, as the sense of Communist solidarity wanes, the communist society which had once been the movement's inspiration is tending to recede further and further into the distance, and while its attainment may still preoccupy certain other members of the Marxist fraternity, it is by no means evident that it remains on any Communist political agenda. Certainly, not since Khrushchev or Mao has any leader put forward a plan for achieving communism in the foreseeable future, and with so many rifts and divisions among Communists it would clearly be difficult to obtain any consensus on what such a prospectus should contain.

It is, however, worth conjecturing that if the changing fortunes and different dimensions of 'Communism' – as an ideology, a movement, and a way of life – had been better understood by its antagonists, the history of the past 40 years might have been different. That so many western policy-makers and their advisers continued to believe until recently that the movement, which had effectively ceased to be unified and homogeneous when Tito broke with Stalin more than 40 years ago, was still 'monolithic' can hardly have been conducive to rational decision-making. Had they had a better grasp of the realities of Communist organization and power in countries such as Vietnam, Chile, Angola, Nicaragua, and, even Afghanistan, perhaps some of the bloodshed might have been avoided and the cold war phased out somewhat earlier. Certainly, it is the underlying purpose of this volume to encourage the kind of informed reflection on 'Communist' history, problems, and prospects not always done in the past, so that some of the lessons might be learned and mistakes avoided in the future.

NOTES

1. Richard Staar (ed.), *1988 Yearbook on International Communist Affairs*, (Stanford, 1988). See Introduction pp. XXXI–XIV.
2. *Nationalism and After* (London, 1945), p. 19.

PART I

Laying the Foundations

1.   The Marxist Base

Contrary to popular belief, the man generally regarded as the founder of modern communism, Karl Marx, was not the world's first communist. Nor did he invent the notion of a communist society. Ironically, when as a young philosophy student in Bonn he was introduced to some of the 'communist' theories then circulating among the radical intelligentsia of western Europe, he showed little interest. And when later the liberal democratic paper he edited in Cologne was charged with 'flirting with communism', he dismissed both the claim and the ideas his journal was accused of promoting. 'The Rheinische Zeitung does not concede even theoretical validity to communist ideas in their present form, let alone their practical realization . . . and will subject these ideas to fundamental criticism', was his reply.[1]

Nevertheless, within two years of that article, written in October 1842, he had dubbed himself a 'communist' and, together with fellow 'communist' Friedrich Engels, with whom he was to begin a lifelong intellectual partnership, had embarked on his first major works of exposition.[2] If the Marxist approach that eventuated was significantly different from those of fellow 'communists' or 'socialists', their ideas had, nonetheless, helped him in fashioning his own. Moreover, as a voracious reader with a penchant for libraries and research institutes, he was able to bring to his studies the benefit of his wide knowledge of texts and treatises, both old and new.

From Marx's first essays in communism, it is clear that he regarded the concept as of ancient lineage. For, he speaks of 'primitive communism',[3] and though he left it to Engels to fill in the details,[4] he strongly implies that before the neolithic revolution, which introduced sedentary village communities, agriculture, and the domestication of plants and animals, the pattern of life could hardly have been other than communistic. In this sense, 'communism' may be taken to mean a form of society without private property, accumulations of wealth, or a ruling caste, and in which rewards for labour are on the basis of some estimation of needs. After all, the hunting and gathering activities of primitive man must have depended on close and continued cooperation and sharing of the proceeds according to some general and understood principle of reciprocity, and it is not inconceivable, judging from evi-

3

dence derived from primitive societies surviving to our own day, that
many neolithic villages also retained a communistic structure for some
considerable time.[5] Unfortunately, however, the historical record concerning such early forms of society is somewhat meagre, and conse-
quently Marx's view of 'primitive communism' was never convincingly
elaborated. There was, however, no corresponding shortage of material
on later communist manifestations. And from his publications and copi-
ous, if barely decipherable notes, it is evident that Marx was well versed
in the literature. What, then, of 'communism' before the age of Marx?

   The earliest major text dealing with the subject is Plato's *Republic* –
a work with which, as a Greek scholar, Marx was very familiar. In the
Platonic state, the small ruling elite – the guardians – are to live a
frugal existence in which they are housed in barracks; eat in communal
mess halls; 'agree to receive from the citizens a fixed rate of pay,
enough to meet the expenses of the year and no more'[6]; and hold
everything – women and children included – in common. From the
perspective of the nineteenth and twentieth centuries, this would seem
more a nightmare than the vision of the good life, but to Plato, rule
by those raised in such a system was an answer to the strife, disruption,
and division then characterizing much of Greek society. For, it would
ensure that the guardians would be imbued with moral excellence as
well as skill in the arts of government, since, 'as they have nothing but
their persons which they can call their own . . . they will be delivered
from all those quarrels of which money and children or relations are
the occasion'.[7]

   Nor was Plato's austere 'communism' a mere abstraction, for, in
Sparta, Plato had a practical model on which to base his ideas. For,
the Spartans, plagued with enemies within as well as outside the state,
had been conditioned, in the words of Plutarch, 'to have neither the
wish nor the ability to live for themselves; but like bees they were to
make themselves always integral parts of the whole community'.[8] Here,
then, was the ultimate communist experience – but one whose ends, to
which the individual was completely subordinated, were largely determined by the exigencies of warfare. It was not the kind of 'Communism'
that was likely to commend itself to Marx, Engels, or, indeed, anyone
far beyond the confines of ancient Greece.

   Far more pervasive and enduring as an impetus to the communal life
has been the quest for inspiration or sanctity in terms of some religious
or metaphysical belief. Even before the time of Plato, groups of
ascetics, especially in Egypt and Mesopotamia, but also in the Far East,
south and south-east Asia, had sought spiritual enlightenment through
the monastic life and the forswearing of property and marriage. Some

had even taken their devotions to the point of self-mutilation[9] (again, not the kind of thing to appeal to the anti-religious sentiments and worldly appetites of Marx and Engels). In the years after Plato, the Middle East produced a number of such movements, from the Essenes – a small Jewish sect which consigned wages and possessions 'into the common stock', allowing 'the benefits thus accruing to be shared'[10] – to those early Christians who felt called upon to surrender their worldly goods both for the benefit of their fellows in Christ and to enhance their chances of entry to the Kingdom of Heaven. Soon life in the Christian monastery was based on the supposition that property was 'a vice' and that, as in the Rule of St. Benedict, a monk 'should have nothing at all: neither a book, nor tablets, nor a pen. . . . All things should be common to all, as it is written, "Let not any man presume or call anything his own" '.[11]

Towards the end of the Middle Ages, as the main body of the Church in Western Europe began to reject the communal approach, various dissident Christians, generally as learned in the classics as in the biblical texts, became attracted to it. To those in Britain, like the influential philosophers Duns Scotus and William of Ockham, and the radical cleric John Ball, who preached to the rebellious peasants of 1381, the economic and other ills of society stood in marked contrast to an earlier age – the age of equality which, supposedly, existed before the Fall. And, of course, such a conception served as justification for an alternative model of society – one in which property was communally owned.[12] If such ideas had comparatively little immediate impact, they helped to create a climate of thought which in the sixteenth century led to a major work of social criticism – one quoted appreciatively by Marx in the first volume of *Capital* and whose author he lists as the first English communist – *Utopia* by Sir Thomas More.

Prompted by the plight of the new poor, who had been dispossessed of their lands by the growing enclosure movement, More's seminal work contains both a searing exposé of what he calls the 'conspiracy of the rich' to 'oppress' the poor, and a trenchant critique of private property, which he sees as the chief cause of crime. For it compels the poor to steal, though they risk the gallows in the process. Even if More does not expect his 'Utopia', with its strict regulations on dress, occupations, and preoccupations; on the size of the family; and on the number and distribution of cities, to have real existence, it is a powerful plea for political and spiritual regeneration and was the progenitor of several other such works by Western European would-be reformers.[13]

A similar combination of religious nonconformity and secular humanism produced a spate of communistic writings during and after the Civil

War in seventeenth-century England. This time, however, they took the form, not of literary fantasies written in elegant Latin, but of political manifestos in colloquial and robust English. Drawing on the ideas of the constitutional Levellers, who had championed the claims of the common man against arbitrary authority and demanded greater equality and accountability, men like Gerrard Winstanley and William Everard sought a yet more thoroughgoing levelling of society.[14]

Radicalized by the failure of Cromwell to extend the franchise, introduce social reform, or solve the country's mounting economic problems, such men began to believe that true liberty was incompatible with the right to accumulate property, and called upon those being dispossessed of their commons to help secure the return of land to the 'common treasury'. If, in this way, they anticipated more recent appeals to 'class solidarity', they were also ahead of their time in their willingness to carry their theories into practice. Identifying themselves with the Digger movement, which had staged a series of risings against the enclosures, Winstanley and Everard established two small agrarian communes on wasteland, first in Walton-on-Thames and then in Cobham, Surrey, and by the beginning of 1650 other Digger colonies had begun to appear in the Home Counties and the Midlands. Because of harassment from official and unofficial sources, none lasted more than about a year, but the fact of their existence was an example to future generations of radical activists, not least in France a century or so later.

It was, however, in the second half of the eighteenth century that the 'communist' idea finally broke the religious connections by which it had been sustained for nearly 2000 years. Here the work of Jean-Jacques Rousseau was of crucial importance, for even if he did not advocate communal ownership, preferring instead to see a society in which a smallholding of land was available for every family, he laid the intellectual groundwork for a host of revolutionary ideas. His epigram, 'Man is born free, and everywhere he is in chains',[15] expressed the despair of millions. Another epigram, 'So long as a people is constrained to obey and does obey it does well; but so soon as it can shake off its yoke and succeeds in doing so it does better',[16] sounded the clarion of revolt.

Rousseau's starting point was the descent to inequality from the equalitarian order by which he believed society had once been characterized. In his view, it was a transformation precipitated by the institution of private property, and in a pithy sentence resembling those of Marx in tone, Rousseau expresses the outrage of the aggrieved: 'It is plainly contrary to the law of nature, however defined . . . that the privileged few should gorge themselves with superfluities, while the starving multitude are in want of the bare necessities of life'.[17] Rousseau does, however, suggest a solution – even if one raising almost as many questions as it answers. For he argues that a more equitable social system can be reinstated through an act of will by a community acting in concert.[18] Exactly how this 'general will' is to be secured, articulated, and manifested and what is to happen to those who dissent are not altogether clear. But if his vision, based as it is, not on public ownership, but on the equal distribution of individual ownership, belongs to the realms of discourse associated with what Communists call 'bourgeois democracy', his vast and diverse corpus of writings have a revolutionary edge and, hence, an abiding appeal to those advocating a thoroughgoing transformation of society.

If Rousseau left a somewhat ambiguous legacy, that of his younger contemporary and former disciple, François Noël 'Gracchus' Babeuf, was much more clear cut. A provincial journalist with a background of rural poverty, he had been bitterly disillusioned by the failure of successive leaders of the French Revolution to effect social equality, extend the franchise to the urban workers or eliminate extremes of wealth, and in his radical journal *Le Tribun du peuple* – in effect, the tribune of the nascent urban proletariat – he called for a much more drastic remedy.

From the broadly held eighteenth-century theory that Nature had intended men to be equal as regards rights and needs, Babeuf derived the justification for a total and necessarily violent transformation of society, even more drastic than anything advocated by Robespierre, Marat and the other Jacobins. The rich, who were seen as having declared war on the poor and stolen what was rightfully theirs, were to be expropriated, and a new system introduced in which each person was to work at what suited him best, the fruits of his labours were to be deposited in a central storehouse, and the proceeds were to be distributed among the collective producers on a strictly equalitarian basis. But since any such system was clearly inconceivable without the capture of political power, Babeuf, in both his writings and activities on behalf of the clandestine 'Conspiracy of Equals' (for which he was guillotined in 1797), sought an insurrection to wrest control from the bourgeois holders of power, a regime of terror to prevent their reestablishing their authority, and a dictatorship by an enlightened and dedicated elite on behalf of the poor.[19] In his thoughts and actions, Babeuf became the prototype of the kind of 'professional revolutionary' later to strive to implant Marxist solutions on the alien soil of tsarist Russia.

Despite the collapse and overthrow of the Revolutionary government in 1799, France remained for more than half a century the hub of radical theory and practice. There had been another attempt at revolution in 1830, and a third was widely expected in the 1840s – which was one of the reasons for Marx's two-year stay in Paris, which began within a few months of his leaving his editorial post in Cologne.[20] In the meantime, left-wing intellectuals, still under the spell of the French Revolution, were developing their doctrines, manifestos, and blueprints for a better world, and by the 1830s they were being depicted as 'socialist' or 'communist', both terms generally being used interchangeably. Yet the Revolution had left two quite distinct radical legacies – one, based on constitutionalism and the parliamentary road, and associated with the early days of the Revolution; the other grounded in armed insurrection as propounded by the Jacobins, Babeuf, and their disciples.

Having at first rejected this latter approach, Marx found himself increasingly drawn to it, as he familiarized himself with the history of communist and socialist thought and experience. Indeed, as he took on the mantle of 'communist', which he came to regard as having a more dynamic and uncompromising connotation then the word 'socialist', he devoted much of his energies to rebutting the ideas of many of his 'socialist' predecessors and contemporaries, dubbing them 'Utopian', i.e. offering blueprints but no practical means of implementation.[21]

On the other hand, for all his criticisms, Marx had clearly assimilated some of their ideas. From Claude-Henri de Saint-Simon, for example, he derived the notion of the planned economy; from Pierre-Joseph Proudhon, the aphorism, 'Property is theft', and from Louis Blanc, the precept, 'From each according to his ability to each according to his need', while many other historians and economists of the time contributed to his understanding of 'class struggle'.[22] For a brief period he also sympathized with the conception of revolutionary terror associated with Louis-Auguste Blanqui, who is also credited with the concept of 'dictatorship of the proletariat', even if his idea did not at the time find its way into print.[23] But he probably garnered even more from his contacts with the workers of Paris, regarded as the vanguard of revolution in Europe, and by the mid-'40s he and his close collaborator, Friedrich Engels, were developing a concept they believed more rigorous, thoroughgoing and practical than anything the 'Utopians' had to offer – 'scientific socialism'.[24]

This was a shrewd use of terminology, for in the mid-nineteenth century, 'science' was beginning to be regarded with enormous reverence. In an age of rapid industrial and technological advance, scientists were seen as harbingers of progress – people whose training and understanding had given them the potential for solving the world's problems, satisfying all needs, and transforming the material and moral conditions of existence. Thus, in appending the term 'scientific' to their method of analysis, Marx and Engels were claiming to be the possessors of incontrovertible knowledge of present and future events whose ideas deserved to be taken much more seriously than those of their socialist rivals. On the other hand, using the term 'scientific' to differentiate their socialist ideas from all the others was not simply a matter of public relations. It reflected their own understanding of what they had achieved – the correct diagnosis of the present ills of society and the appropriate remedy. What, then, was the nature of 'scientific socialism'?

Any attempt to summarize the work of a leading theorist is fraught with difficulty. In the case of Marx, however, the task is especially hazardous, not least because of the ambiguous legacy he left to his disputatious devotees. Part of the problem lies in the fact that his writings were as diverse as they were prolific. He was, by turns, philosopher and historian, classicist and chronicler of current events, economist and political sociologist – and more besides. And because he is at one time the dispassionate researcher; at another, the 'infallible' prophet; and in yet another guise, the polemicist, oversimplifying and exaggerating for political effect, what he says in one context is not always consistent with what he says in another, and scholars may differ in their assessments of what constitutes the essence of his thought. Nor has the problem been made any easier by the recent publication of many of his hitherto unpublished manuscripts – most of them early works – raising fresh queries and conundrums for the modern interpreter.

Above all, there is the problem of disentangling Marx the man from Marx the myth. The trouble is that many so-called Marxists do not know their Marx very well. In the Communist countries, for example, people have tended to learn their 'Marxism' from texts specially selected by governments to suit national purposes, while in many a developing country it is the idiom, rather than the ideology, of Marx which has appeal. In the process, many of the ideas widely attributed to Marx did not originate with him at all, but with his disciples, who sometimes distorted and misrepresented his views. For example, when Engels inherited the mantle of Marxist orthodoxy following Marx's death in 1883, he gave the ideology a more deterministic, if somewhat less revolutionary complexion than many find in the original texts, while much Marxist theorizing about the 'dictatorship of the proletariat', the role of the Communist Party, or the distinction between 'socialism' and 'communism' has more to do with Lenin and Stalin than with Marx.

Many of the concerns which were to preoccupy Marx for the whole
of his adult working life can be traced back to his childhood in Trier –
the Rhineland market town where he was born in May 1818. Once a
provincial capital of the Roman Empire, Trier abounds in ancient
remains, and Marx's formative years spent in a house directly opposite
the magnificent Porta Nigra (the ancient gateway to Trier) clearly fired
his historical imagination. Moreover, many of the ideas to which Trier
had been exposed during its brief period under Napoleonic rule had
filtered through to the young Marx by way of such people as his father
and several teachers at his high school, who had eagerly espoused the
principles of the French Revolution. And from lengthy discussions
with his learned and much travelled near neighbour, the Baron von
Westphalen (later to become his father-in-law), Marx learned about
the socialism of men like Saint-Simon.

In the meantime, though the son of reasonably well-to-do parents –
his father, Heinrich, was a lawyer; his mother, Henrietta, of independent means – Marx had found his radical sympathies engaged early.
For, in the late 1820s, the vagaries of the economic system had led to
a sudden slump in the Moselle wine trade, which meant ruin for the
thousands in Trier and the surrounding districts who depended on it.[25]

Such early influences notwithstanding, it was a philosophy professor
at Berlin University who had perhaps the greatest impact on his intellectual development – Georg Wilhelm Friedrich Hegel. Hegel had, in fact,
died 5 years before Marx took up his studies in Berlin, but his ideas
were very much alive, promoted by his former students, who had
formed themselves into rival left- and right-wing Hegelian groups. What
had originally gripped Marx as a young man already searching for 'the
truth' about humanity, was the all-encompassing nature of the Hegelian
approach. After all, it seemed to offer a comprehensive answer to all
or many of the ultimate questions philosophers have tended to pose –
questions as to the nature and causes of things, the meaning of existence, the destiny of mankind, and so forth. Another attraction was the
optimism and dynamism of the underlying theory. For central to it was
the idea of progress. Nothing in nature was static. Everything was in
the process of moving forward. It was an idea that seemed to fit the
mood of nineteenth-century western Europe, as did the related notion
that the forward movement depended on the overcoming of obstacles.

For Hegel, the pattern of progress written on the pages of history
itself followed a predetermined course, the essence of which was dialectical – that is, characterized by a series of conflicts and their temporary
resolutions. According to this view, everything undergoes a process of
transforming itself into its opposite. Every 'thesis' generates an oppos-

ing force – an 'antithesis' – the tension between the two becoming eventually resolved in a 'synthesis'. But each 'synthesis', while resolving the former contradiction, assumes the role of a fresh 'thesis' and, hence, becomes confronted with another 'antithesis'. Yet, from the dialectical process comes progress, as each succeeding 'synthesis' is of a higher order than its predecessor and, hence, nearer to the blissful moment when the final synthesis is realized and the ultimate purpose of existence stands revealed.

Thus far, Marx and Hegel were in accord.[26] But Marx parted company with his spiritual mentor, firstly, on the political implications of the Hegelian dialectic. For, as a young radical, Marx was not going to be persuaded that the sociopolitical order in nineteenth-century Prussia represented the climax of human endeavour – in effect, the final synthesis. Political differences apart, Marx and Hegel also disagreed about the nature of the forces whose antagonisms determine the content of history. For Hegel, the contradictions existed in the world of ideas, and the essence of the dialectic lay in the opposition of logical categories and concepts. 'Is' implies 'is not'. 'Being' implies 'not being', the antagonism between the two being reconciled by the idea of 'becoming', which itself takes on the guise of a new 'thesis'. For Marx, on the other hand, the dialectical conflict revealed in history was not one of abstractions, but of material factors. Hegel has posited ideas, philosophies, cultures and moralities as things-in-themselves; Marx saw them as human creations, subject to change as material circumstances change perceptions of interests and needs. This, in essence, was what Marx called 'the materialist conception of history', which others have dubbed 'historical materialism' or – so as to distinguish it clearly from the 'idealism' of Hegel – 'dialectical materialism'.[27]

If Marx had done no more than formulate his somewhat esoteric 'materialist conception of history', his impact on the world might well have been small. As it was, however, this theory became a peg upon which to hang a number of socioeconomic theories with revolutionary political implications. At the same time, it gave to these theories the appearance of logical consistency, objectivity and 'scientific' validity, which is perhaps why so many intellectuals have been attracted to them at one time or another.

It was in analysing the development of social relationships that Marx made the most telling use of the dialectical method. First, he held that while societies might comprise several diverse elements they were basically polarized into two antagonistic classes. One would predominate and exploit the other, establishing a 'superstructure' of social, political, legal and religious institutions to justify the system of which it was the major beneficiary. At the basis of this division was a conflict of material interest between the few owners of the means of production and the many who had no such title. But what determined the dynamics of their struggle were the particular socioeconomic conditions obtaining in that society, in terms of forms of property relations and dispositions of 'forces of production', by which Marx meant everything contributing to the creation of material goods – tools, technologies, raw materials and manpower.

Marx contended that the dynamics of production put even the most stable socio-political systems at risk. For, new technologies eventually prove incompatible with existing modes of production and require new kinds of property relationships. As Marx puts it: 'The windmill gives you society with the feudal lord; the steam mill, society with the industrial capitalist'.[28] But the transition from new technology to new socio-economic system is not automatic. In between, the defenders of the old order try to resist the implications of technological advance, while the oppressed class, on whose exploitation the old system depends, rises up and eventually overthrows it. But the success of the new ruling class in establishing a new socio-economic order can only be temporary since it, too, is destined to be toppled when technological change makes an anachronism of the system it has introduced. Only when communism – the final synthesis – is attained will the class conflict and its attendant contradictions cease.[29]

Like its Hegelian predecessor, Marx's theory of history was designed to have universal application. Hence, when he talks of society, his conception relates to human society as a whole rather than to national societies, any national references serving merely to illustrate the general pattern of socio-economic organization in a given historical epoch. In fact, Marx identifies several such systems, each of which is, in some sense, of a higher order than its predecessor.[30] Unfortunately, his writings on the earliest forms of social organization are ambiguous. Generally, he speaks of 'primitive communism', suggesting a society in which the means of production are held in common, but in his *Critique of Political Economy*, written in 1859, he identifies a specifically 'Asiatic' mode of production, in which self-sufficient, isolated and egalitarian village communities subsist within a highly centralized and despotic framework of political control.[31] However, both kinds of society are in jeopardy when commercial criteria are introduced, and surplus wealth is accumulated by a minority who enslave those whom they have disinherited or conquered. In such 'ancient' societies, the slaves work for the profit of their masters, who have united to form settled urban communities. But soon the cities are engulfed in war and the initiative passes from town to country, where a new class of landed gentry challenges and eventually destroys the old order and establishes feudal rule. Here serfdom, involving compulsory labour in return for land and protection, replaces the still more arbitrary institution of slavery. Eventually, developments in technology and trade make untenable the relationship between lord and serf, and feudalism falls to a new bourgeois order in which the capitalists own all the means of production, save one – labour.

From this presumption of a dialectical pattern in history, Marx concluded that capitalism was likely to be no less transitory than the preceding socio-economic systems. For it had brought into being a new exploited class – the proletariat – and Marx prophesied that when capitalism reached its apogee the workers would rise and eventually destroy the system that had oppressed them. They would then establish a socialist/communist order characterized by common ownership of the means of production, the elimination of classes, and, therefore, the elimination of class conflict and the withering away of the state – the instrument of class oppression.[32]

In its original and most detailed formulation, the materialist conception of history seemed so deterministic as to leave little room for individual initiative and choice. On the other hand, had Marx believed that the individual was but a plaything of impersonal forces he would have merited the scorn he levelled at other philosophers for merely interpreting and failing to change the world. In fact, he was able to reconcile his political instincts with his theoretical approach by distinguishing between the general and the specifics of the historical process. The overall pattern was given, but how and when the relevant changes occur is not determined – a conception giving ample scope for political educators and activists who could tap the revolutionary potential of the working class and, hence, 'give history a push'.

Since it has been, above all, what Marx had to say about the capitalist system and its disintegration that has had the greatest impact on the world, it seems appropriate to consider this aspect of his thinking in greater detail. Together with Engels, Marx had from the early 1840s been closely studying the working relations between labour and management in countries under capitalism. From his investigations he concluded that the workers – and here he was concerned mainly with urban rather than rural labour – did not receive an adequate return for the only commodity they had to sell, i.e. their labour. In Marx's view, they were grossly underpaid since what was in their wage packet was far less than the value of the labour they had expended in production. In fact, their employers had creamed off 'surplus value' from their labour, by which Marx meant, roughly speaking, the difference between what capitalists could expect as profit and what they had actually paid in wages for the commodities produced. At the same time, the amount of 'surplus value' represented the degree to which the worker was 'exploited'.[33]

To Marx, such exploitation, was, of course, repugnant; yet he laid no blame on capitalists as such, since they were merely products of a system that had conferred unequal relationships on the groups comprising it. They were bound to view life in terms of the role their class played in the production process. As he says in the preface to his *Critique of Political Economy:* 'It is not the consciousness of men that determines their being, but, on the contrary, their social being that determines their consciousness'.[34] To this theory that class origins constrain thought, the twentieth-century German theorist, Karl Mannheim, accorded the name 'the sociology of knowledge', though perhaps 'the sociology of perception' might have been a more accurate appellation.

But if capitalists must necessarily exploit labour, the oppressed wage-earners must necessarily resent that exploitation. And in delineating the depth of that resentment, Marx employed another Hegelian concept that had seized his imagination in his student days – 'alienation'. Literally 'estrangement', this concept is used by Hegel to depict a process whereby man is prevented from being his true self until he achieves full understanding of his nature and destiny.[35] With Marx the concept loses its metaphysical, even somewhat mystical overtones and becomes an objective condition affecting labour psychology. As he sees it, under capitalism, the workers are alienated in a multiplicity of ways. Since they do not work for themselves, fabricate not more than a part of any product, and are paid less than their labour is worth, they are alienated from their work. Moreover, in the very act of production within a capitalist system, the worker becomes depersonalized, and, therefore, alienated from himself. Furthermore, by virtue of the class struggle, he becomes alienated from the communal life that is the desire and destiny of his social essence, or 'species-being'. In addition, since he is treated simply as a marketable source of labour power to be bought and sold like a commodity, he becomes dehumanized and finds himself alienated from other men.[36] It is this profound and multifaceted sense of alienation which propels labour to discover (or possibly rediscover) that state of happiness from which humankind has been estranged, and this, of course, spurs the working class to wrest political and economic power from its capitalist masters.

If Marx's strictures on the capitalist system seem unduly harsh today, it has to be remembered that his was an age of almost unfettered,

laissez-faire capitalism and that he had empirical evidence for much of
what he had to say about low wages, long hours, and overcrowded
factories and dwellings. The Blue Books published by the British
government went into great detail on these matters, and he could also
rely on the independent researches of Engels – himself, ironically, a
factory owner on whose profits the Marx household came to depend.[37]

In addition, Marx had learned from the classical English economists
Adam Smith and David Ricardo that booms and slumps, the bankruptcy
of the inefficient, subsistence wages, and the sweatshop, conveyor belt,
and production line were necessary components of a system geared to
increasing social wealth. Indeed, it was their defence of the system and
their attempt to produce theories to explain its operation that prompted
Marx to elaborate his own 'laws of motion of the capitalist mode of
production'.[38] That these laws were formulated at a time of unparalleled
boom, which appeared to benefit employer and wage-earner alike, in
no way dented his confidence in their predictive value since, as in the
case of his materialist interpretation of history, they were meant to
signify long-term, not short-run, tendencies.

To Marx, as, indeed, to the classical economists, the chief characteristic of capitalism was its competitive nature. The economics of the
market place held sway, with millions of producers seeking to outsmart
their rivals in obtaining custom. On the other hand, in order to survive
in this competitive environment, the capitalists would eventually have
to instal labour-saving machines so as to increase output. To this process
Marx applied the term, 'the law of capital accumulation'. However,
once installed, the labour-saving devices would increase supply relative
to demand, and profits would tend to fall. As a consequence, several
capitalists, unable to make a profit or raise credit, would go out of
business, and capital would be concentrated into fewer and fewer hands.
According to this 'law of the concentration of capital', ultimately only
monopoly concerns like cartels and trusts could survive such cutthroat
competition.

The net effect would be to create a glut in the labour supply as
unsuccessful former capitalists swelled the ranks of the working class
at a time when mechanical power was increasingly displacing manpower. But with a declining number of buyers relative to the number
of sellers of labour power, exploitation of the worker, over whom there
was the constant threat of unemployment, could only intensify. There
was a 'law of increasing misery', according to which those in work
would receive a diminishing share of the value they produced; their
employers, an increase in the surplus value extracted. The rest of the
workforce, constituting a 'reserve army of the unemployed', would be

left to languish until required in the service of one of capitalism's intermittent booms.[39]

But did Marx mean that the worker's misery would increase absolutely or relatively? In *The Communist Manifesto*, he seems to imply the former: 'The modern worker . . . instead of rising with the progress of industry, sinks ever deeper beneath the social conditions of his own class. The labourer becomes the pauper, and pauperism increases even more rapidly than population and wealth'.[40] But the *Manifesto* was a political tract, hastily and collectively compiled, not a work of scholarship, and in later, more considered works, Marx implies that his concept of 'misery' is both relative and, to some extent, independent of the general wage level.[41] It was, for example, the classical economist David Ricardo, and not Karl Marx, who subscribed to an 'iron law' according to which wages must always fall to subsistence.

But whether their misery is relative or absolute, the workers, according to Marx, see an increasing gap between their living conditions and those of the bourgeoisie and feel a growing sense of wretchedness, even if there is a temporary rise in their economic fortunes. For nothing can compensate for the growing alienation they feel in a system which deprives them of their roots and of their individuality. Thus, Marx's 'law' has a psychological as well as an economic dimension, and in *Wage Labour and Capital*, written in 1849, the emphasis is clearly on the former:

> A noticeable increase in wages presupposes a rapid growth of productive capital. The rapid growth of productive capital brings about an equally rapid growth of wealth, luxury, social wants, social enjoyments. Thus, although the enjoyments of the worker have risen, the social satisfaction that they give has fallen in comparison with the increased enjoyments of the capitalist, which are inaccessible to the worker.[42]

This was, however, a situation which, according to the Marxist prospectus, could not long endure, since capitalism, at once the most inventive and the most dehumanizing system to date, was doomed. Like every system before it, it contained the seeds of its own destruction, which would germinate when 'the monopoly of capital becomes a fetter upon the mode of production',[43] and private ownership an impediment to efficiency. And in creating an ever more numerous and discontented industrial workforce who had learned in the process of production the habits of cooperative effort, the bourgeoisie had produced 'its own grave-diggers'.[44] Though it might try to deflect the revolutionary process by allowing the workers to combine in trade unions and by occasionally meeting some of their demands – higher wages, shorter hours, and, possibly, even the vote – such tactics in the long run could only increase revolutionary class-consciousness. In time, the workers would learn to use the strike weapon and to ascertain the degree of violence 'necessary' to attain their goals – the abolition of bourgeois property and the destruction of capitalism.

Generally speaking, Marx envisaged the transformation from capitalism to communism as occurring in stages. Where the vestiges of feudalism remained, Marx expected the urban proletariat to join with the bourgeoisie in liquidating all traces of a social order less efficient and more iniquitous than capitalism. To accelerate the process, at least in the larger feudal empires, Marx thought it might be expedient for the proletariat to identify itself temporarily with the national inspirations of, say, the Poles, Hungarians and Italians. Later, when capitalism's contradictions reached a critical stage, he anticipated that the urban proletariat, together with the radical intelligentsia and other sympathetic elements, would intensify the struggle against the bourgeoisie until they eventually succeeded in overthrowing it.[45]

Following the downfall of capitalism, Marx envisaged a transitional period in which some of the residual features of the old order, such as the apparatus of the state and the existence of monetary rewards, would remain, while others, such as alienation and the boom/slump cycle with its attendant crises of overproduction and underconsumption, would be mitigated. In political terms, this interim phase was to be 'a dictatorship of the proletariat' – an ill-defined term, by which Marx appears to have meant an administration along the lines of the short-lived Paris Commune of 1871, with its elected officials, subject to recall, and deprofessionalization of governmental functions.[46] In economic terms, the interim phase appeared to involve state planning, with production and distribution rationalized in the common interest[47] – an arrangement which Stalin, amongst others, would depict as 'socialist', as distinct from 'communist', in character.[48] Not until communism was achieved would the state and its apparatus disappear, money be dispensed with, and members of society receive according to need rather than 'social value'.[49]

Such, in outline, is the central core of 'scientific socialism'. But, like many other theoretical approaches, it was free of neither ambiguity nor inconsistency. Did the destruction of capitalism necessitate the use of violence? Almost the whole of Marx's teachings suggested a firm attachment to the view that force was 'the midwife of every old society pregnant with the new one'.[50] Yet, he came to reject revolutionary terror as a sign of political immaturity and weakness, and towards the end of his life, he conceded the possibility of a peaceful transition in countries like 'America, England, and . . . Holland'.[51] Could capitalism reform itself? Marx denied it, dismissing, as attempts to deflect the workers from their true purpose, any temporary concessions made to ease working conditions. Yet, in his inaugural address to the First Working Men's International in 1864, he himself became an advocate of reform, commending, for example, the Ten Hours Act and the growth of a cooperative movement.[52] Could socialism occur in a country with only a small bourgeoisie? The materialist conception of history seemed to deny that possibility, yet in 1848, Marx prepared himself for a socialist revolution in a number of semi-feudal countries, and subsequently surprised Engels by his hopes of a transition to communism in tsarist Russia, despite the pre-capitalist nature of its system.[53]

Notwithstanding their ambiguities and contradictions and the fact that this advocate of a totally integrated world-view never fully systematized his ideas, Marx's writings were to have enormous posthumous appeal. And the attraction was clearly able to survive the invalidation in practice of some of his assumptions and predictions. To the poor, the unemployed, and the underprivileged and alienated, Marxism offered an explanation of their plight and a ray of hope for the future. To middle-class intellectuals, it appeared to provide a coherent method of examining social problems, a plausible critique of capitalism, and a blueprint for an efficient, though just and ultimately peaceful world. To those with a taste for political activism, it was an ideology with which to arouse and excite the masses.

But Marxism's very appeal to a diversity of peoples at different levels of sophistication – many living in conditions far removed from those of nineteenth-century Europe in which the theories first took root – brought its own problems. In particular, there was the difficulty of securing agreement on the interpretation and practical requirements of theory. Lacking accord on these matters, the political movements inspired by Marx have tended to manifest a dialectic of their own, splitting into disputatious factions as soon as they acquire some degree of order. Unity, it seems, is as far from attainment among the Marxist as it is among the Christian or Muslim fraternity. Nonetheless, for some considerable time the Communists were able to constitute an apparently cohesive group in an otherwise faction-ridden movement. What distinguished them from their fellow Marxists (at least until recently) was their highly disciplined and centralized form of political organization, Soviet support, and the belief that Lenin, the architect of the October Revolution in Russia, had the blueprint for the socialist transformation of the world.

But the idiosyncratic organization and perspective of the Communist movement, and, in particular, the tendency of its members to pronounce as hostile to socialism alternative Marxist interpretations, merely engendered in an already much divided Marxist fraternity a fundamental rift, which only an equally fundamental change in approach by either side could bridge. If, in today's ideologically uncertain climate, such a political accommodation is much more feasible, in the days when Lenin was laying the foundations of what became known as international Communism, any lasting compromise between Communists and other sorts of socialists would have seemed virtually inconceivable. But to be able to assess the dimensions of the ideological chasm between one group of Marxists and the rest it is necessary first to comprehend the diverse currents existing in Marxist thought even before Lenin's attempts to give Marxism a new orthodoxy.

NOTES

1. K. Marx, *Selected Writings*, trans. and ed. D. McLellan (Oxford, 1977), p. 20 (hereafter referred to as *KMSW*).
2. In the 'Economic and Philosophical Manuscripts' of 1844, Marx makes his first positive reference to 'communism'. *KMSW*, p. 89.
3. See, for example, 'The German Ideology', *KMSW*, p. 164.
4. For the fullest, if somewhat disorganized, analysis of 'primitive communism', see F. Engels, 'The Origin of the Family, Private Property and the State' in K. Marx and F. Engels, *Selected Works* in 1 vol. (London 1969), pp. 461–566 (hereafter referred to as *MESW*).
5. For a recent scholarly analysis of 'primitive communism', see Kenneth Rexroth, *Communalism: From its Origins to the Twentieth Century* (London, 1975).
6. *The Republic*, book III, as quoted in Alexander Gray, *The Socialist Tradition: Moses to Lenin* (London, 1963), p. 19.
7. *The Republic*, ibid., book v, p. 23.
8. 'Life of Lycurgus', ibid., section xxv, p. 12.
9. See H. G. Wells, *A Short History of the World* (London, 1943), esp. ch. 36.
10. From Philo, 'Quod omnis probus liber sit', sections 12–13, quoted in Gray, p. 37.
11. Trans. F. A. Gasquet (London, 1936).
12. See, for example, K. Feiling, *A History of England* (London, 1970), pp. 250–1.
13. More's *Utopia*, together with Francis Bacon's *New Atlantis* and Thomas Campanella's *City of the Sun*, appears in *Ideal Commonwealths*, with an introduction by Henry Morley (London, 1885).
14. See, for example, Christopher Hill, *The World Upside Down* (London, 1975).
15. *The Social Contract*, trans. Gerard Hopkins (Oxford, 1953), p. 240.
16. Ibid.
17. *Discourse on the Origins of Inequality*, trans. G. D. H. Cole, J. H. Brumfitt & J. C. Hall (London, 1986), p. 117.
18. *The Social Contract*, especially pp. 258–62, 269–76 and 285–90.
19. For a brief introduction to the life and ideas of Babeuf, see, for example, Gray, pp. 100–9.
20. David McLellan, *Karl Marx: The Legacy* (London, 1983), p. 20.
21. *The Communist Manifesto* contains a critique of 'Utopian' socialism as well as other forms of socialism. *KMSW*, pp. 239–45.

22. For a general discussion of the views of the French writers who influenced Marx, see Gray, pp. 136–256.
23. 'The Class Struggles in France', *KMSW*, p. 296.
24. Though the term 'scientific socialism' is associated more with Engels, Marx clearly understood their joint approach as a contribution to 'science'.
25. The early influences on Marx's thinking are traced in I. Berlin, *Karl Marx, His Life and Environment* (Oxford, 1939) and D. McLellan, *Karl Marx: His Life and Thought* (London, 1973).
26. Though Marx sets out the dialectic in these terms only in *The Poverty of Philosophy*, and then only as a rebuke to Proudhon for his 'pseudo-Hegelianism', it remained the basis of much of his thinking.
27. The phrase, popularized by Lenin's teacher, Plekhanov, first appeared in the 1870s, but was never used by Marx or Engels.
28. 'The Poverty of Philosophy', *KMSW*, p. 202.
29. 'The Economic and Philosophical Manuscripts', *KMSW*, p. 89.
30. In 'The German Ideology', written in 1846, historical materialism receives its first and most comprehensive expression.
31. *MESW*, p. 182. For a more comprehensive analysis, see L. Krader, *The Asiatic Mode of Production* (Assen, 1975).
32. In *The Communist Manifesto*, the prognosis is set out with dramatic clarity. *MESW*, pp. 35–63.
33. Those unwilling to 'plough through' the 3 volumes of *Capital* (Moscow, 1954) might consult a much shorter and more readable book on the subject: B. Fine, *Marx's Capital* (London, 1975).
34. *MESW*, p. 181.
35. For an analysis of the relations between the Hegelian and Marxist conceptions of 'alienation', see, for example, S. Hook, *From Hegel to Marx*, 2nd ed, (Ann Arbor, 1962).
36. 'Economic and Philosophical Manuscripts', *KMSW*, pp. 29–30.
37. D. McLellan, *Karl Marx: The Legacy*, pp. 39–56.
38. Marx's debt to the English classical economists is explored in M. Howard and J. King, *The Political Economy of Marx* (London, 1975).
39. For a painless introduction to *Capital*, see Fine, op. cit.
40. *KMSW*, p. 231.
41. For example, in *Capital* vol. I (Moscow, 1954), p. 654 he argues, 'In proportion as capital accumulates, the lot of the labourer, be his payment high or low, must grow worse'.
42. *MESW*, p. 83.
43. *Capital* (Moscow, 1954), vol. I, p. 763.
44. From *The Communist Manifesto*, *KMSW*, p. 231.
45. These are traced in sections 1 and 2 of *The Communist Manifesto*, *MESW*, pp. 35–53.
46. See, for example, his 'Address on the Civil War in France', *KMSW*, pp. 541–5.
47. See, for example, *The Communist Manifesto*, *KMSW*, pp. 237–8.
48. See his *Foundations of Communism* (Moscow, 1947), pp. 498–506.
49. The distinction is clarified in the 'Critique of the Gotha Programme', *KMSW*, pp. 568–9.
50. *Capital*, vol. I, p. 750.
51. 'Speech at Amsterdam' 1872, *KMSW*, pp. 594–5.
52. Text in Said K. Padorev, *The Essential Marx* (New York, 1979), pp. 81–9.
53. In the 1882 preface to the Russian edition of *The Communist Manifesto*, Marx declares that 'the present Russian ownership of land may serve as the starting point' for a communist development, *KMSW*, p. 584.

2. The Leninist Edifice

Despite his prodigious output and interest in virtually every aspect of life, Marx left no systematic doctrine, and it was for others to spell out and popularize his ideas. But immediately there were problems of interpretation. The bulk of his output had been unfinished and unpublished when he died in 1883, and his almost indecipherable handwriting, combined with his tendency to scrawl in a number of different languages simultaneously, made comprehension somewhat difficult. Furthermore, the sheer range and volume of his writings were far greater than the capacity of most of his followers to master them, but the need for selection inevitably led to the development of different Marxist currents. The potential for diversity was further increased when 'the tide of history' generated social, political and economic developments which had been neither described nor analysed by Marx.

For a time, the latent divisions were kept in check by Engels who, fortunately for the movement, survived Marx by a further 12 years to become the acknowledged fount of Marxist orthodoxy. In fact, the mantle of Marx could hardly have fallen on more diligent and conscientious shoulders. After all, the two men had worked together closely for nearly 40 years – Engels having been an invaluable informant and, in many respects, Marx's superior in his attention to historic and current detail. Yet, given that he was of a more practical cast of mind than his erstwhile collaborator, it is perhaps somewhat ironic that he should have devoted much of his latter years to the exposition of ideas which squeeze the flow of history back into the Hegelian corset of thesis, antithesis, and synthesis from which Marx had begun to extricate himself.

Engels's renewed emphasis on historical necessity appears not merely in such learned treatises as *Anti-Dühring* (1877)[1] and *Ludwig Feuerbach and the End of Classical German Philosophy* (1886).[2] It is a constant theme in his correspondence with socialist friends and was the intellectual leitmotif of his address at Marx's graveside. Summing up Marx's achievement, he declared, 'As Darwin discovered the law of evolution in organic nature, so Marx discovered the law of evolution in human history'[3] – i.e. the 'law' that material forces shape man's consciousness. Admittedly, Engels acknowledges in a letter written many years later that he and Marx may have overstressed the importance of the economic factor, 'in opposition to our adversaries who denied it'.[4] Nonetheless, Engels continued to insist that material forces conditioned thought processes and social institutions – a view which coloured the version of Marxism adopted by the German Social Democrats during his lifetime and by Lenin and Stalin years later. If Engels returned to the economic determinism of his younger days, he also seemed to be shedding much of his earlier relish for revolution. In one of his last publications, he enthuses about the electoral successes of the German Social Democrats and concludes that 'the mode of struggle of 1848 is today obsolete from every point of view'.[5]

After Engels's death in 1895, the rifts he had tried to stem grew apace, the main Marxist tendencies – as if in deference to the materialistic conception of history – reflecting the socio-political conditions in the countries from which they emerged. By the end of the nineteenth century, the workers of western Europe – generally far more advanced economically and politically than their counterparts to the east and south – were increasingly receptive to reformist notions, and though the revolutionary overthrow of the state still had many adherents, the analysis of capitalism on which it was based sounded less convincing than it had in 1848.[6] For, though the industrial working class was rapidly increasing in numbers, the Marxist prediction that its conditions of life must worsen was already being disproved in practice. Despite the world economic recession in the last quarter of the nineteenth century, trade-union activity helped to secure higher wages and better working conditions, while political agitation in parliament and through the press produced protective legislation, free education, and other social services. Thus, whilst the Marxist slogan, 'Working men of all lands unite!' might still prove an effective rallying cry, the idea that they had 'nothing to lose but their chains' was much more difficult to sustain in western Europe.

In such circumstances, the revolutionary implications of Marxist theory seemed to many to be outmoded, and immediately after Engels's death, his friend Eduard Bernstein, a leading German Social Democrat, spearheaded a movement for revision.[7] In Bernstein's view, a reformulation was essential, since Marx had made too many false prognoses. His predictions regarding the pauperization of the workers, the disappearance of the peasantry and of the small businessman, the shrinking of the middle classes and the growth of class antagonisms did not accord with the facts. Nor was there any evidence that capitalism was moving towards its final crisis. There were, on the contrary, indications of increasing order, a more equitable distribution of wealth, more widespread ownership of property and greater freedom. To such criticisms, orthodox Marxists had a ready reply. Capitalism had entered a phase of temporary stabilization, but its downfall was no less inevitable.

But Bernstein had more fundamental objections to the orthodoxy, objections which could not be so easily dismissed. He contended, for example, that Marx's materialism was neither scientific nor appropriate as a foundation for socialism. For, it claimed as inevitable something not susceptible of proof and denied any objectively ethical basis for a better society. Social democracy, Bernstein declared, 'should find the courage to emancipate itself from a philosophy which has, in fact, long been outmoded, and be willing to show itself for what it really is – a democratic socialist party of reform'.[8] In practical terms, this meant working for the advancement of socialism through working-class political parties, trade unions, cooperatives, and other such organizations permitted in a democracy, and it meant not trying to cripple or smash the democratic state through which workers' conditions are improved. It was an approach not dissimilar to that of the Fabians and to that of those reformist socialists in France and Italy who had never espoused Marxism.

Not surprisingly, Bernstein's 'revisionism' unleashed a storm of controversy, engendering, in the Second International of working-class organizations, the kind of acrimony which had virtually crippled the First, which had collapsed in 1876.[9] Radical leftists, such as Rosa Luxemburg, made common cause with more centrist Marxists, such as Karl Kautsky and August Bebel, in fiercely attacking a formulation which critically undermined orthodox Marxism. It was their contention that Bernstein's faith in 'bourgeois' democracy was entirely misplaced. No matter what the current situation, the crises of capitalism would mount, and eventually lead to imperialism and, ultimately war, during which a revolutionary situation might well arise[10].

The bitter controversy between 'revisionist' and 'revolutionary' split the Second International movement, and at the same time revealed an increasing divergence between theory and practice. The German Social Democratic Party, for example, refused repeatedly to abandon its revolutionary platform; yet, in practice, as the largest and most highly organized of Europe's working-class parties, it was moving rapidly in the direction of 'revisionism', espousing parliamentarianism and political reform.[11]

In July 1914, as European war loomed, the revolutionary credentials of Europe's Marxists were put to the test. In theory, war arose because of the capitalist urge to secure colonies, protect markets or eliminate foreign trade competitors. The workers of different countries, having no conflicting interests, could not possibly support a bourgeois enterprise which would set them against one another, and without working-class participation wars could not be successfully prosecuted. So much for the theory. But, of course, if the workers in one country chose to support the war while their fellow workers abroad refused to participate, this would produce a one-sided victory, not an end to armed conflict. It seemed an almost insuperable dilemma, and after hours of agonized debate most orthodox Marxists in European parliaments decided to throw in their lot with the 'revisionists' and to vote for war credits. The only formal opposition came from the Social Democrats in the Serbian parliament, while the 12 Social Democrats in the Russian *duma* (including five supporters of Lenin) made an ambiguous statement about defending 'the cultural treasures of the people from attack . . . whether from abroad or inside the country', and then walked out without casting a vote.[12] But the die was cast. The proponents of 'internationalism' had become, in Lenin's words, 'social patriots', and socialism had itself become nationalized.

It was a critical turning point in the history of organized Marxism, not least because it strengthened the conviction of Lenin, then exiled from his native Russia, that the Marxist movement had betrayed the ideals of the First and Second Internationals to which it had belonged and would have to be entirely reconstructed on a revolutionary and insurrectionist platform.

But why should a comparatively little-known Russian political exile with a relatively small following have taken it upon himself to regenerate organized Marxism? The answer lies not merely in Lenin's supreme self-confidence and indomitable will. It is to be found, too, in the kinds of sociopolitical conditions that could turn a minor Russian nobleman, whose eldest brother had been executed in the struggle against tsarist autocracy, into a professional revolutionary.

The fact is that the society that produced the first revolution in the name of Marx was not an obvious candidate for a socialist transformation. For far from being a country of advanced capitalism, Russia was one of the most backward societies in Europe. It had undergone neither Reformation nor Renaissance, and had remained largely untouched by the Enlightenment and the ideas of the French Revolution. Until 1905, the concepts of free speech and movement, and of freedom to join political parties and hold demonstrations were almost unknown, save among a small, westernized elite. Moreover, any attempt at political organization was impeded by government repression, on the one hand; illiteracy, superstition, and apathy, on the other. And, in contrast to the growing industrialization and democratization of western Europe,

Russia had remained throughout the nineteenth century a semi-feudal society under a despotic, if inefficient autocracy.[13]

On the other hand, long before Marxism had made its impact, Russia had acquired a revolutionary tradition. For, now and then, the impoverished and illiterate peasantry, who were virtually slaves until 1861, would rise in revolt against their desperate conditions, and the resort to violence was in no way diminished after the freeing of the serfs. On the contrary, there was to be an upsurge of turbulence in the countryside as hopes of a significant change in the lot of the peasantry after emancipation were dashed. In fact, by the late 1860s, many Russian villages were harbouring cabals of zealots prepared to use terror tactics in the hope of securing redress of popular grievances.

Such groups were generally led by professional revolutionaries, often of middle-class origin or of the lesser nobility, who claimed absolute obedience from their followers and believed that in pursuit of a more just society any means is permissible – even the killing of innocents. For some, the aim was agrarian reform, in particular, more land for the peasants and an end to the crippling burden of taxes and redemption payments. Others, however, sought a much more radical transformation of society.[14] The so-called Narodniks, or Populists, believing the Russian peasantry to be potentially the most revolutionary class in Europe, envisaged the transformation of the rural commune, or 'mir', into the basic unit of a socialist society. In their view, Russia could attain socialism without having to suffer the evils of capitalism which had corrupted the West.

It was a conception grounded more in hope than experience. For the peasants were more interested in land than in socialism, and distrusted these strange missionaries from another class. In any case, the 'mir', which the Narodniks had lauded as a form of nascent socialism, was, in fact, a tsarist device for keeping the peasantry under control, and acted as a brake on revolutionary endeavour. When, moreover, an extensive terror campaign mounted by the more extreme Narodniks culminated in the assassination of Tsar Alexander II in 1881, it merely provoked widespread revulsion among the peasantry and the severest repression by the authorities. Though the cause of agrarian socialism was to revive with the creation, in 1901, of the Social Revolutionary Party, it was in retreat for the last two decades of the nineteenth century, and into the intellectual vacuum created by its decline came another revolutionary doctrine with a belief in mass action and a strong messianic element – Marxism.

It was in the 1860s that a clandestine edition of *The Communist Manifesto* first appeared in Russian translation, and it was in 1872 that a Russian translation of the first volume of *Das Kapital* was allowed to circulate freely. It had passed the censors on the grounds that it was an almost incomprehensible treatise on economics and, therefore, not politically dangerous. But the development of Marxist ideas in Russia was, of course, the product of belated industrialization in the wake of the emancipation of the serfs.[15] Though the industrial working class remained only a tiny fraction of the total population, its size was rapidly increasing during Russia's first industrial revolution at the end of the nineteenth century. From 1887 to 1900, the number of factory workers, miners, and railway employees rose from 1.5 million to 2.8 million,[16] and, since working conditions were far from satisfactory, the urban workers constituted a potential source of recruitment to the Marxist cause. But they needed a recruiting officer and an organization to which they could have regular access, and in the conditions then obtaining in Russia, with its extensive network of bureaucrats, censors, and spies, this was clearly going to be difficult.

Nonetheless, by the 1890s, most major cities contained cells of Marxists, though, like the Narodniks who had organized in the countryside, they were compelled to function in secret. Unlike the Narodniks, however, they lacked any clear sense of direction for some considerable time since their leaders – former Narodniks, Georgi Plekhanov, Paul Axelrod, and Vera Zasulich, who in 1883 had founded a Marxist group known as the Liberation of Labour – had all been forced into exile abroad. This meant, of course, that the leaders could exert influence in their native Russia only to the extent that their writings could be smuggled in – and the limitations this imposed were obvious. Hence their desire to see a more durable organization created within Russia itself, and in 1898 it looked as if their hopes might be realized, as the representatives of several indigenous Marxist groups met in Minsk to form a Russian Social Democratic Labour Party on the western European model. The results were profoundly disappointing. Most of the delegates were arrested shortly after their clandestine congress, so no effective organization was set up. In the aftermath, Russia's infant Marxist movement was thrown into confusion. Rival émigré organizations claimed to be the true voice of Russian Social Democracy, while Marxists within and outside Russia disagreed on strategies and tactics.[17]

Some of the issues in contention were of the kind already hotly debated among western European Socialists. There were, for example, 'revisionists' – among them, 'legal Marxists' such as Pyotr Struve who, like Bernstein, called for a critical revision of Marxist economic theory and believed that Marxists should cooperate with bourgeois elements in a programme of reform. Other 'revisionists' included the 'economists' associated with the journals *Rabochaya Mysl* ('Workers' Thought') and *Rabochaya Dyelo* ('Workers' Cause') who held that the struggle for better conditions should take priority over the fight for political emancipation. Opposing them were those of a more orthodox hue, who continued to believe in revolutionary socialism. But the 'revolutionaries', too were divided. Georgi Plekhanov, 'the father of Russian Marxism', took the standard Kautskyan position in favour of a 'significant interval' between bourgeois and proletarian revolutions. He argued that a thoroughgoing socialist programme required careful preparation, since any premature seizure of power could degenerate into dictatorship, so discrediting the very idea of social democracy. Among the 'revolutionaries' who disagreed with this analysis was the man who was to become Plekhanov's most distinguished disciple, Vladimir Ilyich Ulyanov, known from 1900 onwards as Lenin.[18]

An active Marxist since 1893, Lenin had come to believe that the belated growth in Russia of large-scale capitalist enterprise amid political and economic backwardness called for strategies somewhat different from those appropriate for western Europe. In 'Our Programme', probably written in 1899 at the end of a period of enforced exile in Siberia, Lenin appeared to return to a notion outlined by Marx nearly 50 years earlier – that a highly class-conscious, if numerically small proletariat, might speed the revolutionary transition to socialism by taking the lead in the antecedent struggle for bourgeois democracy. He writes

In the political struggle the workers do not stand alone. The people's complete lack of rights and the savage lawlessness of the bashi-bazouk [literally, Turkish mercenary soldiers not in uniform] officials rouse the indignation of all honest educated people who cannot reconcile themselves to the persecution of free thought and free speech; they rouse the indignation of the persecuted Poles, Finns, Jews and Russian religious sects; they rouse the indignation of the small merchants, manufacturers and peasants who can nowhere find protection from the persecution of officials and police. All these groups of the population are incapable, separately, of carrying on a persistent political struggle. But when the working class raises the banner of this struggle, it will receive support from all sides. Russian Social Democracy will place itself at the head of all fighters for the rights of the people, of all fighters for democracy and it will prove invincible.[19]

But such a prospectus required planning, organization, and, above all, leadership, and after serving his time in Siberia, Lenin devoted himself to the creation of a party that could lead Russia towards its socialist destiny.

His first priority was to found a journal to publicize his views on party organization, and in December 1900 he achieved his ambition

with the first edition of *Iskra* (The Spark). Published on thin cigarette
paper in Munich, Leipzig, and elsewhere, it was smuggled into the
great industrial centres of Russia and distributed by a network of agents.
Though Lenin shared the editorial board with Plekhanov, Axelrod, and
Zasulich, with whom he frequently disagreed, the first issues of the
journal reflected his thinking. They contained bitter denunciations of
'legal Marxism' and 'economism', as well as his ideas on party organization, later to be spelled out in his crucial essay, '*What is to be Done?*'
(1902).[20] Basically, he argued that in an autocracy like Russia, the
revolution required a clandestine party comprising a compact group of
militants agreed on first principles and their implementation, not a
large, amorphous and easily detectable organization with its inevitable
compromises and fudging of issues. As to its membership, Lenin argued
for a tightly knit, underground elite of dedicated and hardened professional revolutionaries possessing the cardinal military virtues of
obedience, loyalty and self-denial, and prepared to sacrifice everything
– family, friends, personal happiness and moral standards – for the
cause. As for those who fell short of what was required, Lenin showed
his own ruthless sense of dedication. 'The organization of real revolutionists will stop at nothing to rid itself of an undesirable member.'[21]

Though Lenin's text of 1902 on political organization was rooted in an
historically grounded and specifically Russian situation and addressed to
a particular Russian problem, i.e. how to create a viable party in an
authoritarian state, it also had wider implications. For, Lenin was already beginning to feel that 'economism' was not just a failing of Russian
Marxism, but had permeated the working class of western Europe,
impeding the growth of revolutionary class-consciousness. By implication, therefore, he was arguing that in western Europe, no less than
in Russia, there was need for a vanguard party with a considerable
leavening of revolutionarily inclined intellectuals to serve as the
advanced guard of a socialist transformation.

If some of his fellow Marxists may have disapproved of Lenin's
somewhat un-Marxist disdain for the working class and his preoccupation with the professional revolutionary, there was no mistaking his
identification with the Russian revolutionary tradition – in particular,
his debt to Pyotr Tkachev, one of the most zealous of the underground
Narodniks, who had declared three decades earlier, 'Neither now nor
in the future will the common people by its own power bring on a
social revolution. We alone, the revolutionary minority, can and should
do that as soon as possible.'[22] Where Tkachev had spoken of 'the
people', Lenin now substituted the words 'working class'.

The history of all countries shows us that the working class, exclusively by its own effort, is able to develop only trade union consciousness; i.e. it may itself realise the necessity for combining in unions to fight against the employers and to strive to compel the government to pass necessary labour legislation, etc. The theory of Socialism, however, grows out of the philosophical, historical and economic theories that were elaborated by the educated representatives of the propertied classes, the intellectuals. The founders of modern, scientific socialism, Marx and Engels, themselves belonged to the bourgeois intelligentsia[23]

To those people who held that Marxism was about extending democratic accountability, Lenin had a ready response. 'Only an incorrigible utopian would want a wide organization of workers, with elections, reports, universal suffrage, etc. under [tsarist] autocracy',[24] which meant, of course, that he was envisaging for the foreseeable future the cooption, not the election, of leaders (a proceeding which so appealed to Stalin, that Lenin's text of 1902 was made compulsory reading for Soviet students of Marxism-Leninism).

Lenin's departure from orthodox Marxism prepared the ground for the critical split that was to emerge in 1903 when Russia's Social Democrats attempted to reconstitute the party which had been stillborn in 1898. Meeting in a rat-infested warehouse in Brussels and then in a trade-union hall in London, the 40 or so disputatious 'delegates' (most of them 'professional revolutionaries') had, in effect, to adjudicate between the conflicting theories of the party's better known personalities as regards its constitution and leadership. Lenin wanted membership restricted to activist professional revolutionaries. His old friend and colleague on *Iskra*, Julius Martov, accepted that the political situation then obtaining in Russia made conspiratorial methods necessary, but did not agree that conditions of party membership need be so onerous, and his view carried the vote.

On the other hand, Lenin scored a narrow victory in the elections both to the editorial board of *Iskra* – now the official party organ – and to the Central Committee, and it was this slender advantage that earned for Lenin's faction the ascription 'Bolshevik' (the Russian for 'majority') and for Lenin's opponents, 'Menshevik' ('minority').[25] For some time, however, this was no hard and fast division, and one already celebrated Social Democrat, the political orator and trade union activist, Lev Davidovich Bronstein, better known as Trotsky, stayed aloof from both factions until 1917.[26] Indeed, since he had warned that Lenin's theory of organization would lead to a situation in which 'the Party is replaced by the organization of the Party, the organization by the Central Committee, and finally the Central Committee by the dictator',[27] the wonder is that Trotsky ever gravitated to Bolshevism.

Soon the divisions among Russia's Social Democrats had been overtaken by events. In 1904, the Tsar embarked on a costly and mismanaged war against Japan, and, for the first time, a basically European power found itself facing defeat at the hands of an Asian neighbour.

As the autocracy became increasingly discredited, Russia experienced the first general strike in its history, and, as tensions rose, Social Democrats joined with agrarian Social Revolutionaries, bourgeois liberals, progressive nobles, and clergy to plead for a parliamentary constitution. The regime's answer was to fire on a peaceful group of demonstrators who had come to petition the Tsar on 9 January 1905.[28] For many of the country's disaffected citizens, 'Bloody Sunday' was the last straw, and over the next few months Russia became the testing ground for the theorists of revolution. The towns were in turmoil, with strikes, demonstrations, and riots daily occurrences, while the countryside was ablaze with peasant risings and the burning and pillaging of the estates of the landed gentry. Meanwhile, a mutiny on the battleship *Potemkin* indicated the low state of morale in Russia's armed forces.

By the second half of the year, the government had been forced to concede a national parliament (*duma*), albeit with limited powers and on a restricted franchise. At the same time, it relaxed the censorship and allowed political parties openly to compete for popular support. The result was a burgeoning of public discussion and debate quite unprecedented in Russia. In the process, Bolshevik and Menshevik were able to establish in St. Petersburg rival daily newspapers to plead their respective causes.[29]

Ironically, the revolutionary upheaval had caught Russia's leading Social Democrats by surprise. Trotsky was one of the few to have been in the country since the start of the disturbances, and he used his formidable rhetorical and organizational skills, learned while a strike leader in Odessa in the 1890s, to help establish in St. Petersburg a soviet ('council') of workers' delegates and to publish a newspaper – *Izvestia*. The initiative for this and the many other proletarian parliaments that were to be set up in various parts of the country had come from the Mensheviks and the Social Revolutionaries (SR), while in the countryside the latter were active in encouraging peasant risings, conducting terror campaigns against officials and agitating for the nationalization of land.[30] Yet, Lenin – the man who had preached and organized for revolution since the early '90s – missed most of the action. Until November, he remained abroad in a vain attempt to undermine the Mensheviks and to secure a provisional revolutionary government through a Bolshevik-led insurrection.[31] By the time Lenin returned to Russia, the high tide of revolution had passed, but the first significant breaches in the ramparts of absolutism had been made, and the new situation seemed to demand a new strategy.

To begin with, much of *What is to be Done?* seemed curiously dated by the events of 1905. In the first place, the masses of workers and peasants, unbidden by any self-selected elite of professional revolutionaries, had amply demonstrated a capacity for revolutionary spontaneity. Secondly, with the increased opportunities for open organization, membership of the Russian Social Democratic Labour Party (RSDLP) had grown considerably, and the conception of an elitist, conspiratorial party was clearly going to be more difficult to sustain or justify. In the circumstances, Lenin qualified his earlier views of party organization. He now welcomed the party's enlargement to include tens of thousands of what he saw as revolutionary workers and accepted that conspiratorial forms must give way to the more open concept of 'democratic centralism',[32] in which Central Committee decisions, binding on all members, are preceded by free discussion among the membership.

Contrary to received opinion, 'democratic centralism' was not a Leninist invention. It had originated at a Menshevik conference in November 1905, during a discussion on political accountability.[33] But when Lenin insisted on its incorporation into the party's statutes at a congress in 1906 temporarily reuniting the two factions, he clearly envisaged it as being sufficiently flexible to enable a tilt in the balance between 'democracy' and 'centralism' as the need arose. On the other hand, his commendation in 1906 of the principle that 'all party functionaries must be elected, accountable to the party and subject to recall'[34] was as forthright as his condemnation in 1902 of democratic procedures in the conditions then obtaining. Indeed, until some four years after the revolution of 1917, Bolshevik organization maintained an element of accountability in fact, as well as in aspiration.

But the revolution of 1905 and its gradual extinction, after the failure in Moscow in December of an armed insurrection (which Lenin came to regard as a 'dress rehearsal' for the future revolution),[35] led him to a reappraisal of tactics. Though he agreed with the Mensheviks that the coming revolution would be 'bourgeois' in character, as in France in 1789, he held that the Russian bourgeoisie, with whom the Mensheviks favoured an alliance, had compromised too readily with absolutism and would, hence, be wholly unreliable in any revolutionary struggle. By contrast, the furious violence unleashed in the countryside had led him to a somewhat un-Marxist regard for the revolutionary potential of the peasantry and to a belief in the efficacy of a 'revolutionary-democratic dictatorship of the proletariat and the peasantry' in lieu of a 'bourgeois revolution'.[36] To Lenin's Menshevik opponents, the idea of a revolution bourgeois in social and economic form (in that it would promote capitalist development), but socialist in political form (in that it would be spearheaded by the RSDLP even though it included SRs) seemed a contradiction in terms, and they remained totally opposed to it.[37]

Over the next few years as the revolutionary impetus waned and the government's policy of 'pacification' of the revolutionary groups sent leading Social Democrats into jail or exile, Bolshevik and Menshevik failed to combine against the common enemy and drifted further apart. At the same time, serious fissures appeared within, as well as among, the warring Social Democratic factions. There were disagreements on, amongst other things, participation in the work of the *duma*; collaboration with other left-wing parties; and the efficacy and propriety of armed robberies, bank raids, extortion and marriages of convenience with wealthy heiresses to increase party funds.[38] In addition, there were the problems created by the clashes of abrasive personalities, some of whom seemed to regard their left-wing critics as even more inimical than the forces of the Tsar.

For example, when charged at a party tribunal in 1907 with having slandered the Menshevik leaders by accusing them of having 'sold out to the bourgeoisie', Lenin confessed: 'I purposely chose that tone calculated to evoke in the hearer hatred, disgust and contempt for the people who carry on such tactics. That tone, that formulation is not designed to convince, but to break the ranks, not to correct a mistake of the opponent but to annihilate him, to wipe him off the face of the earth'.[39] It seems that Lenin's former close colleague, Alexander Potresov, was right when he said of him, 'He could not bear any opinion different from his own. It was foreign to his nature to be just to someone with whom he was in bitter disagreement'.[40] Intolerance of criticism was, of course, a characteristic Lenin shared with his mentor, Marx, and not the least of their joint legacies was the especial vehemence injected into subsequent squabbles among Marxist–Leninists and the difficulties of reconciliation.

In 1912, Lenin decided both to unify his own organization and finalize the rift with the Mensheviks, and at a congress in Prague that year he constituted the Bolsheviks into a separate party with its own newspaper, *Pravda* (Truth) – which remains the official organ of the Soviet Communist Party today. It was a decision which angered not merely the Mensheviks, but also much of western European socialist opinion, since Lenin rejected all offers of mediation.[41] And when, in 1914, most of Europe's parliamentary socialists voted for war credits, the Bolsheviks felt further estranged.

On the other hand, the 'apostasy' of mainstream Marxism was Lenin's opportunity. It confirmed him in the view, forcefully expressed in *What is to be Done?*, that a handful of dedicated revolutionaries was worth more to the socialist cause than a mass of 'revisionist' workers or bourgeois intellectuals, and, of course, for Lenin, political rectitude was always much more important than popularity. Since, moreover, he was beginning to feel that a successful revolution in Russia would be contingent on the support of revolutionaries in the countries of advanced capitalism, he considered it imperative to organize for the revolutionary transformation of not just Russia, but the whole of western Europe. Hence his call for the restructuring of the international socialist movement.

But first he had to explain how it was that 'social patriotism', rather than 'world revolution', had emerged victorious in 1914. Studies of 'imperialism' by such Marxist theorists as Rosa Luxemburg, Rudolf Hilferding and Nikolai Bukharin, as well as by the British liberal economist J. A. Hobson seemed to provide the answer.[42] Imperialism, Lenin argued, was a relationship of inequality enabling states at the monopoly stage of capitalism, when financial interests predominate over the commercial, and the rate of return on domestic investment is low, to gain undue economic advantage from the export of capital to backward countries where 'profits are usually high, for capital is scarce, the price of land is relatively low, wages are low, raw materials are cheap'.[43] The effect was to divide the world, *de facto*, into various spheres of influence, making capitalism a world phenomenon, despite the uneven economic development of the various countries. But it also drew a wedge between the workers in the metropolitan countries and those in the colonial dependencies, the former benefiting at the expense of the latter. Hence the former's support of leaders who bribed them with the spoils of imperialism while betraying their real interests as proletarians.

But Lenin believed that as the coffins came home from the war their leaders had decided to support, the workers would realize they had been betrayed, and in their anger turn to revolution. From exile in Switzerland, he exhorted European socialists to turn the European war into a European civil war through a strategy of 'revolutionary defeatism'. By this he meant working for the defeat of all the belligerents through mutinies, desertions, strikes in munitions factories, and so forth. It was a policy which at first did not even have the wholehearted support of his own, now scattered party, let alone of the Social Democrats of Europe. And in a small gathering of antiwar socialists in the

Swiss village of Zimmerwald in September 1915, Lenin's strategy was rejected in favour of Trotsky's formula of a 'peace without annexations or war indemnities'.[44] Nevertheless, at the next antiwar conference in Kienthal, Switzerland in April 1916, Lenin's 'revolutionary defeatism' gained a measure of acceptance among socialists – Russian and non-Russian – who would later help to form the nucleus of a Third (Communist) International.[45] Meanwhile, his presentiment that the masses would grow to resent the war seemed well founded.

In France and Germany, left-wing socialists grew increasingly vocal in their opposition to the war, whilst in many parts of central and western Europe, periodic work stoppages in war-related industries were intensified as hostilities progressed.[46] But, of course, it was in Russia that 'revolutionary defeatism' had its greatest impact (even if some of its practitioners had never heard of the expression or, indeed, of the man who had coined it). Towards the end of 1915, there were conscription riots in several cities and attacks on the police, who did not have to serve.[47] In 1916, record casualties in a grossly mismanaged and unpopular war caused thousands of ill-trained, underfed peasant soldiers to desert from the front, while strikes hit many of the major towns.[48] But it was at the beginning of 1917 that the years of mounting discontent reached their revolutionary climax. Amid a series of military disasters and after two weeks of strikes in the capital, the Tsar was compelled to abdicate, and the autocracy collapsed on 15 March 1917.[49]

Once again, however, Lenin had been taken by surprise. Only six weeks before, he had sadly prophesied to an audience of young Swiss workers, 'We of the older generation may not live to see the decisive battles of this coming revolution'.[50] But this time he was not going to let nearly a year elapse before his return to Russia, and in the meantime, from his Swiss refuge, he followed with increasing satisfaction Russia's relapse into what seemed like anarchy.

For, whilst Russia was beginning to experience what a British eyewitness called 'the fullest democracy ever known',[51] politically the situation was confused. It was not at all clear, for example, where the real seat of authority lay. On the one hand, there was the provisional government, composed largely of former members of the *duma*, in which liberal and other centrist parties predominated. But there was also the revived Petrograd soviet of workers' and soldiers' deputies – most of them Social Revolutionaries or Mensheviks, the Bolsheviks being small in number, having played only a minor role in the downfall of tsarism.[52]

Nor was the situation made any easier when the soviet instructed all military units to obey its commands rather than those of the provisional government, and then, influenced by the Menshevik notion that the bourgeoisie must hold the reins of power for the time being, refrained from exercising the authority it claimed. Thus, when the provisional government announced that it intended to continue Russia's involvement in the war, the soviet did not immediately dissociate itself. Indeed, some of its Bolshevik members – among them Stalin and Kamenev – were quite prepared to continue hostilities to defend the new order against external threat.[53] But Lenin saw things differently, and in April he returned from exile (in a train sealed by courtesy of the German high command) and spelled out his ideas to a Party congress in Petrograd.

Though Lenin had originally been critical of the soviets when they sprang into existence in 1905, believing that their lack of disciplined organization could harm the revolutionary cause,[54] he had changed his mind. He now held that the soviets, consisting largely of politically inexperienced and untutored workers and peasants, would be more fertile ground for Bolshevik agitation than any parliament of experienced and committed politicians. And in his 'April theses'[55] he announced that capitalism could soon be replaced by a proletarian order if socialists denied support to the provisional government, which he believed to be the instrument of the bourgeois revolution, and helped strengthen the soviets in the capital and provinces. And to win mass support for the Bolsheviks, then a minority in virtually every soviet, he suggested the slogan, 'All power to the Soviets', and urged his supporters to adopt as their motto, 'Peace, Land, and Bread'.

In the meantime, the Mensheviks and Social Revolutionaries were being increasingly drawn into the work of the provisional government, and, in June, Lenin's call at the First All-Russian Soviet of Workers', Soldiers', and Peasants' Deputies for the government's overthrow was decisively rejected.[56] A further setback to Lenin's hopes occurred in July with the publication of documents purporting to 'prove' that he had been sent to Russia as a German agent and had the backing of the German general staff. Following a half-hearted insurrection against the provisional government, Alexander Kerensky, a Social Revolutionary who had succeeded to the premiership in July, took the opportunity to intern the Bolsheviks as defeatists and agents of the Germans.[57] As a result, Lenin fled to Finland, where his ardour for the soviets rapidly cooled. But the failure in August of a coup by the army commander-in-chief, General Kornilov, which the Bolsheviks helped to quell, led to a rise in their fortunes.

Amid mounting chaos, the provisional government lost its nerve, while the Bolsheviks, who had not always displayed that iron unity their leader demanded of them, became increasingly cohesive. Soon they were able to secure majorities in the Petrograd and Moscow soviets,[58] and towards the end of October Lenin slipped back into Russia, confident that the time for a revolutionary bid for power was fast approaching. In this he had the backing of all but two of the Bolshevik hierarchy,[59] as well as the assistance of a recent recruit to Bolshevism – Trotsky, then president of the Petrograd Soviet. His support was invaluable, as he was to prove himself an outstanding organizer of the military committee set up to prepare for the seizure of power.

Less than two and a half weeks after Lenin's return, armed Bolsheviks, enjoying the support of no more than 240,000 followers throughout the country,[60] started taking over key public buildings in Petrograd. There was little resistance, save from the Winter Palace, where the provisional government was besieged. But the cruiser *Aurora*, whose crew had gone over to the revolution, trained her guns on the nearby palace while the ratings stormed it. At 2 a.m. on 7 November 1917, the members of the provisional government, save for Kerensky, who had gone to seek in vain for reinforcements, were arrested and the Bolsheviks were installed. Lenin's victory had been almost bloodless.[61] There were reportedly even fewer casualties than in the making of Eisenstein's film reconstruction a decade later, but whether or not it had been a 'proletarian revolution', as Lenin claimed, is an issue still hotly debated among Marxists today. For socialists like Kautsky, what Lenin had wrought in Russia was no revolution Marxist-style, but a successful coup d'état in conditions of near anarchy.[62]

In *The State and Revolution*, written during his last days of exile, Lenin had outlined the kind of society supposed to emerge after the Bolshevik capture of power.[63] Here he speaks of introducing a 'dictatorship of the proletariat', defined as 'a state of the armed workers', which 'would create for the first time democracy for the people'. Though this would be no 'workers' paradise', it would give the working masses administrative responsibilities and end the exploitative private pursuit of profit, rent or interest. Though the instruments of coercion would be retained, they would be used only against 'counter-revolutionaries' – an ever dwindling minority as a communist order began to take shape. Such were Lenin's hopes, and though he knew that winning over the whole country to his vision of society would be difficult, he assumed that he would have the help of the advanced western European countries, whose imminent transition to socialism he believed assured. He was, of course, mistaken, and was soon left with a situation in Russia he neither anticipated nor wanted.

In the first place, though the November Revolution established Bolshevik rule in Petrograd and, shortly afterwards, in Moscow, much of the country continued to elude its control for some time. And the process of reincorporating much of the former Russian Empire was complicated by the self-determination of some of its nationalities and by the territorial sacrifices that had to be made at Brest-Litovsk in March 1918 as the price for peace with Germany. In fact, Finland was never reintegrated; eastern Poland, the Baltic states and Bessarabia did not return to Russia until the Second World War; and it was not until the early '20s that Bolsheviks (now calling themselves Communists) finally took charge of the Russian and Ukrainian countryside and of the Transcaucasian, central Asian and Far Eastern territories. In the intervening period, a bitterly fought civil war took a heavy toll of lives.

To add to the regime's troubles, there was military intervention from the USA, France, Britain, Japan, and at least 10 other countries, at first, ostensibly, to try to persuade Russia to continue the struggle against the Germans, and later, manifestly, to give encouragement to Lenin's enemies. At the same time, the Allied powers had instigated a blockade against Soviet Russia which was not to be lifted until 1920, when all but the Japanese decided to end their intervention.[64] A further difficulty lay in making viable a country devastated by world war and civil war, and one economically, politically and culturally retarded, compared to most other European states.

Under these circumstances, Lenin came to establish what scholars such as Leonard Schapiro believe he had intended all along – a Party dictatorship.[65] As justification, he used the tactic of identifying Communist Party and proletariat. 'Proletarian rule', in the form of 'the dictatorship of the proletariat', would be exercised through the party – the vanguard of the proletariat. In theory, therefore, whatever the Party did was right because it always acted in the interests of the workers. In practice, however, many workers in the Soviet Union and elsewhere suffered greatly under the 'dictatorship', for, soon the Party's leading officials could order the detention or destruction of those – no matter how long or devoted their service to communism – they chose to label as 'counter-revolutionary'.

The arrest of the provisional government on the day of the Bolshevik coup was an indication of what was to come. Within three days, the Soviet government had issued a decree curtailing freedom of the press, and from then on political power became increasingly concentrated.[66] A potential centre of opposition was destroyed in January 1918 when troops acting on Lenin's instructions forcibly dispersed the constituent assembly – Russia's first and only popularly elected parliament – after elections giving the Social Revolutionaries, with their massive support in the rural areas, an overall majority.[67] To Trotsky, Lenin confided, 'The dissolution of the constituent assembly by the Soviet government means a complete and frank liquidation of the idea of democracy by the idea of dictatorship. It will serve as a good lesson'[68] – though a lesson to whom, Lenin did not specify. Soon, after a brief coalition with left-wing Social Revolutionaries, he began to subject all opposition newspapers and parties to a process of slow strangulation. In the meantime, the old organs of local self-government – the *zemstvos* – were dissolved, and the soviets remodelled so as to be more amenable to Party control.[69]

Lenin's most notorious agency for forging his dictatorship was the Extraordinary Commission for Combating Counter-Revolution and Sabotage – better known as the Cheka. Created in December 1917, this was Lenin's secret police – the forerunner of the OGPU, the NKVD, the MVD and the KGB – modelled, to some extent, on the tsarist Okhrana. Designed to root out threats to the regime – real or imagined – and prepare for the show trials of prestigious opponents, the Cheka unleashed a wave of terror, which was to be intensified after an attempt on Lenin's life in August 1918. As the periodical *Red Sword* explained, 'To us everything is permitted, for we are the first in the world to raise the sword not for the purpose of enslavement and oppression but in the name of liberty and emancipation from slavery.'[70]

In the late spring of 1918, the 'dictatorship' moved to encompass economic as well as political life, as Lenin inaugurated 'War Communism'. Amid the exigencies of civil war and blockade, he accelerated the socialization of agriculture and industry, hoping to arrive at the classless society through military discipline and a spirit of self-sacrifice. In early June, the government set up 'committees of poor peasants' to 'carry the class war to the village' by fighting 'kulaks' (rich peasants), and to requisition grain to feed the towns. Subsequently, all the major industries were nationalized without compensation, with workers' committees taking over all managerial functions. And, in October, all private shops, both great and small, were closed and their merchandise confiscated.[71]

The effect of these measures on an economy already in the process of disintegration was disastrous. The peasants were embittered, and many chose to slaughter their cattle and burn their crops rather than yield their surpluses to a government which had tried originally to win their confidence by parcelling out the land. Though the 'committees of poor peasants' were abandoned in November 1918, the damage had been done. When troops were sent to force the villagers to deliver their grain, there were many armed uprisings, and thousands of peasants joined the counter-revolution.[72]

The disorganization of industry and domestic trade in the wake of government measures was no less catastrophic. As thousands of urban workers fled to the countryside to find food, hundreds of factories had to close, and many still in operation suffered because of the ineptitude of the new workers' committees. Before long, the authorities were forced to reappoint some of the former managers of these enterprises, albeit as state employees supervised by political functionaries.[73] But these doctrinaire experiments brought about neither economic recovery nor the desired social consciousness. And, by March 1921, when one of the bulwarks of Bolshevism – the sailors of Kronstadt – had deserted the cause, and mutinied, only to be gunned down on Trotsky's instructions,[74] Lenin decided to abandon 'War Communism'. To combat economic chaos and civil strife, it was necessary to make a temporary retreat from socialism on several fronts.

Internally the major change in 1921 was the introduction of Lenin's New Economic Policy (NEP).[75] This began with the abandonment of forced requisitioning of agricultural surpluses, in favour of a tax in kind set at a fixed percentage of production, the peasants being allowed to dispose of the remainder on the free market. A year later, peasants were permitted to lease land and hire labour. There was greater freedom, too, for the industrial sector. Though the 'commanding heights' of the economy – large-scale industry, transport, and the banks – remained state-owned, entrepreneurs with small industrial and trading concerns were permitted to resume operations. Trade unions, denied the right to strike under nationalization, were now allowed to advocate withdrawal of labour from private concerns. And foreign capitalists were invited to invest in the Soviet state. Though the NEP was not able to solve all the country's economic problems, it did help to secure a change in the country's fortunes. By the mid-1920s, production was again generally up to the best pre-war levels.

Yet, while this had been brought about by a considerable relaxation of the economic dictatorship, the political dictatorship was, if anything, further tightened. Having suppressed all opposition parties during the later stages of the civil war, Lenin set about prohibiting the formation of opposition groups within the ruling party itself. The 10th Party congress in 1921, which had authorized the NEP, also gave the Party authority to expel all those engaging in 'fractionalism'.[76] No longer were Party dissidents to be allowed to organize factions to campaign for the adoption of their views, even though such matters as national self-determination for the peoples of the Soviet Republic, the role of trade unions in a socialist society, and the dangers of 'bureaucratism' elicited deep divisions of opinion within the Party.

But the new ruling, by undermining the independent voice in the

Party's congress and Central Committee, further strengthened the role of the Politburo – the chief decision-maker in both Party and state. By the time of Lenin's death in January 1924, the central organs between them controlled a Party apparatus that was to keep in check all the professional and interest groups in the country. Henceforth, no social organization – not even the armed forces or the Church – could escape Party control.[77] But the retreat of 1921 was to affect not only domestic policy, but also external relations.

For some four years after the revolution, the Bolsheviks had tried to break with traditional foreign political ambition and the pursuit of national interest. They had refused to accept the established modes of diplomatic intercourse, rejected international law as an instrument of European bourgeois domination, and had repudiated the international agreements of their predecessors, including the debts and liabilities incurred. Likewise, they had no use for the League of Nations, and had revived the French Revolutionary technique of appealing to peoples over the heads of governments. As if to demonstrate the iniquities of the old diplomatic system, Lenin had thrown open the foreign office archives, published the secret treaties of the war years, and abolished diplomatic rank. And at Brest-Litovsk in March 1918, the Bolsheviks underlined their revolutionary approach by distributing political litera-ture from the train window to the assembled German officials.[78] Within a year, the Soviet leaders had set aside several million roubles in order to establish the Third (Communist) International, or Comintern, with a headquarters in Moscow, to train leaders, coordinate revolutionary activity and create throughout the world disciplined Communist parties along the Leninist model.[79] Nonetheless, even in the early years of the revolution, it became apparent that the traditional aims and methods of statecraft could not be abandoned altogether. After all, the Soviet state needed to be defended against the interventionists, while some accords with foreign powers would serve as a useful holding operation until Germany and the rest of Europe sustained a successful revolution.

Under the impact of events, however, Lenin began to take a more long-term view of foreign policy. By 1921, the country had survived its early tribulations and was no longer in a state of siege. Save for the Japanese, who remained in Sakhalin until 1925, the interventionists, together with their blockade, had gone. By contrast, the anticipated revolutionary tide seemed to be fast receding,[80] and, in June 1921, Lenin had to admit that capitalism had survived the first revolutionary advance. To meet the new situation, he was now to advocate adjust-ments in the policies both of the Soviet state and of the Comintern. The Comintern was to be prepared for the 'long haul', and the Foreign

Office to seek temporary agreements with capitalist powers in the interlude between 'inevitable' wars. This was the basis of Lenin's policy of
'cohabitation' (*sozhitel'stvo*) or 'coexistence' (*sosuchchestvovanie*) with
capitalism. Stalin was later to describe the new approach as building
'Socialism in one country', i.e. the creation of a strong, industrialized
socialist state in a non-socialist world (a concept that would have been
inconceivable to Marx).

Such dramatic changes in policy came as no surprise to those more
orthodox Marxists, such as Kautsky and Plekhanov, who had claimed
all along that Lenin's seizure of power was premature. But, for Lenin
himself, such adjustments were both painful and dispiriting, and
towards the end of his life, much of the optimism of his first few months
of office had gone. 'Russia', he was eventually led to confess, lacked
even the basic prerequisites for 'the building of a really new state
apparatus, one worthy to be called socialist'.[81] Too many of its 'revolutionaries' were 'Great power chauvinists with a Bolshevik veneer'.
Above all, 'powerful forces' were driving the revolution 'from its proper
road'.[82] Thus, in the eyes of its founder, the system had become little
more than a temporary and rather unhappy expedient. It is ironic,
therefore, that it should have been presented to the world as some kind
of model with Marxism-Leninism becoming widely regarded as the
'science' of how a communist society might be brought about.

NOTES

1. Moscow, Foreign Languages Publishing House, 1959.
2. *MESW*, pp. 584–622.
3. *MESW*, p. 429.
4. Quoted in R. Carew Hunt, *The Theory and Practice of Communism* (London, 1963), p. 76.
5. *MESW*, p. 645.
6. See, for example, James Joll, *Europe since 1870* (London, 1976), pp. 56–70.
7. His critique of Marxist orthodoxy is explored in J. Braunthal, *History of the Inter-national 1864–1914* (London, 1966). ch. 18.
8. *Evolutionary Socialism* (London, 1963), p. 199.
9. On the ideological and political rifts in the First International, see Braunthal, ch. 12–15.
10. See David Childs, *Marx and the Marxists* (London, 1973), pp. 46–60.
11. See, for example, C. Schorske, *German Social Democracy: 1905–1917* (Cambridge, Mass., 1955).
12. Bertram D. Wolfe, *An Ideology in Power* (London, 1970), pp. 99–100.
13. The extent of Russia's backwardness is traced in Alec Nove, *Political Economy and Soviet Socialism* (London, 1979), ch. 2.
14. The Russian revolutionary tradition is explored in Abraham Yarmolinsky, *Raod to Revolution* (London, 1957).
15. Lionel Kochan, *The Making of Modern Russia* (London, 1963), pp. 201–4.

16. James Mavor, *An Economic History of Russia* (London, 1925), p. 386.
17. For an analysis of the differences within the Russian Social Democratic movement, see, for example, David Shub, *Lenin: A Biography* (London, 1966), pp. 55–60.
18. L. Schapiro, *The Communist Party of the Soviet Union* (London, 1960), p. 146.
19. *Selected Works* (London, 1969), p. 36 (hereafter referred to as *LSW*).
20. Quoted in Helmut Gruber, *International Communism in the Era of Lenin* (New York, 1967), pp. 25–34.
21. Ibid., p. 38.
22. Quoted in Shub, p. 73.
23. From *What is to be Done?* quoted in Gruber, p. 27.
24. Ibid., p. 33.
25. See Shub, pp. 78–83.
26. For an explanation, see Leon Trotsky, *My Life* (New York, 1960).
27. From *Our Political Tasks*, quoted in E. H. Carr, *The Bolshevik Revolution 1917–23* (London, 1950), vol. i, p. 33.
28. Edward Crankshaw, *The Shadow of the Winter Palace* (London, 1976), pp. 337–43.
29. Shub, pp. 98–104.
30. See Crankshaw, pp. 317–19.
31. Shub, pp. 99–103.
32. Michael Waller, *Democratic Centralism: An Historical Commentary* (Manchester, 1981), p. 23.
33. Ibid., pp. 21–2.
34. Ibid., p. 23.
35. Shub, p. 106.
36. He elaborates this theory at length in 'Two Tactics of Social Democracy', *LSW*, pp. 50–147.
37. See H. Seton-Watson, *The Pattern of Communist Revolution* (London, 1960), pp. 26–7.
38. Shub, pp. 122–31.
39. Ibid., p. 117.
40. Quoted in ibid., p. 74.
41. E. H. Carr, *The Bolshevik Revolution 1917–23* (London, 1950), vol. i, pp. 63–5.
42. V. G. Kiernan, *Marxism and Imperialism* (London, 1974), esp. ch. 1.
43. From *Imperialism, the Highest Stage of Capitalism*, *LSW*, pp. 169–263.
44. B. Lazitch and M. M. Drachkovitch, *Lenin and the Comintern* (Stanford, 1972), vol. i, pp. 12–13.
45. G. Nollau, *International Communism and World Revolution* (London, 1961), pp. 35–6.
46. See. J. Braunthal, *In Search of the Millennium* (London, 1945), pp. 207–8, and Joll, pp. 225–6.
47. H. Rogger, *Russia in the Age of Modernisation and Revolution 1881–1917* (New York, 1983), p. 260.
48. Bertram Wolfe, pp. 126–37.
49. See Kochan, pp. 240–4.
50. N. K. Krupskaya, *Reminiscences of Lenin* (Moscow, 1959), p. 335.
51. Robert Bruce-Lockhart in a BBC broadcast, 'Russia 1917: The Bolshevik Triumph' (12 November 1957).
52. In fact, the majority of Bolshevik leaders were either abroad or in Siberian exile when the March Revolution occurred. See Shub, p. 205.
53. Ibid., pp. 206–8.
54. Ibid., p. 102.
55. Quoted in ibid., pp. 221–3.
56. Ibid., pp. 229–35.
57. Ibid., ch. 11.
58. Kochan, p. 250.
59. Kamenev and Zinoviev. See Carr, vol. i, p. 94.

60. Lenin's own estimate in 'Can the Bosheviks Retain State Power?' written on the eve of the Bolshevek Revolution; *LSW*, p. 380.
61. Carr, vol. I, pp. 98–9.
62. See, for example, his anti-Leninist diatribe: *The Dictatorship of the Proletariat*, written in 1918 and trans. H. J. Stenning (Manchester, 1920).
63. *LSW*, pp. 264–351.
64. Donald Treadgold, *Twentieth Century Russia* (Chicago, 1959), pp. 165–87.
65. See, for example, L. Schapiro, *The Origins of the Communist Autocracy* (London, 1955).
66. Shub, pp. 310–13.
67. Ibid., pp. 314–27.
68. Ibid., pp. 327–8.
69. See, for example, M. Liebman, *Leninism under Lenin* (London, 1975).
70. Quoted in Shub, p. 368.
71. Ibid., p. 368.
72. Ibid., p. 370.
73. Treadgold, pp. 164–5.
74. Shub, pp. 405–11.
75. Kochan, pp. 271–3.
76. Ibid., pp. 275–6.
77. The concentration of power in the central organs of the party is traced in Carr, vol. I, ch. 8–9.
78. G. Kennan, *Russia and the West under Lenin and Stalin* (New York, 1961), p. 45.
79. Carr, vol. III, ch. 25–26.
80. Ibid., ch. 30.
81. Better fewer, but Better, in *LSW*, p. 701.
82. For an elaboration of Lenin's doubts, see Louis Fischer, *The Life of Lenin* (London, 1965), pp. 578–88 and 634–71.

3. The Comintern

At one time, it would have seemed inconceivable that one of the most authoritarian and backward countries in Europe could become, for many, the hub of world socialism, securing from the international movement a degree of control and discipline unprecedented since medieval Christendom. For, the Marxist dialectical pattern required socialism to spring from the loins of advanced capitalism, spread from one advanced country to another, and generate the free exchange of ideas – at least among socialists. And it seemed to defy both the logic of Marxism and common sense that some of western Europe's querulous socialists, noted for their attachment to democratic procedures, discussion, and debate should willingly subject themselves to the dictates of those whose concept of socialism bore the unmistakable imprint of the despotism from which it emerged. Nonetheless, for years after November 1917, the Soviet Union and its leadership retained the respect, admiration, and unquestioning loyalty of millions of socialist activists and sympathizers throughout the world. How was it achieved?

In the first place, there was the sheer dramatic impact of the revolution, combined with the astonishing audacity of its agenda. That such a large country had fallen so easily to such a small body of dedicated men was remarkable in itself. That the self-selected elite now presiding over one of the world's most backward countries claimed to be holding power in trust for the world's most progressive forces was breathtaking in its effrontery. Nonetheless, a potent political myth had been created that was to captivate not only many Marxists, but also a substantial number of non-Marxists who had become thoroughly disillusioned with a system which had produced four years of seemingly senseless warfare. To Marxist and non-Marxist alike, the events in Russia appeared to give promise of a better tomorrow.

To Marxists more interested in revolutionary practice than in theories of historical determinism, Lenin seemed to offer the benefits of a new civilization and a blueprint for eradicating the evils of existing society. Furthermore, his faith in the spread of the revolutionary impulse appeared amply justified, not least in view of the upheavals that had occurred in Russia's vicinity even before Lenin's seizure of power. For, the Japanese victory over the Russians in 1905 had given the anti-imperialist movement in Asia a boost, as had the nationalist revolutions in countries such as Turkey (1908), Persia (1909) and China (1911), while the anti-colonial revolts in the wake of the outbreak of war in 1914 seemed to imperil the whole concept of western imperialism, which, in Lenin's view, had temporarily stabilized European capitalism.

Meanwhile, developments in the European heartland appeared to enhance prospects for revolutionary advance. Many of the Social Democrats who had originally approved the vote for war credits were becoming increasingly restive, and as people tired of mounting casualties, food shortages and spiralling prices, their discontent sometimes took the form of strikes and mutinies. Significantly, when an anti-war protester assassinated Austria's prime minister, Count Stürgkh, in October 1916, there was almost as much sympathy for the assailant as for his victim,[1] while, in April 1917, Germany appeared to take a step towards revolution as a disaffected minority of socialists formed themselves into the Independent Social Democratic Party (USPD), encompassing the revolutionary Spartacus group.[2] Named after the celebrated slave revolutionary of Roman times, it was led by Rosa Luxemburg – whose writings and exploits on behalf of revolutionary democracy had been acclaimed for more than two decades – and Karl Liebknecht, the first German deputy to vote against the renewal of war credits. With the European conflagration having clearly radicalized many of Europe's soldiers and civilians even before the Bolshevik revolution, Lenin's prospectus for the European proletariat appeared, to many, to be as feasible as it was desirable.

Events, moreover, seemed to be playing into the Bolsheviks' hands. The antiwar and anti-imperialist propaganda accompanying their calls to revolution soon began to produce results. Clearly, not a few of the two million or more Germans, Austrians, and Hungarians on strike in early 1918 were in sympathy with Bolshevism,[3] while Berlin's Revolutionary Shop Stewards were manifestly trying to prevent the German government from imposing punitive peace terms on revolutionary Russia.[4] And, as Germany's own defeat was in prospect, the country found itself in the grip of a political convulsion reminiscent of the Russian revolution of March 1917.[5] It began with a naval mutiny in Kiel on 30 October 1918, and within hours, sailors, soldiers and workers had seized control of most of the German Baltic ports and established councils on the Soviet model. Soon red flags flew over the town halls of most north German cities. On 9 November the turmoil spread to Berlin, where Kaiser Wilhelm II, having lost the support of his now thoroughly demoralized troops, was forced to follow his cousin, the late Tsar, into abdication. By nightfall, the Social Democrats were vying with the Spartacists for leadership of the German revolution – a Social Democratic republic having been proclaimed from the Reichstag, and a Soviet Germany having been promulgated from the Imperial Palace a mile away.[6]

While the restructuring of German society was in prospect, the country's main wartime ally, Austria-Hungary, was disintegrating, as the Habsburg Empire's Polish, Czech, Slovak, Croat, Slovene, and other subject peoples sought their own political destiny. Soon, what had been a coherent administrative and economic entity was parcelled out to Poland, Czechoslovakia, Yugoslavia, Romania, Italy, and Hungary itself, while Austria remained but a tiny rump of a country. Mutually antagonistic and generally unstable as these new or reconstituted states were, they appeared to offer ample scope for Soviet penetration.

But the potential for political upheaval was not confined to the defeated countries of Europe or their territorial successors. There were disaffected elements, too, among the victorious powers – even in Britain, where the authorities had responded to left-wing agitation by bringing tanks on to the streets of London and surrounding Glasgow with troops.[7] Nor was neutral Switzerland spared the contagion of discord and disaffection that was infecting virtually every other European country after years of warfare.[8] Meanwhile, short-lived, Soviet-style regimes had been established in Finland, Latvia, Lithuania, Estonia, the Ukraine and Byelorussia – each in the process of detaching itself from the Russian Empire.[9] By the end of 1918, moreover, Communist parties along Leninist lines had been established in several other countries. Already, therefore, many were regarding Lenin as the man who could give practical application to Marxism and hasten the world revolutionary process.

More surprisingly, perhaps, Lenin also had devotees outside the Marxist fraternity. For, there were non-Marxists for whom the Russian revolution had become a 'fashionable cause', to be regarded with the same kind of indulgence as many were later to show towards such countries as Cuba and Vietnam. After all, whatever its faults, the Bolshevik regime had extricated itself from a war that was none of its making, and, by comparison, seemed, to many, less unattractive than the failed autocracy of tsarism or the flawed and faltering democracy under Kerensky. Moreover, despite the country's current difficulties, its well-educated and cosmopolitan leader appeared to have the self-confidence, drive, and ability to put through a programme that would, at least, modernize the country. And the perception that Russia's new rulers might hold the key to the development of an underdeveloped society was already beginning to arouse interest in Leninist theory and practice among non-Western intellectuals.

Amid the fund of foreign goodwill towards the new regime, there was also much concern for its future. And, as the powers launched their intervention and blockade in support of the counter-revolution within Russia itself, many sympathetic to Bolshevism tried to render practical assistance. In Britain, for example, there was strong trade-union support for a 'Hands-off Russia' campaign, with dockers refusing to load ships carrying munitions for the interventionist forces, and disaffected soldiers, impatient for demobilization, forming soviets at the ports of Glasgow and Belfast, and in mechanical depots such as Grove Park, near London.[10] In France, 26 warships and the war-weary troops of 14 regiments refused orders to go into action against the infant Soviet regime.[11] Similar displays of solidarity with the Bolsheviks were to occur in most of the other western European countries and also in North America, where many recent immigrants retained the radicalism that had forced their flight from tsarist Russia in the first place.[12]

If some of the enthusiasm for the new regime stemmed from ideological commitment, much of it, too, was based on a mystique, which, in turn, rested on widespread ignorance of Bolshevism and its background. After all, comparatively few foreigners were familiar with the language, culture or history of Russia, or with the peculiarities of Russian Marxism, while the difficulties of communicating with the country during the intervention and blockade ensured that outsiders remained largely uninformed regarding the current situation. For the beleaguered regime, an ill-informed foreign public was a mixed blessing. On the one hand, the sympathizers were receptive to the favourable accounts accorded developments in Russia by western correspondents such as John Reed,[13] M. Philips Price, and Arthur Ransome,[14] who shielded their readers (and, to some extent, themselves) from some of the painful realities of the system – including the terror, the lack of a viable economic strategy and the mounting opposition among former supporters.

On the other hand, Bolshevism's opponents were given free rein to exercise their imaginations on the iniquities of the regime, safe in the knowledge that their allegations would be difficult to disprove. The claims, for example, that Lenin was a paid German agent, or at the hub of a Jewish conspiracy to dominate the world, surfaced early, to be followed by lurid tales of women treated as common property in accordance with the 'new morality' propagated by the Bolsheviks.[15] And, of course, such allegations merely served to intensify the apprehensions of those already alarmed by what they understood as the Bolshevik prospectus – the destruction of all established political and economic systems. In this sense, lack of an informed perspective on the situation in Soviet Russia played into the hands of those anxious to liquidate 'the Bolshevik conspiracy' by any means.

But, for Lenin, the mere counting of heads on either side of the barricades was no reliable guide to the future of the revolution. For, within Russia, its fate had depended not on numbers, but on organization, leadership, doctrine and dedication, and Lenin concluded that these must also determine the destiny of the revolution abroad. For, though, as a Marxist, he believed that the ultimate success of world revolution was assured, he had still not lost his earlier mistrust in the revolutionary credentials of the working class. In any case, he had seen too many setbacks to the revolutionary process, both in his own country and throughout Europe. Interminable wrangles and the lack of international solidarity in time of war had destroyed the first two Internationals, and, after hearing of the 'betrayal' of socialism on the outbreak of war in 1914, he had devised a plan for a Third International which was to be much more centralized and disciplined than its predecessors:

> The Second International is dead, overcome by opportunism. Down with opportunism and long live the Third International . . . To the Third International falls the task of organizing the proletarian forces for the revolutionary onslaughts against the capitalist governments, for civil war against the bourgeoisie of all countries, for the capture of political power, for the triumph of socialism.[16]

Though his call – made public in November 1914 – was to receive qualified support from the so-called 'Zimmerwald Left', a small revolutionary faction among Europe's anti-war socialists,[17] it had made little headway elsewhere. Once in power, however, Lenin had both the authority and the resources to attain his objective, and within days of taking office he had begun to work towards this end.

Believing a Third International both politically and morally imperative, Lenin and his fellow Bolsheviks began to act as if it had already attained *de facto* existence on the inauguration of the Soviet state. To them, Petrograd was not the capital of a national state but the staff headquarters of the revolutionary proletariat, and Russia was destined to merge into some European or worldwide federation of socialist republics. This was a conception which, like so many other Leninist concepts proclaiming as fact things existing only in idea, had important practical consequences. It meant, firstly, that people of any nationality prepared to profess ideological loyalty and class solidarity with Bolshevism could regard themselves as citizens of the Soviet Republic; secondly, that, by the same token, any Bolshevik was entitled to see himself as a citizen of a much wider socialist world; and, thirdly, that there was little or no place for the customary procedures of diplomacy and statecraft.

The new People's Commissar for Foreign Affairs, Trotsky, expected to have little more to do than 'issue a few revolutionary proclamations to the peoples of the world and then shut up shop',[18] and during his brief tenure of office he remained largely true to his word. Beyond replacing most of the leading Russian envoys abroad with dedicated Bolsheviks, publishing the secret treaties of previous governments, selling off the contents of the diplomatic bags which arrived full of costly personal gifts from abroad, and taking charge of the protracted negotiations leading to the onerous Treaty of Brest-Litovsk,[19] he largely eschewed foreign policy. Under Trotsky, the Commissariat of Foreign Affairs (Narkomindel) was concerned less with diplomacy than with fomenting revolution abroad and establishing, *de jure*, the Third International.

Working closely with Lenin and the Party's Central Committee, and Stalin at the Commissariat of Nationalities, Narkomindel organized the indoctrination, recruitment and financing of foreign nationals for a variety of tasks. Some were recruited into the Russian Bolshevik Party and into the Red Army, now regarded as the international army of the world proletariat. Others, including prisoners of war and migrant workers, were sent back to their countries of origin to distribute revolutionary literature, act as couriers and informants, make contact with sympathetic political groups, form Communist parties and work for the overthrow of bourgeois or feudal rule. Still others remained in Moscow to form the nucleus of an international Communist apparatus. Divided into sections, each claiming to 'represent' its people, it was a Comintern Executive in embryo and was to play a considerable role in organizing and staffing the 'independent' Soviet-style governments of the Ukraine, Byelorussia, Latvia, Lithuania, Estonia, and the eastern borderlands and beyond which were enjoying a short-lived existence in the wake of the Red Army's advance.[20]

Just how close was the connection between the Russian Communist Party (Bolsheviks) and these 'independent' governments is attested by a Soviet account of the formation in December 1918, of the White Russian (Byelorussian) Soviet Socialist Republic under local party chief A. F. Myasnikov – an Armenian by birth.

Comrade Stalin informed Myasnikov of the decision of the Central Committee of the Communist Party about the foundation of a White Russian Soviet
Socialist Republic and summoned [him] to Moscow . . . The instructions of
Comrade Stalin . . . formed the basis of the construction of the White Russian Soviet Socialist Republic and Communist Party and guided the Bolsheviks of White Russia in their struggle against bourgeois White nationalists.
The government of the White Russian Soviet Socialist Republic was to consist
of 15 persons. Comrade Stalin also concerned himself with the personal
recruitment of those concerned.[21]

The creation of a Soviet Communist Republic in the neighbouring
Ukraine, in March 1919, followed much the same pattern, save that
Moscow's first appointee as leader of the new government was at least
a Ukrainian by birth. On the other hand, his credentials as spokesman
for the Ukrainian nation were not very substantial, and he was, in any
case, soon to be replaced by a Bolshevik of Romanian origin, with a
cabinet predominantly Great Russian in spirit and training and hostile
to the use of Ukrainian as an official language.[22]

But Narkomindel was equally active promoting revolution and
advancing the cause of the Third International beyond the Soviet orbit.
Trotsky and Grigori Vasilevich Chicherin, who became Commissar for
Foreign Affairs in the spring of 1918, dispatched prominent Bolsheviks
as 'ambassadors' to countries selected for their revolutionary potential.
Their brief was to make converts for the cause and, in effect, subvert
the governments to which they were accredited. Once established,
they would acquire staffs whose expertise in propaganda, agitation,
espionage, and sabotage were at least equal to their more conventional
diplomatic skills. A sympathetic observer has described the work of
Adolf Abramovich Ioffe, who held the key post of Ambassador to
Berlin between April and November 1918:

Acting in perfect bad faith – he admitted it in January 1919 – he worked
assiduously against the Imperial government. More than ten Left Social
Democratic newspapers were directed and supported by the Soviet Embassy
in the German capital. The embassy bought information from officials in
various German ministries and passed it on to radical leaders for use in
Reichstag speeches, in workers' meetings, and in the press. Anti-war and
anti-government literature was sent to all parts of the country and to the
front. Tons of literature were printed and clandestinely distributed by Ioffe's
office . . . Leaders of the German Independents discussed most matters of
revolutionary tactics with Ioffe, who was an experienced conspirator. In a
radio message dated December 15, 1918, broadcast by Ioffe to the revolutionary Soviets of Germany, he admitted having paid 100,000 marks for the
purchase of arms for the revolutionists and announced that he had established
in Germany a 10,000,000 ruble fund for the support of the revolution.[23]

Ioffe's clandestine activities may have been especially frenetic since Lenin and his fellow Bolsheviks still expected the revolutionary headquarters to be transferred to Berlin. Yet some of his fellow 'ambassadors' were scarcely less industrious. For, they were all charged with encouraging dissidence, disruption and disaffection abroad; organizing and distributing Bolshevik propaganda; creating Bolshevik movements; building up bureaux and agencies of trusties and sympathizers, and collecting and utilizing information relevant to the revolutionary cause. Moreover, to ensure that they honoured their revolutionary obligations, Lenin kept in regular contact. And, from December 1917, when his government resolved that 'the sum of two million roubles shall be placed at the disposal of the foreign representatives of the Commissariat of Foreign Affairs for the needs of the Revolutionary Internationalist Movement',[24] there was never any shortage of funds. As Lenin wrote to the Italian Socialist Angelica Balabanov in Stockholm, on behalf of the nascent Third International: 'The work you are doing is of the utmost importance . . . Do not consider the cost. There is plenty of money at our disposal'[25] – money which would be made available either through the diplomatic bag or by means of special couriers.

Thus, well before its *de jure* existence, the structure of the Comintern could already be seen in outline. But it would be some time before it would become a pliant tool of Soviet foreign policy. For, the Bolshevik Party was itself not yet monolithic, and the line conveyed through its envoys, unofficial agents, couriers, conference and congresses, press releases, pamphlets and personal contacts was not always consistent or clear. Moreover, since many foreign adherents had arrived at their political position independently of Soviet prompting, bringing to their Bolshevism a political culture different from that of Soviet Russia, they had not yet learned the habit of obedience and were not infrequently at odds with Moscow.

In the long run, perhaps the most significant disagreements involved the passionate Polish revolutionary Rosa Luxemburg, who had moved on to Germany to become the leading intellectual of the socialist Left. Though, like Lenin, she had fought tirelessly against what she saw as the iniquities of capitalism, she also firmly believed in democratic accountability and freedom of choice, and, like Marx, she regarded revolution as a product of spontaneous mass action.[26] As such, she found Lenin's fetish for organization and discipline repugnant and all too reminiscent of the German trade-union bureaucrats and reformist parliamentarians who made their careers out of the Social Democratic Party machine. As it happens, she had been at one with Lenin in viewing the war in 1914 as a consequence of imperialist rivalries, and in appealing to the workers everywhere to oppose it.

About the Russian Revolution, however, she had serious misgivings. On the one hand, she believed, as against Kautsky, that a revolutionary situation did obtain in Russia in 1917 and that Lenin had been right, therefore, to take power. On the other hand, having years before chided Lenin for proposing to confine Social Democracy to a 'bureaucratic straitjacket' and 'immobilise the movement and turn it into an automaton manipulated by a Central Committee',[27] she had the gravest doubts about how he would behave once in office, and, in a pamphlet written shortly before her untimely death in 1919, she took a generally critical view. She deplored what she perceived as a lack of socialist principle in his handling of the peasantry, in his espousal (no matter how disingenuous) of national self-determination and in his forcible dispersion of the Constituent Assembly. And, in her strictures against Lenin's system of government after the revolution, she proved strangely prophetic:

> Freedom restricted to the supporters of a government, freedom only for the members of one party, however numerous, is no sort of freedom. Freedom is always and only the freedom of those who think differently . . . Without the right of free speech, the life of public institutions will wither away, become a shadow and a masquerade and only bureaucracy will remain as the active component. Public life will gradually become anaesthetised while a few dozen leaders with unquenchable energy and boundless idealism direct, a dozen of the best brains rule and a working class elite is assembled in official meetings from time to time to applaud speeches of the leaders, to vote unanimously for resolutions put before them . . . Under such conditions public life will take on a new savagery and will lead to political assassinations, the shooting of hostages, and so on.[28]

Perhaps her apprehensions might have been eased had Lenin been prepared to countenance, among the wider revolutionary fraternity, approaches to the conquest and maintenance of power he was loath to admit at home. But he was not. By the second half of 1918, when he was satisfied that 'we have never been so near to world proletarian revolution as we are now',[29] he was calling for the Bolshevik revolution to be regarded not simply as a pioneering venture, but as a blueprint. In a diatribe against Karl Kautsky, whom he had regarded as a reliable interpreter of Marxism until the 'betrayal' of 1914, he claimed that 'Bolshevism has created the ideological and tactical foundations of a Third International, of a really proletarian and Communist International . . . Bolshevism can serve as a model for all.'[30] Lenin's insistence on prescribing Bolshevik 'solutions' for a variegated world went totally against Rosa Luxemburg's convictions and, despite her own deep differences with Kautsky and the doyens of the Second International, she was unwilling to contemplate the immediate creation of a Third International. One political colleague recalls her as saying, 'Founding it now would be premature. The Communist International should be definitively established only when, in the course of the revolutionary mass movement gripping nearly all the countries of Europe, Communist parties have sprung up'.[31] It was her view that the situation was not yet ripe and that the formation of a Communist International in the absence of mass revolutionary action could result only in a centralized institution organized along Leninist lines.

Though Rosa Luxemburg's stand against Lenin was sufficiently powerful to have led Communist circles to ban her writings throughout the Stalinist period and beyond, she never lived to see her worst fears regarding the Third International confirmed. Tragically, in mid-January 1919, she and her colleague, Karl Liebknecht, were murdered by a *Freikorps* of ex-officers and NCO's, after taking part in a week-long Berlin insurrection she had considered ill-advised, on behalf of a party – the Communist Party of Germany (KPD) – whose designation she had originally opposed in view of its associations with Moscow.[32]

In retrospect, her death can be seen as a symbol of the fate of the revolution for which both she and Lenin, in their different ways, had been striving. The Soviet leaders had failed to appreciate the differences between Russia in 1917 and Germany a year later. In contrast to the situation in Russia, the old organs of German administration remained intact; the non-revolutionary Left had taken over the government and been confirmed in office at a free election, while the Communists had remained a small party lacking both mass support and Lenin's conviction that such a minority movement could and should seize power. Though other attempts at Communist risings soon followed – most seriously in Munich, on 17 April, when, after a failed attempt at revolution by the non-Communist Left, the Communists began a two-week reign in which they armed the workers, nationalized the banks, expropriated a number of large estates, and proclaimed solidarity with Moscow, 'where happiness is, where the sun has risen' – the Freikorps put these down as easily as they had the January insurrection in Berlin.[33] Germany's Communists, it seemed, could win neither an election nor an armed struggle.

As in Germany, the revolutionary drive in its neighbours appeared to lose impetus or change direction altogether. Once again, false hopes had been pinned on false analogies. In Hungary, for example, where a Social Democratic government had taken control in most difficult circumstances – in the aftermath of defeat, occupation, and a punitive peace – the prime minister, Count Michael Károlyi, was seen as another Kerensky.[34] Faced with often violent opposition from both Right and Left, and pressurized by predatory neighbouring nations he was finding it increasingly difficult to govern, and when, in February 1919, he arrested several Communist leaders after a half-hearted attempt at an insurrection, some compared it to the 'July days' in Petrograd in 1917, when the Bolshevik revolution was only a little over three months away.

But Hungary was not Russia. Though its social structure had certain similarities, with its powerful landowning class, small proletariat and politically conscious intelligentsia, it was different. If, like Russia, it had once been part of a vast multi-ethnic empire, it was now a small, landlocked and relatively homogeneous state. Moreover, unlike Russia, Hungary lacked a revolutionary tradition, and its tiny Communist Party, many of whose leaders were Jews who had learned their Marxism in Russia as prisoners of war, tended to be regarded as alien to the country. More importantly, the Party chief, Béla Kun, who had formed a coalition with left wing Social Democrats in March 1919, was certainly no Lenin, and his Soviet Republic was undermined from the start by external as well as internal opposition.[35]

The western allies remained committed to the support of the succession states – Romania, Czechoslovakia, and Yugoslavia – with territorial claims on Hungary, while the government's lack of unity and incompetence merely compounded its unpopularity. It alienated the peasants by refusing them the land the Social Democrats had originally promised them. It alienated the Catholics by its uncompromising attitude to religion. It alienated the workers by its economic austerity and unparalleled political terror. Deprived of the military assistance proffered when the Soviet state was on the advance, and in the face of a Romanian intervention backed by the western Allies, the Hungarian Soviet Republic collapsed after 133 days, amid a general revulsion for Communism that was to span the generations. By the end of 1919, any revolutionary spirit that survived in Hungary was to be channelled into a movement acutely hostile to Communism – National Socialism.

In the meantime, Kun's hopes of expanding the revolution abroad had met an equally decisive rebuff. An attempt to establish in northern Yugoslavia a 'Soviet Republic of Baranya' had been no more successful than other efforts at revolution in Slovenia, Croatia and Serbia. A 'Soviet Republic of Slovakia', which had appeared in the wake of a Hungarian military advance, had disappeared after the Hungarian retreat. And the revolution in Austria, which had been an urgent priority for Kun, was stillborn. Hungarian-inspired uprisings in mid-April and mid-June had failed to dislodge the ruling coalition of Austrian Social Democrats and the left-inclined Christian Social Party not least because few of Austria's miniscule Communist Party would agree to support actions they perceived as ill-judged and ill-prepared.[36]

The fate of the revolution in countries of such strategic significance at such a crucial period in history was to have a critical effect on the Bolsheviks' twin ideological struggle – against capitalism and against Social Democracy. Yet, neither in Moscow, nor in the anti-Bolshevik capitals of the West were people drawing the requisite conclusions – that the prospects for revolution in Europe were no better than Soviet Russia's ability to promote it. Instead, Lenin continued to insist, even after one foreign Communist débâcle after another, that 'the social revolution is moving forward day by day, hour by hour', and it would be some time before western statesmen lost the fear, which surfaced at the peace conference at Versailles, that 'Bolshevism is gaining ground everywhere'.[37]

Amid these exaggerated expectations and apprehensions, Lenin issued the summons he had been contemplating for nearly four and a half years, calling on 'all parties opposed to the Second International' to attend a conference in Moscow with a view to establishing a Third International. The invitation, broadcast on 24 January 1919, had become a matter of urgency following a call by the British Labour Party for the revival of the Second International, but it also came less than a month after the foundation of the German Communist Party, which was expected to provide the essential nucleus of an international Communist organization. Signed on behalf of the Russian Communist Party and several other pro-Communist groups, it named 39 political organizations as eligible to attend – all but one of them based in Europe – and at the beginning of March 1919 more than 50 'delegates' accepted the invitation.[38]

If the congress had met at a more propitious time the outcome might well have been different. For, many of the parties called to attend had emerged out of a left-wing tradition which, for all its internationalism, reflected certain national preoccupations and styles. As it was, however, the conference took place when Soviet Russia was at its most isolated, and this inevitably affected the attendance and, hence, the general tenor of the meeting. For with Kolchak's White offensive approaching the Volga, and Bolshevik territory largely cut off by the intervention, it was difficult for foreign sympathizers to obtain the necessary accreditation and transportation to participate – all of which prevented the congress from being representative.

Undaunted, Lenin pressed ahead regardless, employing a stratagem with which students of the Communist movement were to become familiar – the creation of the non-delegated 'delegate'. Though Soviet propaganda was to describe the Moscow meeting as a representative conference, most of the participants were, in effect, nominees of the organizers. All but four of the 34 foreign 'delegates' were either émigrés residing in Russia or former prisoners of war who had become Communists, but had not yet returned to their own countries. Most either had no authorization to represent movements whose delegates they purported to be, or represented 'movements' specially created by Lenin for the purpose of inflating the numbers.

Nonetheless, this sparsely attended, largely unrepresentative forum was to take a decision with momentous consequences for the labour movement. Neutralizing the views of German Communist Hugo Eberlein, one of the four genuine delegates from abroad, who had been instructed by the late Rosa Luxemburg to oppose the immediate establishment of a Communist International, the assembly proclaimed itself the founding congress of the Third International. Furthermore, it entrusted Lenin, together with Trotsky and Bukharin, with the task of drawing up a programme, and called on all members of the International to sever their ties with other left-wing movements and follow the Soviet revolutionary model, which was deemed to make irresistible the world revolutionary movement.[39]

Already, therefore, the Third International was distinct from the other two. For, it was going to be no mere 'talking shop' or propaganda forum. It was going to act as a political general staff from which revolutionary activity throughout the world would be planned and coordinated, and rules of discipline established that would suppress the kinds of national preoccupations that had brought its predecessors to grief.

It was also going to be different in another crucial respect. For, it seemed to shift the revolutionary focus away from western Europe, on which it had been traditionally fixed. After all, the First Working Men's International, founded in London, in 1864, on the initiative of British, French, and German socialists, tended to be dominated by their preoccupations. And, speaking of the Second International, which had come into existence in 1889, Trotsky had written that the German Social Democratic Party 'was for us not one of the parties of the International, but *the* party'.[40] With the Third International, western Europe soon lost its claim to being the hub of revolutionary endeavour, for, as E. H. Carr notes,

What had taken place in Moscow in March 1919 was not in fact the fusion of a number of national Communist parties of approximately equal strength into an international organisation, but the harnessing of a number of weak, in some cases embryonic and still unformed, groups to an organisation whose main support and motive force was necessarily and inevitably the power of the Soviet state.[41]

And, although it had been the Bolshevik aim to see the Comintern's headquarters moved to a Soviet Germany, the establishment of a central organization in Moscow ensured that, in the absence of a transfer, the Soviet Communist Party would hold sway. For, it had been agreed at the 'founding congress' that a major share of executive responsibility would be borne by the representatives of the country in which it was situated, and as its Russian members were obliged to implement the decisions of their own Politburo, while the non-Russians were under Soviet jurisdiction and subject to the same pressures and constraints as their Soviet counterparts, Moscow's political will was almost bound to prevail. And if, as Angelica Balabanov suggests, most of the non-Russian functionaries were, in any case, 'ignoramuses who trembled before authority', Moscow's predominance was even more assured.[42]

But Moscow's role in the Comintern was to be affected not just by organizational forms, but also by the broader political situation as perceived in the Kremlin. Between March 1919 and July 1920, when the Comintern had its second, and more representative congress, the revolution had mixed fortunes. On the one hand, there had been the failures in central Europe and in the Baltic states. On the other hand, the attempt to revive the Second International was foundering, while membership of the Third International was growing apace. If most of the new adherents were small sectarian groups, some enjoyed more substantial support. These included Socialist parties from France, Norway, and Czechoslovakia, and the Communist Party of Bulgaria – the only mass party other than the Russian of indubitably Bolshevik credentials.

Moreover, in at least two other countries, the revolution seemed imminent. In Italy, where the war and its aftermath had occasioned widespread disillusionment with parliamentary democracy, the activities of several varieties of revolutionaries – socialist, syndicalist, and anarchist – had caused Lenin to draw his customary analogy with Russia in 1917. In Poland, where Trotsky's Red Army, having repulsed an invading force hoping to seize the Ukraine and White Russia, was rapidly advancing on Warsaw, the Communist Party was expected to take power within a matter of days. In addition, within Russia itself, the Communists could claim to have won a decisive victory in the civil war, even if mopping up operations were still continuing. Drawing up a revolutionary balance sheet, Lenin became convinced of the need to bring what he saw as the 'objective' and 'subjective' factors in the revolutionary process into line. 'Objectively', the situation was ripe for revolution. 'Subjectively', no party other than the Bolsheviks had proved equal to the task of restructuring society. To correct the imbalance, it was, hence, necessary to transform the Comintern into a 'single Communist Party' organized on the basis of 'democratic centralism' with membership restricted to those who would accept the strictest discipline, along the lines already operating within the Russian Party.[43]

According to the 'Twenty-one Conditions of Membership' drawn up by Lenin, adherence to the Comintern meant adopting the appellation 'Communist' and a complete break not only with reformist Social Democracy, but also with leftist parties such as the German USPD, who sought a compromise between Communists and Social Democrats. And since 'the Communist Party will be able to fulfil its duty only if its organization is as centralized as possible, if iron discipline prevails and if the party centre . . . is equipped with the most comprehensive powers', periodic purges of the membership were imperative. Further, 'unconditional support to any Soviet Republic' was demanded, as well as unquestioning obedience to the decisions of the Comintern leadership, on pain of expulsion from the movement. In addition, though each party was given the right to participate in the 'democratic' process prior to a decision, in practice its independence was qualified. For, the Comintern's Executive Committee – a third of whose 18 votes were directly under Russian control – was given the statutory power to make policy between congresses, to compel errant parties to come into line, and to oversee all political communications between members. Clearly, Lenin was taking a risk in making such demands of the revolutionary left. But so strong was the faith of those in attendance in the Bolshevik formula that the proposed 'conditions' and 'statutes' were overwhelmingly approved.[44]

The projection on to the International of basic Bolshevik principles set the tone for the future development of the movement. But the very stringency of the conditions of membership lost the Comintern much of the support it had recently gained. As Lazitch and Drachkovitch have pointed out: 'Generally speaking, the numbers rallying to the Communist International were in inverse proportion to the numerical strength of the organizations in question'.[45] Mass Socialist parties, like the French and the Czech, were either seriously split or, like the Italian and Norwegian, withdrew altogether. If the Soviet leaders took comfort from the fact that a small but hardened adherent would be more pliable than a mass organization, it was much more difficult to come to terms with the failure of their hopes for Italy and Poland. For, the Italian Socialist Party's withdrawal from the Comintern merely intensified existing factional struggles on the left, undermining the chances of revolution and giving the former Socialist, Benito Mussolini, an opportunity for his newly created Fascist squads to wreck the Italian labour movement.

Meanwhile, in Poland, the refusal of the workers of Warsaw to rise in support of the advancing Red Army had stiffened military resistance and led not merely to the hasty retreat of the Soviet force, but, in effect, to the most serious defeat to date of the revolutionary cause. Certainly, Lenin was forced to recognize the folly of trying to revolutionize Poland at the point of a bayonet. At the same time, however, it was now apparent that the bureaucratic machinery he had created, as it were, to destroy Soviet predominance in the course of the spread of world revolution was failing to achieve results, and that even if 'subjective' conditions for revolution had improved, the 'objective' conditions were becoming distinctly unfavourable. But, of course, as the prospects of revolution were seen to fade, the structure and functioning of the Third International merely served to codify and confirm Moscow's predominance.[46]

The Soviet Communist Party's effective control of the International movement served to persuade large numbers of left-inclined western Europeans to think and act in ways having their origins in the political conditions of Russia – a country they had always regarded as authoritarian and backward. But, in looking to Moscow for guidance, they were identifying with a political force as hostile to the 'open society' and to western concepts of pluralistic democracy as to capitalism, and, in the process, doing immense damage to the image of Marxism as a harbinger of 'progress'. They were agreeing in the name of 'science' to dispense with 'scientific objectivity' and the disinterested pursuit of truth. They were agreeing in the name of 'proletarian unity' to fracture the labour movement as never before and to subject their left-wing opponents to relentless and unremitting hostility. They were agreeing in the name of 'Marxism' to display an 'un-Marxist' disregard of socio-economic analysis, preferring instead to adulate or vilify particular individuals rather than the class such people were said to represent. They were agreeing in the name of 'internationalism' to put themselves at the service of a state – the Soviet Union – whose national interests were increasingly to take precedence.

In effect, a 'utopia' had been transformed into an 'ideology' for justifying a new status quo, and for the alienated, the guilt-ridden, and the insecure, the Communist movement increasingly took on the appeal of a 'secular religion'. It is, perhaps, for this reason that large numbers of otherwise rational beings who liked to think that they thought for themselves were prepared to sacrifice their intellectual, moral and political integrity and, in the name of the party, agree to forms of political behaviour their consciences might not otherwise have enjoined.

NOTES

1. See J. Braunthal, *In Search of the Millennium* (London, 1945), p. 197.
2. See H. Seton-Watson, *The Pattern of Communist Revolution* (London, 1960) p. 52.
3. F. Borkenau describes it as 'the biggest revolutionary movement of properly proletarian origin which the modern world has ever seen . . . The international co-ordination which the Comintern later so often tried to bring about was here produced automatically'. *World Communism*, (Ann Arbor, 1962), p. 92.
4. H. Seton-Watson, p. 52.
5. J. Joll, *Europe since 1870* (London, 1976), pp. 239–42.
6. George Kennan, *Russia and the West under Lenin and Stalin* (New York, 1961). pp. 148–9.
7. A. Cave Brown and C. B. MacDonald, *The Communist International and the Crisis of World War II* (London, 1982), p. 66.
8. E. H. Carr, *The Bolshevik Revolution 1917–23* (London, 1966), vol. III, p. 135.
9. B. Lazitch and M. M. Drachkovitch, *Lenin and the Comintern*, (Stanford, 1972) vol. I, p. 48.
10. A. Cave Brown and C. B. MacDonald, p. 66.
11. D. Hyde. *Communism Today* (London, 1972), p. 16.
12. See T. Chandra Bose, *American-Soviet Relations* (Calcutta, 1967), esp. ch. 1.
13. Author of *Ten Days that Shook the World* (New York, 1918) and a correspondent for the American socialist journal, *The Masses*.
14. Both Price and Ransome at that time wrote for the *Manchester Guardian*.
15. The American press was particularly alarmist – a fact exploited by US government agencies to justify intervention. See, for example, Department of State *Memorandum on Certain Aspects of the Bolshevik Movement in Russia* (Washington, 1919).
16. Quoted in Lazitch and Drachkovitch, vol. I, p. 6.
17. Ibid., pp. 11–27.
18. Quoted in Carr, vol. III, p. 28.
19. Ibid., pp. 28–59.
20. See, for example, Lazitch and Drachkovitch, vol. I, pp. 129–34.
21. E. H. Carr, vol. I (London, 1950), pp. 308–9.
22. Ibid., pp. 301–7.
23. Quoted in Lazitch and Drachkovitch, vol. I, pp. 40–1.
24. Ibid., p. 32.
25. Ibid., p. 39.
26. See, for example, Lelio Basso, *Rosa Luxemburg: A Reappraisal* (London, 1975), pp. 97–108.
27. From *Leninism or Marxism?*, trans. by Integer and quoted in Helmut Gruber, *International Communism in the era of Lenin* (New York, 1967), p. 51.
28. Quoted in Geoffrey Stern, *Fifty Years of Communism* (London, 1967), p. 24.
29. Quoted in Carr, vol. III, p. 102.
30. From 'The Proletarian Revolution and the Renegade Kautsky', quoted in Lazitch and Drachkovitch, vol. I, p. 46.

31. Ibid., p. 61.
32. Lazitch and Drachkovitch, pp. 59–60.
33. See, for example, Sebastian Haffner, *Failure of a Revolution: Germany 1918–19* (London, 1973).
34. See, for example, Seton-Watson, pp. 58–60.
35. Ibid., pp. 51–3.
36. Lazitch and Drachkovitch, pp. 118–24.
37. Carr, vol. III, p. 128.
38. Ibid., pp. 119–20, and Lazitch and Drachkovitch, p. 56.
39. Ibid., pp. 116–27 and Lazitch and Drachkovitch, pp. 66–88.
40. Cited by I. Deutscher, *The Prophet Armed: Trotsky 1879–1921* (London, 1970), p. 214.
41. Carr, vol. III, p. 125.
42. Ibid., p. 132, n. 1.
43. See Lazitch and Drachkovitch, ch. 3 and 5.
44. The 21 conditions are reprinted in R. V. Daniels (ed.), *A Documentary History of Communism* (London, 1985), vol. 2, pp. 44–7.
45. Lazitch and Drachkovitch, p. 216.
46. Ibid., ch. 10 and 12.

4. Socialism in One Country

When, on 9 March 1919, Lenin concluded the founding conference of the Comintern with the claim that 'the victory of the proletarian revolution all over the world is assured',[1] he was encapsulating a core Marxist tenet. For, Marxists had always believed that capitalism was doomed to disappear, not just from one country, but from the entire globe, since the workers worldwide had a shared interest in the downfall of the socioeconomic system oppressing them and preventing them from achieving their true potential. Where Lenin parted company with the traditional Marxist was in his contention that in the Soviet state the proletarian revolution had already occurred, whereas, for the Kautskyans and Mensheviks, the revolutionary situation that would engender a socialist transformation was yet to come.

Yet, for the Soviet leader, the spread of revolution had become more than an article of faith. It had become a vital necessity. For, the very weakness, isolation and vulnerability of the Soviet state made a Communist uprising in Berlin, Vienna, or Budapest appear as crucial to the future of the revolution as a Red victory in the Russian civil war. And since the Bolshevik understanding of the Labour movement outside Soviet Russia was probably no better than the latter's understanding of Bolshevism, the Soviet leaders had tended to see in the European-wide turmoil in the aftermath of war the irresistible wave of revolution they were looking for.

Yet, Moscow's revolutionary euphoria had already been checked even before the inaugural meeting of the Comintern. For, at Brest-Litovsk in March 1918, the rulers of the infant Soviet state had received their first lesson in political realism. Then had come the now familiar litany of failed revolutionary hopes – Finland, the Baltic states, Germany, Hungary, Austria, Poland, and Italy, and the more temporary defeats in the Caucasus and the Muslim borderlands.

On the other hand, and equally unforeseen by the Bolsheviks, the Soviet state had endured its early years of tribulation unaided. In the process, however, it had been obliged to devise measures – some, arguably, of a non-socialist character – to cope with the problems of survival in a non-socialist world. Internally, these included measures such as 'War Communism' and its successor the 'New Economic Policy'

– the former in response to the civil war, the latter as a prescription for averting the total collapse of the Soviet economy. Externally, they involved a limited return to some of the more traditional practices of statecraft, so as to enhance the Soviet State's security, welfare and standing, even as the Communist movement stood by as a kind of international revolutionary army waiting for the call to action from its headquarters in Moscow.

At first, such measures were regarded as only *ad hoc* expedients, pending completion of the revolutionary process begun in 1917. Gradually however, they took on a more permanent complexion, as the world's proletariat remained stubbornly resistant to what was to have been the lure of Bolshevism. The combined effects of famine, peasant discontent, the Kronstadt mutiny and the formation of a Communist Workers' Opposition within Russia, the Italian Socialist defection from the Comintern, and the failure of a Moscow-inspired attempt at revolution in Germany, in March 1921, marked the turning point. Soviet Russia's rulers had, henceforth, to think in terms of the long haul – involving a shift from international to domestic priorities, to which some party members adjusted more readily than others.

As usual, it was Lenin who seized the initiative, combining the search for foreign expertise, credits, trade, and diplomatic recognition, with a further tightening of discipline throughout the Communist movement to try to silence the doubters. In fact, the political squeeze had begun even before the Comintern's second congress when, in an attempt to bring into line those preferring worker control to Communist organization, street agitation to Communist penetration, and political intransigence to political compromise, he had written, *Left-Wing Communism: An Infantile Disorder*.[2] At the congress itself, his 21 Conditions of membership sought to outlaw both 'ultra-leftist' and right-wing 'opportunist' tendencies from the movement, and in the following year he imposed his ban on 'fractionalism', to forestall organized dissidence within the Party (a ban never fully implemented until Stalin's time).

At the same time, Lenin began to make further amendments to classical Marxist theory, in switching his revolutionary gaze from the European to the Asian theatre. In fact, his interest in the East was nothing new. In his *Imperialism, the Highest Stage of Capitalism*,[3] written in 1916, he had seen the colonies as the 'Achilles heel' of capitalism, since the struggle for national liberation would ultimately destroy the socio-economic nexus that had served to rejuvenate an otherwise decaying capitalist system. In his *National and Colonial Theses*, prepared for the Comintern's second congress (at which there were but 25 'Easterners' out of a total of 218 'delegates'),[4] he translated his theory of imperialism into a prescription for political action, urging Communists to support 'bourgeois liberation struggles' in the colonies and 'semicolonies' (states like Persia, Turkey and China whose sovereignty, in Lenin's view, was nominal only). On the critical question as to whom the Communists were to back in the event of a conflict between 'bourgeois nationalists' who happen to be socially reactionary and the nascent forces of social revolution, he equivocated, while the Indian Communist M. N. Roy, with a rival text on the same subject, came down firmly in support of social revolution.[5]

Lenin's dilemma was in no way resolved at Baku the following September, where the First [and only] Congress of the Peoples of the East brought together some 2,000 Turks, Persians, Armenians, Georgians and others to 'accelerate the upheaval of world capitalism . . . and assure the liberation of the workers and peasants in the whole world'.[6] In calling for a 'Jihad' (Holy War) against British and French imperialism, the hosts, Zinoviev, Radek, and Kun, were on safe ground. But mindful that nearly a third of the 'delegates' were non-Communists, the organizers tended to shift somewhat uneasily between urging all-out opposition to the 'national bourgeoisie' and qualified support.[7] Their ambivalence merely underlined the contradictions in Soviet policy which became glaringly obvious in the months following Baku.

On the one hand, Soviet troops were sponsoring client states in Tannu Tuva and Outer Mongolia (formerly part of Outer China), and helping to consolidate Communist rule in Ghilan, in northern Persia. On the other hand, Soviet diplomats were exchanging missions with the newly installed nationalist governments of Afghanistan, Persia and Turkey – the last under the fiercely anti-Communist Mustafa Kemal Atatürk – to whom they offered economic assistance. At the same time, Soviet propagandists were waging a violent campaign against Menshevik rule in Armenia and Georgia, which the Soviet government had recognized as independent states.[8] Nevertheless, for all its ambiguities Soviet policy had recognized what most Marxists had hitherto tended to ignore – the need to tap the revolutionary potential of the East. In the aftermath of Baku, a Communist University of the Toilers of the East was established for the training of Communist cadres, but, in keeping with Lenin's desire to keep a tight rein on Soviet Russia's volatile Asian neighbours, the 'University' was located in the Soviet capital and put under the direction of the Comintern's newly created Eastern Department, with its predominantly Russian staff.[9]

Having changed economic tack, tightened discipline in the Communist movement, and turned to the East following a series of setbacks to his revolutionary prospectus in 1920–21, Lenin devised for the world's

Communists a new tactic for dealing with the current predicament. Only a year after insisting that the Comintern's adherents split away from other socialist parties, and constitute recognizably distinct Bolshevik-type political organizations, he was urging them to resume ties with the parties from which they had so recently become estranged. Through the 'United Front' policy promulgated after the Comintern's third congress in June 1921, Communists in the West were instructed to give other left-wing groups the kind of support Communists in the East were to give to the 'national bourgeoisie'. It was not, of course, to be collaboration for its own sake. Neither was it expected to be anything but temporary. The Communists were to 'support' the non-Communist Left in their parliamentary, trade-union, and other activities, in Lenin's words, 'as the rope supports a hanged man',[10] or, as one British Communist put it, 'take them by the hand before taking them by the throat'.[11] To try to make the policy more palatable to the revolutionary purists, the experience of the Bolsheviks between 1903 and 1917 was offered as a model, the nature and degree of collaboration to vary in accordance with national conditions.

But the policy, designed to deal with a series of crises, merely succeeded in provoking more.[12] For, to many Communists, the 'United Front' tactics seemed to deny the Comintern's raison d'être as a revolutionary organization. And when, in April 1922, Comintern officials entered into what turned out to be fruitless negotiations with the Second International and representatives of the so-called 'International Two and a Half' of left-wing non-Communists, many Party members felt betrayed. For the first time, they were prepared to challenge and even defy a Comintern directive. The French party rejected it outright, while in the Italian party a strong 'Left' opposition bitterly denounced what it believed to be an erroneous policy.

In the German party, too, there was a formidable 'left-wing' challenge, and soon the KPD leaders, Arkady Maslow and Ruth Fischer, were levelling against the Comintern and its agents the kinds of charges for which, in March 1921, they had drummed a leading Communist, Paul Levi, out of the party. At that time, when some Comintern officials had backed a Leftist call for an ill-judged insurrection in central Germany, Levi had complained that the Comintern's Executive Committee was ill-informed, incompetent, and operating simply as 'a Cheka projected beyond Russian borders'.[13] Now Maslow and Fischer, though starting from the opposite end of the Communist spectrum, were beginning to reach a similar conclusion. In their view, Moscow's desire to avoid the divisions of the First and Second Internationals was leading the Third to an almost total disregard of local feelings and conditions – to the detriment of the world Communist movement as a whole.[14]

By the time of its fourth congress in November 1922, the Comintern was facing its gravest crisis. For, already large numbers of Communists, having originally been attracted because of the Party's revolutionary programme, were preparing to leave it. The failure of world revolution, Kronstadt and the repression in the Soviet state of dissident Communists, the New Economic Policy, and now the United Front had all taken their toll. And those German, French, Italian and Polish Communists that decided to take their opposition to the fourth congress soon found that there was little point in carrying on the fight. For, not only was the United Front policy passed by a sizeable majority, but it was also buttressed by a new disciplinary code, introducing the concept of 'deviation'. This was, as E. H. Carr points out, 'the language not of political differences, but of doctrinal heresy'.[15] Yet, it was a concept based on no fixed principle of 'socialism', but on conformity to Comintern directives.

In addition, there was a new set of Comintern institutions designed to reinforce the central control that had been under challenge. Hitherto, the Comintern had functioned as a federation of Communist parties. Now revisions in its constitution enlarged the central command structure and made its directing role more explicit. Its Executive Committee (ECCI), formerly elected by the congress, was now to be nominated by 'responsible' Comintern officials, while its Presidium was to act as a political bureau and direct, by means of a small organization bureau (*Orgburo*), a host of key administrative bodies charged with selecting and training functionaries, coordinating propaganda, conveying instructions and funds to loyal Communists and disciplining 'deviationists'. Meanwhile, a Comintern directive that national Party congresses be held after, and not before, world congresses meant that the Comintern had ceased to be a forum where collective decisions could be reached through debate and compromise among national delegates. It was now an autonomous directorate whose decisions would be handed down to be interpreted and applied by national leaders.[16] It was thus going to be increasingly hard to oppose the Comintern line and retain Party membership.

As the Comintern's bureaucrats consolidated their influence over the Communist parties, their directives came increasingly to reflect the vicissitudes of power in the Kremlin. For, given the location of Comintern headquarters, as well as the prestige and funds available to Moscow, the Soviet Communist Party was bound to play a key role in the Comintern's apparatus and actions. Unfortunately for the movement, the Soviet leadership had begun to lose its firm sense of direction at the end of 1921 when Lenin first succumbed to the illness that was to paralyse him in little over a year. As he took increasingly to his sickbed, the Party began to divide into factions, but, as in subsequent succession struggles, power political rivalries tended to be expressed as disagreements over policy, and what may have begun as a difference of emphasis was soon made to appear an unbridgeable ideological chasm, with repercussions throughout the movement.

That Trotsky, who had been closer to the Mensheviks than to the Bolsheviks until just before the Revolution, was on the left of the party was incontestable. At home, he advocated greater party democracy, more central planning, and fewer concessions to the peasants. Abroad, he was prepared to take risks in the cause of world revolution. Stalin, on the other hand, played a much more cautious game. He had fewer qualms than Trotsky about the changes in political and economic policy since 1921, and, like Lenin, felt that the Soviet state needed credits, trade and diplomatic exchange in order to be able to deflect capitalist hostility and consolidate Communist power. Yet the differences between them were probably ones of degree rather than of kind. After all, despite his belief in permanent revolution, Trotsky had never advocated a revolutionary offensive regardless of circumstances. Indeed, he had opposed both the Red Army's march on Warsaw, in August 1920, and the insurrection in Germany, the following March. And, as War Commissar, he had helped to forge one of the most controversial links the Soviet state ever made with a capitalist power – the secret deal in 1922 allowing the German *Reichswehr* to manufacture poison gas, planes and artillery shells on Soviet soil. As for Stalin, though he was to become the advocate of 'Socialism in One Country', he was merely expressing in words what Lenin had been forced to concede in practice in proclaiming the necessity for 'coexistence' and beginning the search for a *modus vivendi* with the governments he had been attempting to overthrow. For, the policy that was to lead to Stalin's non-aggression pacts with Fascist Italy and Nazi Germany, had begun with Lenin's agreements with such anti-Communist countries as Finland, the Baltic states, Poland, Persia, Afghanistan, Turkey, and Weimar Germany – all of which were designed as interim measures until capitalism was again destabilized.[17]

The first indications of what was to become a duel to the death between Stalin and Trotsky appeared in 1923. At that time Stalin – a drunken cobbler's son, who had forsaken a theological seminary at the turn of the century to become one of the first Bolsheviks – formed his first political coalition against the brilliant newcomer to the Party. For the latter's meteoric rise and military success had aroused both jealousy and fear. As Hugh Seton-Watson has pointed out: 'To the Bolshevik bosses, who liked to make parallels between their revolution and the French, Trotsky was the obvious candidate for the role of Bonaparte'.[18]

In the event, it was not Trotsky, but Stalin who assumed that role, seizing every opportunity to add to his formidable array of offices in a system which contained few, if any, in-built checks and balances on power. A Georgian who had urged his fellow Bolsheviks to resist the rising tide of 'bourgeois nationalism', Stalin had been put in charge of a programme designed, in effect, to wean the non-Russian nationalities away from the 'bourgeois' concept of 'self-determination', in favour of the Soviet interpretation – by force, if necessary. Later, as one of five members of the ruling Politburo, he had been invited to head the 'Workers' and Peasants' Inspectorate' formed to eliminate corruption and inefficiency from government.

Finally, in 1922, Stalin acquired the post he was never to relinquish and which brought him to the pinnacle of power – that of General Secretary of the Party. With each office, he was able to dispense the kind of patronage that would assure his future. And, though the dying Lenin, increasingly troubled by what he saw as the General Secretary's abuse of authority, had called for Stalin's removal from the office, his plea was to no avail. Stalin used his connections to ensure that Lenin's call never reached the Soviet public during his (Stalin's) lifetime and went on to exercise, by means of the system Lenin had created, the kind of untrammelled authority that Lenin had tried to restrain. The way Stalin outmanœuvred Trotsky and justified the removal of all other potential political rivals had a profound effect on the Comintern, setting the international Communist movement in a mould from which it has only recently emerged.

The ascendancy of Stalin was a triumph for machine politics. In the words of Sheila Fitzpatrick: 'He was not a charismatic figure, a fine orator or a distinguished theoretician like Lenin or Trotsky. He was not a war hero, an upstanding son of the working class or even much of an intellectual. He was . . . a man without personal distinction'.[19] On the other hand, he enjoyed not only unrivalled power, but also singular good fortune. Lenin's incapacity was, for Stalin, literally, a stroke of luck, while his death, in January 1924, removed the only man to threaten Stalin's power and offer advancement to his major rival.

Without Lenin, Trotsky lacked any real power base, while Stalin could increasingly pack key committees with his supporters. At the same time, personal and political differences among other leading officials enabled Stalin to make tactical alliances which would still further enhance his position. In 1923, for example, when he combined with the Petrograd party boss, Grigori Zinoviev, and the Moscow party chief, Lev Kamenev, to form an anti-Trotsky ruling triumvirate, Stalin succeeded in weeding out most of the War Commissar's few remaining followers in the hierarchy. Later, when he joined political forces with the now right-wing theoretician, Nikolai Bukharin, together with Aleksei Rykov, Lenin's successor as Chairman of the Council of Peoples' Commissars, and Mikhail Tomsky, who headed the trade unions, it was with the same end in view – to crush Trotsky and his dwindling band of followers. And, though Trotsky attempted to revive his sagging political fortunes by making common cause with Zinoviev and Kamenev in 1925 after they had fallen out with Stalin, it was too late.[20] Stalin's ascendancy seemed virtually unstoppable, and he was able to have Trotsky removed from the War Commissariat in 1925, removed from the Politburo in 1926, expelled from the Party in 1927, expelled from Moscow in 1928, and expelled from the country in 1929. By this time, the distinction in Soviet Russia between Party and state had been eroded, and the charge of 'fractionalism' was being equated with disloyalty against the state.[21] Yet, this outcome was, in part, a product of the barrage of ideological thrusts and counter-thrusts between the Communist titans which continued throughout the '20s.

If Trotsky's duties had afforded him little time for politicking during the civil war, he was under no such constraint after it and decided to speak his mind on a variety of issues then in contention. While many of his colleagues now regarded 'War Communism' as a regrettable expedient dictated by adversity, Trotsky lauded it as a necessary stage, intrinsic to the development of a socialist economy in a backward country. Indeed, his continued advocacy of the militarization of labour alienated groups such as the Workers' Opposition, who sought worker control of industry and greater autonomy for trade unions. On the other hand, he, like them, wanted greater inner-Party democracy and identified with the Left-inclined Democratic Centralists in their criticisms of the bureaucratic trends in the Party organization. On NEP, he found himself at odds with both Lenin and Bukharin, in that he felt that it involved too many concessions to the peasantry at the expense of industrial development.

The dispute came to a head in 1923 in the aftermath of what became known as the 'scissors crisis', as the Party intervened to try to reverse a downward spiral in agricultural prices as industrial prices soared. Trotsky's response was a bitter attack on the whole thrust of government policy and on those formulating it. His criticisms, in a letter of 8 October 1923 to the Central Committee, were immediately followed by a public 'platform' of support issued by 46 prominent Communists, and for the next few weeks the columns of *Pravda* were open to both protagonists and opponents. But, on 5 December, Trotsky went too far. In an open letter, he warned against the possible degeneration of the revolutionary 'old guard' into 'bureaucratism' and 'opportunism', as had happened to German Social Democracy in 1914. Thereafter, *Pravda*'s columns were closed to the advocates of what Zinoviev dubbed 'Trotskyism', and dogged by illness and increasingly bereft of support, Trotsky went into political eclipse and then exile.[22]

As a theoretician, however, Trotsky maintained the struggle against both Stalinist bureaucracy and the concept of 'Socialism in One Country', by which Stalin was increasingly justifying Soviet policy. For, while he appreciated that the revolutionary tide had ebbed, he could not accept Stalin's proclamation of the self-containment and national self-sufficiency of the revolution, not least because of its implications for the Third International. For, if the Comintern were now to be largely deprived of its revolutionary function, Trotsky feared it would be reduced to an instrument of the Soviet bureaucracy, impeding rather than promoting the objective for which it had been originally designed.[23]

Trotsky's apprehensions regarding the Comintern were well founded. For, by the decision approved at the fifth congress in June 1924 to 'bolshevize' the parties – their leaders to be appointed by Moscow, their rank and file to be divided into political cells and their code of discipline to be tightened still further – the bureaucracy in the Soviet capital had the power virtually to recast the international movement in its own image.[24] Well before Trotsky's own political disgrace, the authorities in Moscow had seen to it that his followers were hounded out of the French, German, Italian and Polish parties.

Moreover, from the tenor of Comintern policy since the United Front, Trotsky could only draw the most pessimistic conclusions. For example, in Germany in 1923, what he had perceived as a revolutionary opportunity had been wasted for want of a coherent and relevant Comintern strategy. For, though Moscow did, indeed, call for revolution, it was only after first urging the KPD to make common cause with right-wing activists (including the Nazis) in a 'National Bolshevist' strategy against the French occupation of the Ruhr, and then to combine in local government with the Social Democratic Left – a succession of policy prescriptions leaving a trail of confusion. He also believed that the cause of revolution in China had been sacrificed on the altar of the United Front and at considerable cost to the Chinese Communist Party, which had to bear the full brunt of the anti-Communist activities of the Nationalists under Chiang Kai-shek.

Meanwhile, in Poland, where Communists had helped to power a radical nationalist, Marshal Pilsudski, who would turn against them, and in Britain, where overzealous Communist support of the 1926 General Strike, through the recently established Anglo-Russian Trade Union Committee, was to lead to a Labour Party ban on Communist infiltration, Trotsky found further examples of the folly of the United Front.[25] Finally, in August 1927, shortly before his expulsion from the party, Trotsky had his worst fears confirmed when Stalin redefined an 'internationalist' as one who 'unreservedly, unhesitatingly and without conditions is prepared to defend the USSR because it is the base of the world revolutionary movement'.[26]

But, in giving his own peculiar imprint to the 'bolshevization' process, Stalin succeeded in neutralizing not just Trotsky and the Left, but anyone – Right or Left – who might oppose what he decreed to be the 'correct' line of the day. By 1926, the list of opponents to be emasculated included both Kamenev and Zinoviev, whom Stalin had recently removed from the presidency of the Comintern, to be replaced by Bukharin, who had accepted the theory of 'Socialism in One Country'.

But Bukharin's tenure of the presidency was to be short-lived, as it became increasingly clear that his conception of building socialism was incompatible with Stalin's. A staunch champion of NEP, he believed that the 'middle peasantry' i.e. those sufficiently well-to-do to be able to hire one or more labourers, held the key to the eventual construction of socialism through its ability to create a secure agricultural base – an essential prerequisite to industrial expansion.[27] Stalin, on the other hand, had no use for Bukharin's socialism 'at a snail's pace'.

And, in 1927, as new challenges confronted the Soviet Union both at home and abroad, came the first indications of what the Stalinist prospectus might contain. In the face of a growing shortage of grain, as the peasants had little incentive to sell their surpluses when consumer goods were scarce and the country's external relations were, in any case, taking a sudden turn for the worse, Stalin rounded on the kulaks (richer peasants). He held that a lack of adequate controls had enabled them to hold the country to ransom, and, in early 1928, designed a series of 'emergency measures' to force them to part with their crop. It was the beginning of the end for NEP. For, Stalin now sought to redirect revolutionary energies into a new and highly ambitious programme for rapid advance towards economic self-sufficiency. It was to mean submitting the whole economy to a central plan and the enforcement of rigid discipline in every facet of life. No longer would the Soviet regime tolerate private entrepreneurs in industry and agriculture, or independent trade unions with the right to strike. No longer would it allow workers the freedom to choose their jobs and places of residence.

In fact, the collectivization of agriculture which proceeded apace from 1928, converted the peasantry into a virtually landless, agricultural proletariat.[28] Henceforth, the Soviet Union would be geared to extracting from the peasantry enough food and manpower to service the demands of heavy industry. And under Stalin's five-year plans, first introduced in 1928, light industry and the satisfaction of consumer needs had only the lowest priority. In order to deter, relocate or punish those who might resist the new order, special detachments of internal security forces equipped with tanks, artillery and machine guns were on stand-by. By the end of the first five-year plan, the kulaks had ceased to exist as a class, many having been driven to the cities or else deported in cattle cars to the country's most inhospitable regions. Meanwhile, up to 10 million Ukrainian, Byelorussian, Russian and Kazakh peasants starved to death – their lives traumatized by the effects of collectivization.

In effect, Stalin had appropriated the Trotskyist thesis that the deliberate exploitation of peasant agriculture would generate sufficient capital to speed Soviet industrial advance,[29] though whether or not Trotsky, who had not hesitated to give the order to fire on the rebellious sailors of Kronstadt in 1921, would have been quite as ruthless as Stalin in implementing such a programme is debatable. Certainly, however, Stalin's turn to the Left, which presaged the downfall of Bukharin and his followers, came too late to save Trotsky.

As with the introduction of NEP, so with its demise, a change of policy in the Soviet state was to be followed by a shift of line in the Comintern.[30] To Stalin, the strategy of the United Front was but a logical corollary of NEP, which had produced a mass of defections from most Communist parties. Accordingly, the Kremlin's turn to the Left domestically would need to be reflected throughout the international movement. Towards the end of 1927 came the first indications of a change of line, as Stalin gave the 'thumbs down' to continued Communist collaboration with the Social Democrats. And at the sixth Comintern congress, July to September 1928, he spelled out the implications. Under the slogan 'class against class', Communists were, henceforth, to make war against Social Democracy – a bourgeois institution masquerading as a movement of the working class, and having more in common with Fascism than socialism. The theory underscoring this startling volte-face was that capitalism's postwar economic difficulties were accelerating to the point of final crisis, but that, in their dying agony the bourgeois power-holders and their 'Social Fascist' dupes

Socialism in One Country   73

would conspire against the USSR in the mistaken belief that it was the source of their troubles. From this, incidentally, it followed that Communists everywhere must work to frustrate anti-Soviet designs and assist the Soviet Union – the base of world revolution. It was a theory which had implications for East as well as West, since it meant that Communists must regard all but the most radical elements of the 'national bourgeoisie' as being as hostile to their cause as the Social Democrats.[31]

Yet, while the shift to the Left in domestic policy was real enough, the shift in Comintern policy was more apparent than real. Notwithstanding the rhetoric and the evident crisis of capitalism in the aftermath of the Wall Street Crash of 1929, Stalin was even less inclined to sanction revolutionary activity in the years following the sixth Comintern congress than in the period preceding it. In Colombia and El Salvador, for example, where local Communists were convinced that a revolutionary situation was in prospect, they looked in vain for a signal from Moscow.[32] In China, Mao Tse-tung was demoted for his overenthusiastic testimony to the revolutionary potential of the peasantry, and received little support from Stalin when he took to the countryside to establish a Soviet Republic on the Kiangsi–Hunan border.[33] In central and eastern Europe, the parties appeared increasingly tolerant of the extreme Right, the major beneficiary of the Communists' often violent manœuvres against Social Democracy in the early '30s.

In Germany, for example, where the effects of the Great Depression were more serious than in any other industrial country, the Communists, having repeatedly refused Social Democratic pleas for a united front against Hitler, reverted to a strategy akin to that of 'National Bolshevism'. Communists and Nazis agreed to disrupt Social Democratic meetings, jointly arranged a transport strike to ease the grip of the Social Democrats on Berlin, and worked together in the Prussian Diet to oust the SPD from government.[34] As Georgi Dimitrov, head of the Comintern's Western European Bureau, explained in January 1931: 'United action of the Communist Party and Hitler will accelerate the disintegration of the crumbling democratic bloc which governs Germany'.[35] It was a strategy the Communists refused to abandon even after Hitler's advent in power. Two months after the inauguration of Hitler's anti-Communist and anti-socialist revolution, the Comintern journal *Rundschau* even managed to sound enthusiastic. 'The Fascist dictatorship, in destroying all democratic illusions, is ridding the masses of noxious Social Democratic influences and hence accelerating Germany's march towards proletarian revolution.'[36]

If such Moscow-approved policies appear paradoxical, they were merely in keeping with a Soviet foreign political approach itself at variance with the Kremlin's most alarmist rhetoric. For, despite its talk of 'capitalist encirclement' and 'the inevitability of war', Maxim Litvinov, Chicherin's successor as Soviet Foreign Commissar, took a high profile in international forums on peace and disarmament and was instrumental in concluding non-aggression pacts with a host of countries antagonistic to Moscow. In attempting to foster good relations with the very countries with which Communism was supposedly in mortal combat, Soviet policy reached a peak of dialectical complexity, though the policy remained explicable in terms of Lenin's concept of 'coexistence'.[37]

To the Trotskyists, however, there was a more sinister explanation for the apparent paradoxes of Stalinist policy. They saw his 'revolutionary' and 'internationalist' programme as merely an ideological smokescreen for the pursuit of 'Socialism in One Country' – a policy they perceived as basically nationalist in orientation. Whether or not one accepts the Trotskyist explanation, there is no question that by 1929 the Comintern had been transformed into an instrument faithfully reflecting Moscow's demands. Bukharin, its last independent-minded president, had been removed, only to be replaced by a directorate of obedient Stalinists – Vyacheslav Molotov, later Stalin's long-standing Foreign Minister; Dimitri Manuilsky, a Ukrainian with years of experience as a Comintern official; and Otto Kuusinen, a Finnish Communist and founder member of the Comintern.[38] In the meantime, Party officialdom had been purged so as to comprise either loyal Stalinists or those whose views happened to accord with current policy. The rank and file had also been cleansed of doubters and sceptics, and there was no room for Communists who refused to accept that their Socialist comrades of yesterday were now 'Social Fascists' and more dangerous than any other 'Fascist' tendency to the Communist cause.

Yet, as in the early '20s, so in the late '20s, the switch in Comintern policy had left a number of committed former Communists without an ideological base. In Germany, for example, right-wingers such as Heinrich Brandler, August Thalheimer and Paul Fröhlich followed left-wingers like Arkady Maslow and Ruth Fischer into the political wilderness. In France, Right-inclined Communists like Paul Marion joined Leftward-looking Communists such as Boris Souvarine and Madeleine Marx (Paz) in political exile. Some of the expellees, unwilling to stake their political fortunes outside the movement, tried to set up 'Communist Opposition' groups of their own, and in Sweden, where most of the party had been expelled for right-wing deviation, an unofficial Communist Party was able to function successfully for several years.[39]

Elsewhere, however, such parties had little more staying power than some of the groups identifying themselves with Trotsky's Fourth International, which he founded in 1938, or the sectarian Marxist–Leninist groups that sprang up in the '60s in the wake of the Sino-Soviet split. In the meantime, many former Communists had begun to repudiate and excoriate the movement to which they had hitherto dedicated their lives.

Soon, however, the baleful effects of the 'class against class' policy were to become only too clear. Though the Communist movement should have been the major beneficiary of the world economic crisis it had predicted and which seemed to provide daily confirmation of the validity of the theory of 'increasing pauperization', the only revolutionaries to take power were Fascists and semi-Fascists. In fact, the sustained attack on Social Democracy had produced a mass of lost opportunities instead of Red Revolution or a power balance in Moscow's favour. Yet, preoccupied as Stalin was with a host of domestic problems – the mounting death toll in the wake of forced industrialization and collectivization as well as the thought of a right-wing 'backlash', to say nothing of the personal crisis induced by the apparent suicide of his young wife – he refused to budge from the line he had laid down at the sixth Comintern congress. Others, however, were beginning to have their doubts, and among French Communists, where a modicum of independent thinking had managed to survive the rigours of party discipline, there was a growing mood of disquiet.

One of the first to raise the alarm was the idiosyncratic Communist writer, Henri Barbusse, whose left-wing journal, *Monde*, became a vehicle for thinly veiled attacks on the sectarian line of the Comintern.[40] In August 1932, Barbusse went a stage further, inviting Socialists, Syndicalists, Trotskyists, and pacifists, as well as Communists, to attend an international anti-war congress in Amsterdam, and securing their general support for such current Communist preoccupations as the need to rally to the defence of the Soviet Union. In effect, the congress had demonstrated the continued value of 'the united front from below', and, having enjoyed the financial support of 'Front' organizer, press baron and publicist for the Comintern, Willi Münzenberg, it became a testing ground for the 'Front' organizations of the future, which would attract thousands of non-Communists to the Communist cause. Barbusse was to chair a second World Congress against War in Paris, in April 1933, and in the following September the now renamed League Against War and Fascism assembled (with a sizeable contingent from the FBI) in New York. Thus, even while the Comintern was at its most intransigent towards the non-Communist Left, the seeds of another United Front were germinating.[41]

By 1934, some of Barbusse's earlier heresies, which had been under attack in the more orthodox Communist journals, began to be incorporated into a new orthodoxy. The moment of truth had come on 6 February when, in the wake of a financial scandal which rocked the French government, Communist demonstrators attached themselves to armed bands of right-wing extremists and brought down the Socialist-Radical administration of Edouard Daladier. Suddenly, it seemed that Paris might be on the verge of a dictatorship on the model of Rome or Berlin – and, increasingly, Communists began to shrink from the consequences. In a matter of days, the French party (PCF) was backing an anti-Fascist strike organized by Socialist trade unions, and the phrase 'United Front' began to reappear in the French journals. On the other hand, while 'class against class' remained the official policy of the Comintern, the French party leader, Maurice Thorez, insisted that any joint action with non-Communists had to be on Communist terms. There was to be no place for a 'united front from above', and only the most stringent conditions for a 'united front from below'. Indeed, as late as 13 April, Thorez was holding that those advocating an open alliance with the Socialists be 'thrown on the rubbish heap of history', and, accordingly, he had a leading French Communist, Jacques Doriot, expelled from the party for protesting to the ECCI about the Communist campaign against Social Democracy.

Ironically, it was at the party congress of June 1934, at which Doriot was expelled, that the PCF finally reversed its attitude to Social Democracy. Claiming this as a change not of policy, but of tactics, the leaders called on members to work for the kind of United Front that Social Democrats could understand. By mid-July this had taken the form of a pact with leading French Socialists for a joint struggle against Fascism, imperialism and war. All references to 'Social Fascism' and 'Social Democratic treachery' had been dropped from the French Communist press. But if the impetus for a change of line had come from individual French Communists it required a change of heart in the Kremlin to give sanction to such a shift.[42]

The belated realization that Germany and Japan might pose an especial threat had already begun to modify Moscow's indiscriminate condemnation of all 'bourgeois' states and to propel the USSR into a closer alignment with anti-Fascist governments. In November 1933, it had managed to secure diplomatic recognition by the USA. In May 1934, Foreign Commissar Litvinov and French Foreign Minister Barthou began discussing proposals for a Franco-Soviet mutual assistance pact, which came to fruition the following year, and, in September 1934, the USSR was admitted to the League of Nations it had shunned for 15 years. Clearly, if the Soviet Union could collaborate with 'bourgeois' states against Fascism, it could hardly object if the Communist parties in those states collaborated with the very same 'bourgeois' politicians who were being conciliatory to Moscow. It was in this context that Soviet disapproval of the 'united front from above' began to crumble.[43] It was Georgi Dimitrov, head of the Western European Bureau, chief defendant in the Reichstag Fire Trial of 1933 and Secretary-General-elect of the Comintern, who gave the green light for the new line. In June 1934, he stressed the need for a review of Comintern tactics to meet changed circumstances,[44] and soon the Czechoslovakian, Austrian, Swiss, Spanish and Italian parties were lining up with the French in seeking unity of action with the Socialists on an anti-Fascist platform.

Even so, the old line had not yet been completely disavowed, and, as late as November 1934, Dimitrov was still warning Communists that united front action did not mean the abandonment of the ideological struggle against Social Democracy.[45] Given the Comintern's somewhat equivocal stance during this period, some Communists chose, perhaps not surprisingly, to maintain rigid adherence to 'class against class'. Even if Willi Münzenberg had effectively anticipated the new line, his party, the KPD, was among the last to change – to its cost. But while the German party dragged its feet, the PCF continued to point the way. In October 1934, it had extended its olive branch to the very same Radical Party it had conspired against the previous February, and in so doing had broadened the United Front concept into what was to become known as the Popular Front.

It was at the Comintern's seventh congress, in July 1935, that its effective head, Dimitrov, finally terminated a policy so damaging to the political health of international Communism.[46] Urging the Communist movement to abandon 'self-satisfied sectarianism', he called for 'joint action with the Social Democratic parties, reformist trade unions and other organizations of the toilers against the class enemy of the proletariat', the precise form of this action to 'depend on the condition and character of the labour organizations and on the concrete situation'. But in singling out the PCF, whose actions had 'helped to prepare the decisions of our Congress', Dimitrov was, in effect, commending particular methods of procedure. These were characterized by the search for the broadest possible anti-Fascist coalition with a view to forming a government, willingness to countenance the amalgamation of Communist and non-Communist trade unions, and a new interpretation of the notion of the 'struggle for peace'.[47] Hitherto, the phrase had connoted uncompromising hostility to war, armaments, armies, conscription, and taxation for military purposes. From now on, it was to signify support for a programme of national rearmament to defend the anti-Fascist powers and deter aggression from Nazi Germany and militarist Japan – the two powers now felt to present the most serious threat to the Soviet state. Once again, therefore, an ideological shift had been grounded in considerations of power.

If the Popular Front policy did nothing to hasten world revolution, it did at least bring positive, if temporary, benefits both for Soviet strategy and for the Communist movement as a whole. It brought Moscow considerable foreign popularity and influence at a time when Stalin's brutal excesses at home might have made it a pariah among the nations. At the same time, it widened the appeal of the party in many countries, bringing to it and to the many 'Front' organizations under Communist auspices a flood of new and often influential recruits. It was in France, China and Spain, where the Fascist threat seemed especially acute, that the Popular Front policy succeeded in bolstering party fortunes and producing its most spectacular, if transitory, successes.

In France, dramatic confirmation of the success of the PCF's negotiations with the Socialists and Radicals occurred on 14 July 1935, when Thorez, Socialist leader Léon Blum, and Daladier marched arm in arm at the head of the Bastille Day parade in Paris. Soon they had agreed on an electoral programme which 'did little to frighten the middle class', and though its lack of provision for widespread nationalization and collectivization disappointed many Communists and Socialists, it propelled the Popular Front to power in April 1936 – the PCF being the major beneficiary. For in four years its parliamentary representation leapt from 12 to 72 seats, its vote from 800,000 to 1,500,000, its membership from 25,000 to 350,000 – making it the most powerful and highly organized party outside Russia. But when Blum, as leader of the largest party in the Front, offered the Communists seats in his new cabinet, they refused – thereby undermining from the start the very government the PCF had helped to create.

Even now, their reasons are still not entirely clear. It is possible that with France immersed in a tidal wave of anarcho-syndicalist unrest by the time Blum had taken office, the Communists had lost faith in his ability to lead an effective government and were hoping to profit from his mistakes. It is equally possible that they would have preferred Daladier to Blum as premier, since the former's foreign policy was more to the taste of a Communist Party now bent on rearmament in the face of Fascism, while the latter represented a party with which it was still in competition for the working-class vote. In any event, once the PCF had failed to rally the country in defence of the Republican cause in Spain, it lost interest in the Popular Front government, hastening its downfall and leaving its partners weakened, divided and embittered. By contrast, the PCF emerged stronger than before and in a position to replace the Socialists as the country's main party of the Left immediately after the Second World War.[48]

In Spain, the rise of Communist influence was, in some ways, even more remarkable, though of shorter duration than that in France. When the militant socialist miners of Asturias raised the red flag of revolt against right-wing government in October 1934, the Spanish Communist Party (PCE), who decided to support them, was one of the smallest Communist parties in Europe. In comparison with the parties of the Spanish non-Communist Left – including the Socialists, Syndicalists, Left Republicans, Trotskyists and Anarchists – the role of the PCE had been almost insignificant, not least because of its uncompromising attitude to the other parties during the 'class against class' period. But when it began to align with other left-wing parties in a Popular Front, which polarized the country after its narrow election victory of February 1936, Communist fortunes began rapidly to rise. From 1933 to 1937, PCE membership burgeoned from 1,800 to 300,000, the party having committed itself, as in France, to a programme of only mild reform.

However, if it had hoped thereby to safeguard the Popular Front against internal or external threat, it was to be sadly disappointed. For one thing, buoyed by the Popular Front victory, some of the Party's much less disciplined colleagues on the Left indulged in an orgy of violence, setting fire to churches and convents, assaulting and even murdering political opponents, sacking newspaper offices, and organizing armed seizures of large properties and enterprises. While Leftist strong-arm squads were at large, Fascist *agents provocateurs* were assisting the spread of disorder to give the Right a pretext for a putsch.

Ironically, it was General Francisco Franco's army revolt against Republican Spain in July 1936, that gave the Communists their chance. For, soon the PCE was playing a key role in defending the Republic, thanks to the economic, technical and military support provided by the Soviet Union, having failed to secure French or British intervention on behalf of the constitution. The Party's position was further strengthened when, after a series of bloody clashes in Barcelona in April and May 1937, contingents of the Soviet OGPU intervened to assist the PCE in what was becoming an increasingly murderous conflict among the various factions of the Left. Soon a Soviet-directed wave of terror against all those opposed to Communist demands for order and discipline had weakened the ability of its left-wing rivals to resist the PCE's efforts to dominate the Republican administration. At the same time, the activities of the International Brigades, which consisted of volunteers from many countries who had come to fight for the Republic, served to camouflage the degree to which the cause had been weakened by the PCE's Soviet-backed purge.[49]

On the other hand, given the PCE's dependence on foreign support, its role could only decline once Stalin, having concluded that German and Italian support had made Franco's victory inevitable, had decided to end Soviet intervention, halt arms shipments, and recall the Soviet officials directing the work of the International Brigades. With the final collapse, in March 1939, of the fast decaying Popular Front, the PCE's future was bleak. Communists choosing to stay in Spain faced summary execution or lengthy prison sentences. Those escaping to Moscow were granted no respite either, since they were soon caught up in Stalin's murderous purges, which were especially brutal towards émigrés who lacked their governments' protection. In fact, many PCE leaders disappeared shortly after their arrival in the Soviet capital, and when Dolores Ibarruri ('La Pasionaria') emerged as the new party chief, Jose Diaz having died in Moscow after a 'fall' from an upper-storey window, she had few followers left in either Spain or the USSR.[50]

Clearly, the Party's decimation in 1939 reflected, as did its resurrection three years earlier, priorities drawn up in Moscow rather than Madrid. But the memory of its close ties with the Kremlin, ultimately so damaging to itself and to the Popular Front it had once helped to promote, made the Party something of a pariah among the Left for many years. It soon became clear, too, that if ever the PCE were to become a viable force in Spain again, it would need to demonstrate that it had an independent existence and that its policies were not made in Moscow.

In China there might have been no Popular Front but for the outbreak of hostilities with Japan. For the Party's previous experience of political collaboration had been disastrous.[51] In 1923, the United Front had been thrust upon a sceptical Chinese party by men in Moscow with no particular expertise on the country and in the midst of a power struggle affecting political priorities. To Stalin, China was a strife-torn, backward society at the mercy of Japanese, British, French, and American imperialism and with no immediate prospect of proletarian revolution. At the same time, Sun Yat-sen's nationalist Kuomintang (KMT) represented, as Lenin had suggested, a 'progressive' force against 'feudal' warlords and foreign interests, and its struggle for 'national liberation' merited Communist support. To Trotsky, on the other hand, capitalism, both domestic and foreign, had corroded China to a far greater extent than Stalin would admit, putting the country within range, given the appropriate leadership, of a proletarian revolution. As such, any Communist pact with the 'national bourgeoisie' could only impede the revolutionary process. Though it was, of course, Stalin who won the argument, the Chinese Communists were to get caught in the ideological crossfire.

At first, all seemed well. Sun had allowed Soviet advisers to remodel his party on 'democratic centralist' lines, giving Communists an opportunity to penetrate the top echelons of the KMT's political, economic and military institutions. But when the KMT's military commander, Chiang Kai-shek, took control of the party to forestall a left-wing coup in the aftermath of Sun's death in 1925, he took immediate action to curb Communist power. In March 1926, Chiang arrested the political director of the Whampoa military academy, Chou En-lai, and several of his Communist colleagues on the staff, disbanded the army's semi-autonomous Workers' Guard, and placed the trade unions under surveillance. Shortly after, as Communists gained mass support in the southern cities which fell to the coalition during a highly successful military expedition, Chiang resorted to more drastic anti-Communist measures. In 1927, having expelled the Communists from the KMT, he unleashed a reign of terror against them. In Shanghai, in April, he staged a veritable massacre of Communist sympathizers, repeating it in Hankow, Changsha, Nanking, Canton and other major cities.

And, until Chiang's troops began raiding Soviet consulates in June, Stalin remained deaf to each successive Communist plea for Soviet arms and for the party's release from the United Front. Adding insult to injury, Stalin blamed the Chinese leaders (who had never wanted the United Front) for the fiasco, and then, as if to prove that Trotsky's insurrectionist tactics were equally flawed, he gave orders for an uprising in Canton – Chiang's home base – resulting in a final bloody defeat for the Communists in December. In effect, the Chinese Communist Party (CCP) had fallen victim to an uncomprehending Soviet leadership, which had failed to locate the prime source of revolutionary endeavour in China – the peasantry. For Mao Tse-tung, who was later to lead the CCP, the lessons of the United Front débâcle were only too clear.[52]

While the much depleted CCP remained urban-based, Mao, increasingly impressed by the revolutionary credentials of the Chinese peasant, took to the countryside to carve out a Soviet base in Kiangsi province. From here he declared war on Japan, called for the overthrow of the

KMT, and devised a strategy to 'encircle the cities from the country-side'. By 1932, he had persuaded the Central Committee to leave Shanghai and join him in Kiangsi. But soon his base was under threat. By 1934, it was at the mercy of KMT troops, backed, according to an article in *Communist International*, by 'imperialist counter-revolution'.[53] If the list of international 'counter-revolutionaries' sounds somewhat far-fetched (they include the British Ambassador, who 'personally, by means of bribery, organized a united front of the generals' to wage war against Soviet China; the Japanese, who 'have their fingers in every pie'; the French, who had wiped out soviets in south China; the Germans, who had supplied military advisers; the Americans and Canadians, who were flying Chiang's aircraft; the Italians, whose warships had joined American, Japanese, and British vessels 'for the purpose of shooting down the revolutionary Chinese soldiers'; and the League of Nations, whose technical aid mission was being exploited for counter-revolutionary purposes), Mao's followers were sufficiently alarmed to make a hasty retreat in October 1934. It was the start of the Long March north-westwards, along 6,000 miles of difficult terrain, to Yenan in northern Shensi – a much more remote area near Soviet-controlled Outer Mongolia.

As the Communists' epic march proceeded to take its heavy toll of lives, another costly historical drama was being played out in the south-east of the country as the Japanese expanded their imperial domain at China's expense. Increasingly alarmed by the wider implications, not least to the Soviet Union itself which shared a frontier with Japanese-controlled Manchuria, Moscow urged a united Chinese riposte. Not surprisingly, in view of the party's earlier experience, Mao, who assumed the leadership of the CCP during the Long March, was reluctant to comply.[54]

What seems to have tipped the scales in favour of a common front was the evident growth within China itself of patriotic indignation, as the Japanese seized more and more of China's homeland. It was a feeling which affected Communists as well as Nationalists, warlords as well as workers, and soldiers as well as students. As a result, some of Chiang's troops began to feel that the fight against the Communists was an unnecessary distraction from the main task, and in the university towns students repeatedly demonstrated for an end to civil war. When these failed to persuade Chiang to change his priorities, the Communists seized the opportunity to pose as 'true' patriots, halted a remorseless campaign against wealthy landlords and endorsed the idea of a 'united national revolutionary front' against Japanese imperialism – a movement strenuously resisted by the KMT's leader. But, in November

1936, the signing of the German–Japanese anti-Comintern pact at a time when Japanese troops were occupying non-Communist areas in China further strengthened the case for a Chinese coalition, and, in December, Chiang was forced to consider united action with the Communists after the 'Sian incident', in which he was arrested by one of his own marshals. In the end, however, it was the start of all-out hostilities between China and Japan, in July 1937, that formalized the long-delayed anti-Japanese coalition.[55]

With a membership of only some 40,000 the CCP had to agree to act as junior partner in the arrangement with the KMT, and, in September, the Communists accepted the KMT's political programme. This meant the formal dissolution of the Yenan-based Chinese Soviet government and of the Red Army, acceptance of the KMT's military authority and an end to such revolutionary activities as land confiscation. It also meant that Soviet military and economic aid, which was to arrive in considerable quantity in the wake of a Soviet–Chinese nonaggression pact of August 1937, went to Chiang rather than Mao, not least because Stalin also regarded the KMT's leader as the senior partner in the anti-Japanese struggle. But the CCP had refused to surrender its autonomy, and the Communists continued to build up their own military cadres, civil bureaucracy and propaganda organizations. Skilled in guerrilla tactics, they soon expanded their political orbit from Shensi province to adjacent areas north of the Yangtse valley and to more distant territory, at a time when the Japanese were forcing the KMT to retreat. The Communists also benefited from the KMT's loss in esteem which went along with the rapid decline of the Nationalists' home base.

But Chiang's increasingly corrupt and unpopular regime never lost its earlier fear of 'Communism', and, by 1940, renewed armed clashes between Communist and KMT forces had brought their uneasy truce to an end. In the remaining years of the war, the KMT's attempt to blockade the Communists in Shensi may have weakened the anti-Japanese struggle, but it enabled the CCP to pose as China's only dedicated and effective anti-imperialist force and the true custodian of the national interest. As in France, therefore, the Popular Front enabled the Communists to lay the groundwork for their postwar successes, though the CCP's strategies, perhaps because of its bitter experiences in the '20s, were less responsive than those of the PCF to the twists and turns of Soviet policy towards Germany and Japan.[56]

If, in China, the Communists retained the goodwill earned during the Popular Front period, in Europe they generally fared less well after its demise. For, since they had attracted support largely on the basis of their (not wholly accurate) claim to have been the only consistent and effective anti-Fascist movement, they stood to lose when that assertion could no longer be sustained. In August 1939, Moscow undermined Communist credibility by apparently reversing its policies and signing a non-aggression pact with Nazi Germany. To those who had closely studied Soviet policy over the years this should not have come as a complete surprise. After all, there is nothing in Marx or Lenin to ban temporary accords with the 'class enemy' if these can be presented as serving the long-term interests of the 'revolution'. In any case, Stalin had always kept his options open, both prior to and during the period of the Popular Front. While he tried to bring such states as France, Britain and Czechoslovakia into an effective anti-Fascist coalition, he also seems to have made strenuous efforts to placate Berlin, regardless of the consequences to the KPD.

One highly placed Soviet source alleges that Stalin was already contemplating an accord with Hitler as early as 1937,[57] while the German Foreign Minister, von Neurath, in a dispatch of February 1937, speaks of frequent 'overtures' from Moscow. In this regard, the German Foreign Office documents are especially instructive. In a revealing memorandum of 13 December 1935, one German official speaks of Stalin's representative, Gnedin, as having been sent

> with direct instructions to work energetically for an improvement in German–Soviet relations . . . He [Gnedin] completely understood and thought it a matter of course that the Germans should take strong measures against the Communists in their own country. But this did not exclude the possibility of close collaboration between the two countries . . . Although the ideologies of the Comintern and of the Soviet Union were the same, the Realpolitik of the USSR had nothing to do with the Comintern.[58]

While such clandestine contacts were continued, trade between Moscow and Berlin rose steadily until 1937, and, although it was Stalin who terminated the collaboration between the Red Army and the *Reichswehr*, he did it reluctantly.[59] Meanwhile, the way for a Russo-German accommodation had been cleared well beforehand with Moscow's disengagement from Spain; the liquidation in the purges of tens of thousands of émigrés from Fascism and of others who might have strongly objected to such a deal; the removal from the foreign office of Litvinov, the Jewish-born enthusiast of 'collective security', and Stalin's signal to Germany in his report to the 18th congress of the Soviet Communist Party (CPSU) in March 1939, that Moscow intended to stay neutral in the event of a 'new imperialist war'.[60]

If the Nazi–Soviet pact had shocked the Communist movement,

bringing the Popular Front (where it still existed) to an unceremonious end, there was worse to follow. For, in less than a month, the Red Army was in eastern Poland 'protecting' the Ukrainians and Byelorussians in the region from the *Wehrmacht*, which had invaded western Poland. Soon the 'protected' areas had 'voted' for inclusion into the Soviet Union and within a year Soviet forces had assisted the transfer to the 'Socialist homeland' of a part of Finland; the whole of Latvia, Lithuania, and Estonia; and the Romanian provinces of Bessarabia and northern Bukovina. Moscow's justification was partly ideological, partly strategic, in the context of recent German military successes. But many suspected, rightly, that Moscow's expansionism had been provided for in a secret 'spheres of influence' clause in the Nazi–Soviet pact.[61]

Even more damaging to the Communist movement were the ideological and political contortions the parties had to undertake to keep in step with Soviet policy. Those, like the British and French, who had originally proclaimed the struggle against Hitler a 'just' war, soon had to change their line. According to Moscow, it was a 'great imperialist war', and Communists were to oppose the war effort and refuse to fight.[62] Still more controversially, but with a certain perverse logic, Communists were told to collaborate with the authorities in countries under Nazi occupation. In occupied Norway, for example, the Communist press advised: 'It is in the interests of the Norwegian people that resistance cease' – a view so congenial to the Quisling government that Communist journals were allowed to function relatively freely during the early months of Nazi rule.[63]

Nor was there to be any Communist resistance in Germany. Writing from the comfort of exile in Stockholm, the Communist leader, Walter Ulbricht, urged the German workers to vent their frustrations against not Hitler, but British imperialism: 'The British ruling class have declared war against the workers. If Germany is defeated, German workers can expect the same treatment. Communists, like many Social Democratic and Nazi workers, regard it as their task not to permit a breach of the Soviet–German pact. [It is] Britain [that] is the most reactionary country in the world.'[64] While Communists were called upon to tolerate Nazi rule, they were also enjoined to endorse every Soviet territorial acquisition as being in accordance with the popular will of the countries concerned. For thousands of Communists, this was stretching credulity and credibility too far, and they left the movement in disgust.

Yet, though Communist fortunes reached their lowest ebb during this period, a hard core of members remained. Most were people who had understood that revolution was not an immediate prospect and were prepared to accept that each change of political direction served to advance the revolutionary cause. But there were others whose allegiance was conditional upon their understanding of the nature of Soviet society – and their continued membership was more problematic. Whilst they were persuaded of the wisdom, justice or necessity of Soviet action, they maintained their allegiance. But if they had reason for serious doubt, they could decide to tear up their party cards, though, because of the importance they had learned to attach to Soviet Russia as the 'base of world socialism', they were often prepared to give Moscow the benefit of any doubts they might entertain. Over the years, however, their fidelity had frequently been put to the test.

For example, Stalin's decision in 1928 to abandon NEP had aroused almost as many Communist misgivings as Lenin's decision to implement it, not least because, by appearing to adopt some of Trotsky's earlier demands, Stalin had injected a further element of confusion into the already confusing, if acrimonious, debate over 'Socialism in One Country'. Subsequently, even among those accepting Stalin's crash programme of modernization, some had had qualms about his methods – in particular, the liquidation of the kulaks, the coercion involved in collectivization, and the draconian labour laws which led to widespread, often forcible separation of families.

But perhaps the issue most exercising the conscience of party members before 1939 was the question of the Great Purges. As indicated above, these had reached well beyond the boundaries of the Soviet Union, maiming the Spanish party and virtually decimating the ranks of the thousands of Polish, Yugoslav and other Communist émigrés who had sought sanctuary in the Soviet Union. That Stalin had also sealed the fate of many 'unreliable' German Communist exiles by ensuring that the Gestapo was apprised of their whereabouts when ordered to undertake missions into Germany was, perhaps, not so well known.[65] But what Stalin was doing to Soviet officialdom was public knowledge.

The first indication of a bloody purge had come in 1934 when over 200 hostages were shot in reprisal for the murder (in which Stalin might himself have had a hand) of Kirov, the party chief in Leningrad. Then, between 1936 and 1939, Zinoviev, Kamenev, Rykov, Bukharin and many other celebrated Old Bolsheviks were subjected to a series of show trials and executed after confessing to a number of 'crimes', some of which they could not possibly have committed. At the same time, many prominent figures in the army, the security police, the republican administrations, the foreign office and the Comintern apparatus were exterminated, allegedly for plotting to overthrow the regime. The Party hierarchy, too, was decimated. According to Nikita Khrushchev: 'Of the 1966 delegates to the 17th party congress of 1934, 1108 were arrested for "anti-revolutionary crimes" and of the 139 members elected by that congress to the Central Committee no fewer than 98 were shot'.[66] Though the magnitude of the purges may not have been fully appreciated outside the Soviet Union, of their existence there was no doubt, and all Communists were obliged to decide whether or not the Stalinist case for a blood purge was credible or consistent with their idea of the 'class struggle'.

Thus, while the fidelity of Communists had been put to the test many times before 1939, the dilemmas posed by the Nazi–Soviet pact and its aftermath were probably the most difficult they had ever had to face, and for many it was the 'last straw'. The price of building 'Socialism in One Country' according to a Stalinist blueprint was for them too high. Though Communist parties had always had a rapid turnover of members, the drain in the two years following the pact was especially marked. For the historian, this had a salutary consequence in that it produced a number of knowledgeable ex-Communists who were later to make their contribution to an understanding of international Communism when its fortunes were on the rise. Were it not for the Nazi attack on the Soviet Union in June 1941, the movement might have gone into terminal decline. As it was, however, what Stalin was now to call the 'Great Patriotic War' was to produce a reversal of Communist fortunes, ushering in an expansion of international Communism and producing what became known as 'Socialism in One Zone'.

NOTES

1. *Selected Works* (London, 1938) vol. 10. p. 28.
2. *LSW* pp. 516–91.
3. Ibid., pp. 169–263.
4. Lazitch and Drachkovitch, vol. I, p. 389.
5. For the rival texts, see X. J. Eudin and R. C. North (eds.), *Soviet Russia and the East 1920–1927* (Stanford, 1957), pp. 63–7.
6. Lazitch and Drachkovitch, vol. I, p. 397.
7. Ibid., pp. 396–406.
8. Carr, vol. I, pp. 339–50; 387–98.
9. Lazitch and Drachkovitch, pp. 409–15.
10. 'Left-Wing Communism: An Infantile Disorder', *LSW*, p. 569.
11. Quoted in Douglas Hyde, *United We Fall* (London, 1964), p. 19.
12. G. Nollau, *International Communism and World Revolution* (London, 1961), pp. 75–8.
13. 'Our Course against Putschism' in H. Gruber (ed.), *International Communism in the Era of Lenin* (New York, 1967), p. 340.
14. For an elaboration of their views, see Ruth Fischer, *Stalin and German Communism* (Harvard, 1948).

15. *The Russian Revolution from Lenin to Stalin 1917–1929* (London, 1987), p. 120.
16. E. H. Carr, *The Bolshevik Revolution*, vol. III, pp. 443–6.
17. For a view on the Stalin–Trotsky controversy sympathetic to the latter, see I. Deutscher's 2-volume biography, *The Prophet Unarmed: Trotsky, 1921–1929* (London, 1970).
18. *The Pattern of Communist Revolution* (London, 1960), p. 89.
19. *The Russian Revolution 1917–32* (Oxford, 1986), p. 99.
20. E. H. Carr, *The Interregnum 1923–1924* (London, 1966), ch. 11–13.
21. Carr, *The Russian Revolution* p. 120.
22. Trotsky's decline and fall are traced in Deutscher, ch. 5–6.
23. See his critique, *The Third International after Lenin* (New York, 1970). For a general commentary on Comintern policy in the 1920s, see H. Gruber (ed.), *Soviet Russia Masters the Comintern* (New York, 1974).
24. 'Bolshevization' and its impact on the parties are traced in Gruber (ed.), and Seton-Watson, pp. 104–6.
25. F. Borkenau, *World Communism* (Ann Arbor, 1962), pp. 272–83.
26. Cited in Robert Tucker, *The Soviet Political Mind* (London, 1971), p. 233.
27. See S. F. Cohen, *Bukharin and the Bolshevik Revolution* (New York, 1973), ch. 5–9.
28. M. Lewin, *Russian Peasants and Soviet Power* (London, 1968).
29. See A. Nove, *Political Economy and Soviet Socialism* (London, 1979), ch. 3.
30. G. Nollau, pp. 105–8.
31. E. H. Carr, *Foundations of a Planned Economy 1926–1929* (London, 1976), vol. III, ch. 68, 70, 71, 72.
32. Stephen Clissold (ed.), *Soviet Relations with Latin America 1918–68: A Documentary History* (Oxford, 1970), pp. 13–18.
33. Stuart Schram, *Mao Tse-tung* (London, 1966), pp. 125–55.
34. Seton-Watson, p. 109.
35. J. Valtin, *Out of the Night* (London, 1941), p. 225.
36. J. Degras (ed.), *The Communist International 1919–1943 Documents*, (Oxford, 1965), vol. III, p. 262.
37. For a cogent analysis of Moscow's external policy during this period, see J. Haslam, *Soviet Foreign Policy 1930–1933* (London, 1983).
38. Borkenau, p. 339.
39. Ibid., pp. 347–8.
40. David Caute, *Communism and the French Intellectuals 1914–1960* (London, 1964), pp. 102–11.
41. See, for example, L. Ceplair, *Under the Shadow of War: Fascism, Anti-Fascism and Marxists 1918–1939* (New York, 1987), pp. 127–9.
42. E. H. Carr, *The Twilight of the Comintern 1930–1935* (London, 1982), ch. 9.
43. See J. Haslam, *The Soviet Union and the Struggle for Collective Security in Europe 1933–1939* (London, 1984), ch 1–4.
44. Degras, vol. III, p. 33.
45. Degras, p. 334.
46. Carr, *Twilight*, ch. 16.
47. Degras, pp. 353–5.
48. For the role of the PCF during the Popular Front, see E. Mortimer, *The Rise of the French Communist Party* (London, 1984), ch. 6–8.
49. Borkenau, ch. 24.
50. A. Cave Brown and C. B. MacDonald, *The Communist International and World War II* (London, 1981), p. 433.
51. Schram, pp. 192–7. See also R. C. North, *Moscow and the Chinese Communists* (Stanford, 1962), ch. 11–12.
52. The lessons are traced in G. Wint, *Communist China's Crusade* (London, 1965), pp. 31–46. See also Carr, *Twilight*, ch. 16.
53. Degras, pp. 310–11.

54. Carr, *Twilight*, ch. 16.
55. Schram, pp. 192–7.
56. C. P. Fitzgerald, *The Birth of Communist China* (London, 1964), pp. 84–93.
57. G. W. Krivitsky, *I was Stalin's Agent* (London, 1939).
58. Extracts in *Survey*, No. 49 (October 1963) 129–31.
59. J. Hochman, *The Soviet Union and the Failure of Collective Security* (Cornell, 1984), ch. 5. For an alternative interpretation of Soviet–German relations in the 1930s, see G. Roberts, *The Unholy Alliance: Stalin's Pact with Hitler* (London, 1989) p. 58.
60. For Stalin's report to the congress, see his *Leninism* (London, 1940), pp. 619–30.
61. A contemporary account of these events is given by D. J. Dallin, *Soviet Russia's Foreign Policy 1939–1942* (Yale, 1942).
62. P. Spriano, *Stalin and the European Communists* (London, 1985), ch. 10.
63. Geoffrey Stern, *Fifty Years of Communism* (London, 1967), p. 54.
64. Ulbricht's article is reprinted in Victor Gollancz, *The Betrayal of the Left* (London, 1941), pp. 302–3.
65. See B. Lazitch, 'Stalin's Massacre of the Foreign Communist Leaders' in M. M. Drachkovitch and B. Lazitch (eds.), *The Comintern: Historical Highlights* (New York, 1966). For recent Soviet revelations, see F. Firsov, 'What the Comintern's Archives will Reveal', *World Marxist Review*, vol. 31, No. 1 (January 1989) p. 8.
66. *Khrushchev Remembers*, trans. by Strobe Talbot (London, 1971), pp. 516–17.

PART II

The Rise of International Communism

5. Socialism in One Zone

Ironically, the man who had argued that war was inevitable, who had predicted an eventual German onslaught, and who had been advised by Soviet and British intelligence when Germany would attack, was not prepared for Operation Barbarossa when it came. On the night of 21–22 June 1941, Stalin's forces were literally caught napping, and some units were overwhelmed before they even had time to dress.[1] Ill-informed, poorly led and low in morale as a result of Stalin's purges, the forces suffered one defeat after another. Worse still, many thousands of Ukrainians, Balts and Russians were greeting the invading Germans as 'liberators'. Stalin's answer was to jettison much of the ideological baggage he had been carrying for the past 20 years or so, to cease persecuting the Church (now reminded of its duty to defeat the 'God-less' Nazi), and to call upon his fellow citizens to fight not so much for socialism as for the Fatherland, and in the name of Russia's 'great ancestors' – Alexander Nevsky, Dimitri Donskoi, and Peter the Great.[2] Once again a change of domestic fortunes had produced a change in Comintern tactics. Calling for a 'Patriotic Front' of peoples and of nations against Fascism, Stalin urged Communists to collaborate with 'bourgeois' resistance leaders to intensify the war effort.

On the other hand, given the exigencies of war, Stalin could no longer maintain the kind of control over international Communism he had exercised hitherto, and in countries such as Yugoslavia, Albania, Greece, China and Indochina, Communist-led guerrillas, often with little or no Soviet help, were able to set up networks of administrative centres constituting Communist-style governments-in-embryo. In the circumstances, the Comintern, for long hardly more than an extension of the apparatus of the CPSU, became more or less redundant and, in May 1943, without warning, Stalin had the organization dissolved. In this, he at once rid himself of an institution in which now autonomous and battle-scarred parties might press for a fair share of power, and misled the western powers into thinking that he would no longer seek to promote revolution abroad. In fact, though the Comintern as an institution had been dissolved, many of its functions and personnel had merely been transferred elsewhere – to a new International Department of the Soviet party's Central Committee. Here former ECCI officials such as Dimitrov, Kuusinen and Thorez continued to serve the Soviet authorities, while the original purposes of the organization – promoting and coordinating revolutionary activity – were not so much abandoned as postponed.[3]

Though many heralded the Comintern's demise as final confirmation of the self-contained nature of 'Socialism in One Country', they tended to overlook the degree to which Soviet power had been expanded under that rubric, and could be still further enlarged. First, there had been the reacquisition, mainly by force of arms, of much of the former Russian Empire, which had disintegrated in 1917. There had also been the absorption into the 'Socialist homeland' of contiguous territories, such as northern Bukovina, which had never been an imperial Russian domain. In addition, there had been the use of the Red Army to secure controlled revolution from above in central Asia – as in Tannu Tuva, west of Outer Mongolia, and Outer Mongolia itself, which in the early '20s became nominally autonomous 'People's Republics' (unlike the khanates of Khorezm and Bukhara, which were incorporated directly into the USSR). In little over a year after the Comintern's dissolution, Soviet troops had helped to establish another People's Republic in central Asia at the expense of the enfeebled Chinese Empire – the Eastern Turkistan Republic in northwest Sinkiang. A year later, two more People's Republics appeared briefly in central Asia – this time carved out of northern Iran, where Soviet troops had been stationed since 1941. Clearly, the Soviets had established in central Asia a *modus operandi* which was later to prove useful in eastern Europe.[4]

As in parts of central Asia in an earlier period, so in eastern Europe at the end of 1944, the military successes of the Red Army raised political as well as strategic issues. For, while it was clearly in Moscow's interests to seek to deny to any potential aggressor the areas liberated by Soviet troops at such heavy cost, there was also the question of the form of administration these countries should be permitted to develop under Moscow's protective umbrella. In the 'autonomous' Soviet republics of central Asia, where local Communists were far outnumbered by indigenous nationalist and anti-imperialist forces, the Soviet system had been modified to allow for their pastoral, non-industrial character, and they remained 'People's Republics', in contrast to the 'Socialist Republics' of the Soviet Union. However, in the strategically more critical area of eastern Europe, from which, historically, Russian security had been repeatedly endangered, the Red Army faced societies at once more developed and diverse, thus complicating the problem of finding an appropriate political framework.

Firstly, eastern Europe had for years been the 'powder keg' of

Europe – a cockpit of inter- and intra-national discord. Moreover, its condition prior to the Second World War had resembled much of Africa and Asia today,[5] given its authoritarian governments, coups and counter-coups, bitter political and ethnic divisions, territorial disputes, oppressed minorities and refugee problems. Above all, its economies – still suffering from the collapse of the Russian, Habsburg, German and Ottoman Empires from one or other of which most eastern European countries had only recently been wrenched – had seemed to lurch from crisis to crisis.

Such a strife-torn and impoverished region should have been fertile soil for Communist advance. Yet in the inter-war period, support for Communism was limited. Only in pre-Hitlerite Germany and in eastern Europe's one stable parliamentary democracy – Czechoslovakia – had the Communists enjoyed a mass following, though the party, organized clandestinely in Yugoslavia and Bulgaria (like Czechoslovakia, Slav states traditionally friendly to Russia) had attracted considerable working-class support. Later Communists had tried to prove themselves in the resistance, but, in countries like Poland, Romania and Hungary, their distinction in battle had not succeeded in overcoming the widespread antipathy to Communism and Communists.

On the other hand, the Kremlin could take comfort from the fact that even without Soviet pressure and the presence of the Red Army, eastern Europe was set for a drastic political and economic overhaul on the onset of peace. After all, capitalism had not brought much benefit to the region. It had led to economic depression and, in turn, to Fascism, together with a war which the western democracies had done little to avert. Moreover, because of the degree of state control and central management of industry involved in prosecuting hostilities, it would, in any case, have been difficult to return immediately to something like a free-enterprise market economy. Nor would it have been possible to restore pre-war patterns of ownership, since vast tracts of land and industrial capacity had now been vacated by the vanquished Fascist occupation forces, by the German minorities expelled at the end of hostilities and, of course, by the millions of war dead.[6]

Furthermore, the fact that in each country the Communists had maintained a separate and distinct political identity within the resistance groups had led them to expect at least a share of political power in peacetime, regardless of Moscow's views. Significantly, in two countries whose victory owed little to the Red Army – Yugoslavia and Albania – Communists took power despite, rather than because of Moscow, and but for British and US intervention, Greece might have had a similar fate.

Yet, apart from Yugoslavia and Albania, which were too far from the Soviet Union to be heavily under its sway, eastern Europe's destiny would ultimately depend not so much on the political inclinations of its peoples and the strength of indigenous Communist parties, as on calculations of interest in Moscow. In turn, these would be influenced by the complexities of the Soviet Union's relations with the West.[7] From his study of Marxist–Leninist dialectics and of Russian historical experience both before and after the Revolution, Stalin had concluded that despite four years of successful common action against the Axis powers, the Soviet Union was likely to remain at risk and should fashion its foreign political response accordingly. For one thing, the unprovoked Nazi invasion, which cost 20 million Soviet lives – one in 10 of its population – and much of the country's treasure, had been only the latest in a series of foreign interventions. From the 14-nation attempt to stifle the infant Soviet state, through the French-backed Polish attack on the Ukraine and the *cordon sanitaire* to the appeasement of Hitler by the western democracies and the explicit support of the Führer by some of the Soviet Union's east European neighbours, 'capitalist encirclement' seemed repeatedly confirmed.

Nor had Stalin's suspicions been much allayed by the assistance furnished by his wartime allies. Given the contrast between America's boom conditions and the USSR's war-ravaged economy, Stalin felt that the US might have been more generous, and his disappointment turned to anger with the abrupt termination of Lend Lease at the end of the war. He had also been incensed at the way his allies had virtually excluded him from any say in the future of liberated Italy. And he had put the worst construction on the western powers' repeated delay in opening up a second front in Europe to relieve the pressure on the Soviet Union. That Washington was unwilling to share her atom secrets either before or after the decision to bomb Hiroshima – which many had seen as an attempt to impress Stalin at least as much as Hirohito[8] – only made matters worse.

On the other hand, Stalin's western allies had awarded him a valuable concession which he could use to advantage in eastern Europe – the decision to divide Europe into two exclusive zones of power. First mooted at a meeting of the Big Three in Teheran at the end of 1943, the 'spheres of influence' idea had been made more explicit in the 'percentages agreement' with Churchill in Moscow, in October 1944, and had become manifest at Yalta in February 1945. In any case, since Soviet troops, who had shouldered the main burden of fighting, were already in control of most of eastern Europe it would have been difficult for the Western powers to have denied Moscow a key role in the region.[9] The crucial questions for Moscow were how to exercise its leverage and to what end?

As the Red Army swept to victory, Moscow-trained political agents, many of them eastern European nationals, were dispatched to the countries in its 'sphere' to convey instructions and furnish assistance to the Communists already in the area. By the end of the war, these had helped to boost Communist fortunes throughout the region at a time when the party's prospects seemed equally bright in many countries beyond the Soviet orbit. Though Stalin could depict these political trends as indicating the 'correctness' of Marxism–Leninism, he was not prepared to countenance uncontrolled transition to revolutionary Socialism. A Bolshevik for more than 40 years, he had learned to distrust revolutionary spontaneity – which had Luxemburgist and Trotskyist overtones.[10] He also feared that precipitate transition to one-party rule would provoke a hostile coalition of counter-revolutionaries from East and West, and put Soviet security at risk. In any case, there would be the difficulty of reconciling Socialism in these countries with the exploitation of their human, material, and strategic resources for the benefit of the now enlarged Soviet state.

Thus, far from encouraging Communist seizures of power, he used the Soviet presence in the area initially to try to prevent them. Both Tito in Yugoslavia and Hoxha in Albania were taken to task for putting Communists in sole charge, while the Greek Communists were ordered to end their armed struggle for power, as soon as the USA gave its backing to the Greek government.[11] (Here there is an instructive parallel with Stalin's policy towards the Spanish republic in face of active Italian and German opposition in the '30s.)

But, while trying to rein in Communists he could not control and to temper the political aspirations of those he could, did he nonetheless have a secret blueprint for 'communizing' the countries of eastern Europe and turning them into Soviet satellites in due course? 'Revisionist' historians of the '60s and '70s doubted it. They saw Stalin's gradual subjugation of eastern Europe as a largely improvised response to an international environment perceived as increasingly threatening. In their view, but for western hostility, he would have been content merely to have exercised in the area the power of veto – as in Finland.[12] But western analysts in the early years of the cold war felt they had good cause to see in Stalin's steady political and ideological squeeze on eastern Europe the fulfilment of a master plan.[13] After all, the Hungarian Communist leader, Mátyás Rákosi, had himself spoken of the 'salami method',[14] i.e. progressing slice by slice, as it were, to Communist victory, while in one eastern European country after another, a broadly similar political scenario was being played out which, many believed, could only have been devised in Moscow.

First, there was Communist participation in a Popular Front coalition on the basis of a relatively uncontroversial programme of reconstruction. At this time, Communists championed the mixed economy, spoke of 'separate roads to socialism', and took an appropriately 'patriotic' line on the major issues of the day – spearheading the expropriation and expulsion of ethnic Germans and upholding the national cause in such regional disputes as those regarding Transylvania, Macedonia, and the Oder-Neisse territories (which, of course, put them at odds with 'nationally orientated' Communists of other countries).

At a later stage, however, their bid for popularity took second place to the drive for increased political and economic control. During this period, Communists in eastern Europe infiltrated the key ministries of security and defence and developed an extensive secret-police network. They further enhanced their power by penetrating political, economic and cultural organizations, and by sponsoring frequent purges of 'Fascists' – a term so loosely defined as to include most of the party's influential opponents. At the same time, they were so successful at exploiting divisions within and among rival political groups that soon they could virtually determine the leadership of the parties with which they now only nominally shared power. By February 1948, when Czech tanks effectively intervened in Prague to bring down the world's first democratically elected, Communist-led coalition, active opponents of Communist rule had been more or less suppressed and what has been called 'monolithic Communism' descended on the region.[15]

Yet, given the complex interplay of domestic and international forces, the transition from coalition to monolith did not occur at a uniform pace. In Yugoslavia and Albania, where Communist-led partisans had waged a successful struggle against their enemies – domestic as well as foreign – Communist rule was achieved too soon to accord with Stalin's requirements.

In Poland – traditionally Catholic and anti-Russian – the process took longer, though because of the executions, deportation or exile of leading non-Communists after the Nazi and Soviet invasion of 1939, and the rout of the non-Communist underground following the anti-Nazi Warsaw Rising of August 1944, there was never any semblance of a genuine Popular Front coalition.[16] Stalin, having broken with the Polish government-in-exile in London, following the controversy in 1943 over the fate of the massacred Polish officers whose graves had been discovered in Katyń forest near Smolensk, had established a government of his own choosing in the liberated town of Lublin and installed it as

Poland's provisional administration in the wake of the Red Army advance in 1944. This was, of course, Communist-dominated, and though it was later diluted by the inclusion of a few members from the London government, a concession secured by the western powers as a price for recognition, its political direction was little affected. The non-Communists were heavily outnumbered and, by 1947, Stanisław Mikołajczyk, one of the four 'London Poles' in the cabinet, had been forced to flee the country. On his departure, his Peasant Party collapsed, and within a year, Communist and Socialist parties had been merged into a single Polish United Workers' (Communist) Party. Though the Peasant and other political parties survived, they served merely as 'transmission belts' for the Communist leadership and played no independent role in the country's politics until more than 40 years later.

The Soviet zone of Germany (i.e. the eastern part of the now divided country), likewise, produced no 'coalition of equals'.[17] After the Communists had failed to win more than 20 per cent of the votes in local elections in the autumn of 1945, the Soviet Union decided on the fusion of the Communist and Social Democratic parties in the zone, and, in April, 1946, set up the Socialist Unity Party (SED) under Walter Ulbricht's leadership. Almost immediately, the other parties tolerated under the Soviet occupation were rendered politically impotent and soon most of the former Social Democrats, who had hoped to gain influence in the SED, were deprived of effective power.

In the ex-Axis states of Romania and Bulgaria, any 'genuine coalition' was of short duration. In March 1945, King Michael of Romania yielded to a Soviet ultimatum and appointed Petru Groza, leader of the leftward-looking Ploughman's Front, as premier of a new National Democratic Front government in place of the former coalition. All the vital posts in the new administration were held by Communists, even though the party's membership in 1944 had barely exceeded a thousand. By November 1946, the Front, after much intrigue and intimidation, was able to secure four-fifths of the parliamentary seats at a general election. Within a year, the King had abdicated, Socialist and Communist parties had been merged, and all effective opposition eliminated.[18]

If there was some logic in the Communist decision to curtail parliamentary activity in countries with a strong anti-Communist tradition, there was much less excuse for treating Bulgaria in like fashion. After all, the Bulgarian Party had enjoyed considerable popularity both before and after 1923, when it was forced underground, and its Soviet connections were no obstacle in a country traditionally pro-Russian.

On the other hand, Bulgaria's pre-war ruling parties had remained largely intact at the end of the war, and the Communist Party felt that it would be necessary to neutralize them to guarantee its own survival. In January 1945, the Communists secured the resignation of a leading official in the Agrarian Union, the most influential group in the Fatherland Front coalition, and increasingly established their own domination of the Front. By October 1946, the government had been placed in the hands of veteran Communist, Georgi Dimitrov, after a Communist-sponsored general election, and active opposition crumbled after the execution, in September 1947, of Nikola Petkov, leader of the Agrarian Union. Shortly afterwards, what remained of his group was merged with the Communists, and the other parties were disbanded in little over a year.[19]

In Hungary, another ex-Axis state, whose experiences under Béla Kun's Soviet-style regime in 1919 had rendered the country strongly anti-Communist, the parliamentary system was allowed to survive unfettered for somewhat longer. In November 1945, a general election in which the Communists polled only 17 per cent of the votes brought the Smallholders' (i.e. Peasant) Party to power, but its authority was soon undermined when the Communists formed a leftist bloc with the Social Democratic and National Peasant parties. In February 1947, Moscow ordered the arrest of the Secretary General of the Smallholders' Party, and, in May, the Communists forced the Prime Minister, Ferenc Nagy, to resign. The ruling party was effectively undermined, and the leftist bloc, having disenfranchised about half a million voters and intimidated others, was able to obtain a small lead over its opponents in the election of August 1947. Within a year, Socialist and Communist parties were fused into a single political organization, and the last independent political party was dissolved in 1949.[20]

It was in Czechoslovakia that a 'genuine coalition' lasted longest. Here the Communists, who had enjoyed both legality and popularity until the Nazi occupation, and who had not been associated with those who 'betrayed' the country to Hitler in 1938, constituted the largest parliamentary party, after obtaining 38 per cent of the votes in a free election in May 1946. With several Communists in the cabinet and their leader, Klement Gottwald, as premier, it seemed as if Communist ambitions were being achieved by parliamentary means. But when the party suffered reverses in local elections in late 1947, it began police operations against its rivals, and several non-Communists resigned from Gottwald's cabinet in protest. But the Communists retaliated with strikes, street demonstrations and the occupation of premises belonging to the non-Communist parties; and, on 25 February 1948, while Czech

tanks ringed Prague, Gottwald staged his coup, creating a new administration which omitted almost all those opposed to his party (a not
especially difficult undertaking since most non-Communists had already
departed). Soon the Communist takeover was complete. On 10 March,
Jan Masarýk, the non-Communist Foreign Minister, died after a fall
(possibly induced) from his office window, and, in June, Eduard Beneš
resigned from the presidency, only to die three months later.[21]

As organized opposition to Communism crumbled in eastern Europe,
it began to intensify beyond the Soviet sphere. By 1947, the watchword
in the West was 'containment', and a series of measures was devised
to check what was seen as Soviet-sponsored 'Communism'. Within two
years of the Truman Doctrine, which pledged aid to Greece and
Turkey, the USA, Canada and 10 western European countries had
joined forces in NATO, Washington having recently reinvigorated western Europe's floundering economies through the Marshall Plan. If Stalin
felt threatened by these moves, he was hardly less disturbed by the
growing tendency of eastern Europe's Communists to pursue their own
line, regardless of Soviet interests. The process had, of course, begun
when Tito and Hoxha, in Yugoslavia and Albania, respectively, sliced
their 'political salamis' far too rapidly for Stalin's comfort. Then Poland
and Czechoslovakia declared an interest in Marshall aid, with all that
that implied, and Yugoslavia and Bulgaria moved to fashion a Balkan
confederation of their own design.[22] In face of such unwelcome initiatives, Stalin took steps to tighten his grip on eastern Europe by strengthening his country's political, economic and military ties with the region.

The creation of the Cominform – an information bureau linking the
CPSU with those European Communist parties (including the French
and Italian) enjoying a share in government – was indicative of the
new trend.[23] For, at its inaugural meeting in September 1947, Andrei
Zhdanov, Stalin's ideological 'watchdog', proclaimed the division of
the world into two hostile 'camps' and spoke of the need to consolidate
the 'camp of socialism, peace, and democracy'. But perhaps more
crucial in the transition from 'Socialism in One Country' to 'Socialism
in One Zone' were the bilateral treaties of friendship and mutual assistance legalizing the presence of Soviet troops in eastern Europe and
serving as a cover for the growth of a vast network of Soviet security
agents and informers.

Fortunately for Stalin, economic conditions merely reinforced the
structure of dominance and dependency. Whereas trade pre-war
between the Soviet Union and eastern Europe had been negligible, by
1948 the USSR was already fast becoming the area's largest supplier
and customer, assisted in no small measure by the western powers'

growing embargo on strategic goods to the Communist-dominated countries. For the West's sizeable list of restrictions, drawn up by a co-ordinating committee known as COCOM, necessitated a reorientation of eastern European trade, enabling Moscow to hold its trade-dependent allies at its mercy. Meanwhile, the creation of an 'iron curtain' of barbed wire, watchtowers, steel helmeted guards and ploughed mine-fields, together with an administrative system effectively isolating the eastern European countries from one another as well as from the West, enabled Moscow to pursue the time-honoured strategy of 'divide and rule!'[24]

Yet, what had become, by 1948, a Soviet bloc was not just the product of Soviet strategems or of docile Communist leaders. For, the Soviet Union did enjoy a certain degree of popular support, even among non-Communists. There was admiration for a country which had emerged victorious against the world's most powerful military machine. There was hope that a country which had apparently pulled itself up by its own bootstraps might enable eastern Europe to do likewise. There was confidence in Moscow's ability to protect eastern Europe from the irredentist claims of West Germany or from the uncertain ambitions of the USA, with its atomic superiority. There was also a general welcome for the transfer to eastern Europe of some of the more positive aspects of the Soviet system, especially as regards education, literacy, health and employment.

Moreover, though both western critics and Communist apologists spoke of the bloc as 'monolithic', it was never quite as uniform, either in alliance terms or even as regards the political organization of its members, as it appeared. There were to be differences of emphasis as well as minor variations in political and economic structures and priorities, reflecting to a degree divergences in national culture and tradition. On the other hand, Stalin did manage to conjure a remarkable degree of conformity from such a diverse and variegated region, and, from 1948 until Stalin's death in 1953, in all essentials of policy and organization similarities outweighed differences.

In practice, this meant that the intimidation which had facilitated the Communist rise to power was extended to party functionaries as well as their foes, in the interests of promoting unswerving loyalty to the Soviet Union. A reign of terror was unleashed throughout the bloc (as in the Soviet Union itself) during which thousands of Communists and non-Communists were arrested, imprisoned, or executed.[25] The Hungarian Minister of the Interior, László Rajk; a Bulgarian deputy Prime Minister, Traicho Kostov; the Czechoslovakian Foreign Minister, Vladimir Clementis and the General Secretary of the Czechoslovakian party, Rudolf Slánský were among those charged with 'national deviationism' and executed after carefully staged show trials. Those imprisoned during this period included Władysław Gomułka, János Kádár, Gustav Husák and Josef Smrkovský, who were to become prominent in post-Stalinist politics. That a score of Bulgarian ministers were purged indicates the extent and severity of the upheaval.

No longer were the parties able to commend 'independent roads to Socialism'.[26] For, Moscow had drawn up a blueprint for what it called a 'People's Democracy' – a halfway house, as it were, to Socialism – and the countries of eastern Europe were called upon to apply it. In effect, each was to bear the imprint of Soviet experience, modelling its constitution on the Soviet constitution of 1936, but, as in the Soviet Union, effectively ignoring its more liberal provisions. Most were to be headed by a dictator who developed his own personality cult alongside that of Stalin – for example, Hoxha of Albania, Gottwald of Czechoslovakia, Rákosi of Hungary, and Ulbricht of the German Democratic Republic (fashioned in 1949 out of the former Soviet zone of Germany following the collapse of the four-power administration, the Berlin blockade, and the creation of the German Federal Republic). All secondary schools were obliged to teach Russian, and strict censorship was imposed on all forms of literature and the arts. Religious activities were placed under state control and several thousand clergymen – including Hungary's Cardinal Mindszenty and Poland's Cardinal Wyszyński – were imprisoned. Moreover, following Moscow's lead, the eastern Europeans took to persecuting Jews under the pretext of fighting Zionism – even though the Soviet Union was one of the first countries to recognize Israel.

During this period, too, the economies of the bloc were reorganized to accord with Soviet requirements. Each country completed the nationalization of industry and trade and adopted central planning techniques along Soviet lines, with its emphasis on heavy industry, especially steel. Labour discipline was tightened, and trade unions became, as in the USSR, mere transmission belts for the party line. In agriculture, the aim was full collectivization, but, as in the Soviet Union, production lagged as the peasants, in effect, deprived of their title to land, lost interest in farming – and everywhere the consumer sector languished.

Given Stalin's preference for bilateral rather than multilateral ties, little use was made of the Council for Mutual Economic Assistance (COMECON) created in January 1949, ostensibly to facilitate economic cooperation among bloc members.[27] Nonetheless, by the time of Stalin's death, the bloc's economic relations had been completely reorientated, largely to Moscow's advantage. With eastern Europe increasingly dependent on the Soviet Union's vast market, technology, trade credits and raw materials, Moscow was able to weight the terms of trade heavily in its favour. Whilst, for example, the Russians generally sold their raw materials at prices above those obtaining on the world market, they bought Polish coal at a fraction of the world price and paid so little for Bulgarian tobacco that they were able substantially to undercut Bulgaria's selling price on the world market. At the same time, Moscow benefited from the joint-stock companies established to manage former enemy property in East Germany, Romania and Hungary, taking the lion's share of the profits even though the eastern Europeans had invested most of the capital. Finally, the heavy reparations exacted from the ex-Axis states together with Poland, which now had title to the former German territories of the Oder-Neisse, in compensation for land lost to the Soviet Union, meant the stripping of eastern European assets and the transfer of resources to the USSR on an enormous scale. In the circumstances, the notion that these countries had become mere 'satellites' of Moscow was scarcely inappropriate.[28]

Stalin's chain of satellite states had one weak link, however – Yugoslavia. Having won national power largely through his own efforts as a wartime partisan leader, Tito did not feel as beholden to Moscow as did many fellow Communists. Moreover, his original admiration for the Soviet party chief began to wane when, towards the end of the war, Stalin and Churchill appeared to be bargaining away Yugoslavia's future behind his back. From then on, the points of friction between the Yugoslav and Soviet leadership began to mount, and, by 1948, the conflict between them was so intense that Stalin could no longer countenance Tito's continued membership of the Communist fraternity. In June, he gave orders for Yugoslavia's expulsion from the organization whose headquarters, ironically, Stalin had centred in Belgrade – the Cominform – and proceeded to batten down the hatches among its remaining members. If Stalin's intention was to isolate and kill the contagion of nationalism emanating from the Yugoslav capital, it failed, for the bacillus refused to die. Indeed, it lived on to infect other members of the Communist body politic and to pose the greatest potential threat to 'Socialism in One Zone' along Stalinist lines.

NOTES

1. J. Erickson, *The Road to Stalingrad* (London, 1975), ch. 2–4.
2. A. Werth, *Russia at War 1941–1945* (London, 1964), part 2, chp. 11; part 4, ch. 6.
3. On the dissolution of the Comintern, see. F. Claudin, *The Communist Movement* (London, 1975), ch. 1.

4. See R. Pethybridge, *The Development of the Communist Bloc* (Boston, 1965) esp. Introduction.
5. See H. Seton-Watson, *Eastern Europe between the Wars* (London, 1962).
6. See M. McCauley (ed.), *Communist Power in Europe 1944–1949* (London, 1977).
7. See Z. Brzezinski, *The Soviet Bloc: Unity and Conflict* (New York, 1961), ch. 1.
8. See, for example, Gar Alperowitz, *Atomic War* (London, 1966).
9. See W. H. McNeill, *America, Britain and Russia: Their Cooperation and Conflict 1941–1946* (New York, 1953).
10. See Y. Gluckstein, *Stalin's Satellites in Europe* (London, 1952), esp. part II.
11. M. Djilas, *Conversations with Stalin* (London, 1963), p. 140.
12. See, for example, G. Kolko, *The Politics of War* (New York, 1968), and G. and J. Kolko, *The Limits of Power* (New York, 1972).
13. See, for example, J. F. Dulles, *War or Peace* (New York, 1950); S. T. Possony, *A Century of Conflict* (Chicago, 1953); and Waldemar Gourian (ed.), *Soviet Imperialism, Its Origins and Tactics* (Indiana, 1953).
14. Cited in A. Fontaine, *History of the Cold War* (London, 1968), p. 306.
15. On political events in eastern Europe after 1945, see R. Betts (ed.), *Central and South-Eastern Europe 1945–1948* (London, 1950); M. McCauley (ed.), *Communist Power in Europe 1944–1949* (London, 1977); T. T. Hammond, *Anatomy of Communist Takeovers* (New Haven, 1973); D. Warriner, *Revolution in Eastern Europe* (London, 1950); and H. Seton-Watson, *The Pattern of Communist Revolution* (London, 1960), ch. 13.
16. On Poland, see A. Polonsky and B. Drukier (eds.), *The Beginnings of Communist Rule in Poland* (London, 1980), and S. Mikołajczyk, *The Pattern of Soviet Domination* (London, 1948).
17. On Germany, see J. P. Nettl, *The Eastern Zone and Soviet Policy in Germany, 1945–1950* (London, 1951).
18. On Romania, see G. Ionescu, *Communism in Rumania 1944–1962* (London, 1964).
19. On Bulgaria, see N. Oren, *Revolution Administered: Agrarianism and Communism in Bulgaria* (Baltimore, 1973).
20. On Hungary, see. G. Schöpflin's essay in McCauley, ch. 6.
21. On Czechoslovakia, see P. Zinner, *Communist Strategy and Tactics in Czechoslovakia* (London, 1963).
22. See Brzezinski, pp. 51–8.
23. See Claudin, ch. 6.
24. I. Deutscher, *Stalin* (Oxford, 1961), p. 564.
25. See A. Westoby, *Communism since World War II* (Brighton, 1981), pp. 71–6.
26. On the Stalinization of eastern Europe, see the texts cited in note 15.
27. See M. Kaser, *Comecon* (London, 1965).
28. T. Cliff, *Russia: A Marxist Analysis* (London, 1970), ch. 9 and 13. See also C. Harman, *Bureaucracy and Revolution in Eastern Europe* (London, 1974), ch. 2.

6. The Yugoslav 'Defection'

Stalin's decision to expel and isolate Tito's Yugoslavia from the Communist fraternity had come as a political bombshell to friend and foe alike – Tito included. Yet, since the Yugoslav party (CPY) had been a thorn in Moscow's flesh almost since its foundation in 1919, its exclusion in 1948 should not have been a total surprise. For, the CPY had always been one of Communism's least manageable parties, having attracted many of uncertain ideology for whom the party was a vehicle of protest against the political contours of a state to which they could feel no loyalty.[1]

For, Yugoslavia had been a creation of the Versailles peacemakers, who had failed to realize that giving the south Slavs self-determination was meaningless since they did not consider themselves to constitute a national self. They were themselves divided into distinct and often conflicting nationalities, most of which resented incorporation into a strongly centralized state run from the old Serbian capital, Belgrade. At times of inter-communal tension, the CPY had tended to become a receptical for regional secessionists who had their own reasons for supporting the Communist aim of overthrowing the state. But the Communists' regional preoccupations had brought them into conflict both with one another and with the party's ideologues, themselves rent between left- and right-wing factions, for which the party was repeatedly censured by the Comintern. Moreover, in the wake of a further rift, between a faction operating from abroad and another from inside the country, the CPY had almost followed the Polish party into oblivion. Certainly, the Comintern had seriously considered its dissolution, as its membership, once in excess of 60,000, had shrunk, by 1937, to little over 1,500 querulous souls. Ironically, what had saved it from the fate of the Polish party was the very factor which was to be so decisive in the CPY's exclusion 10 years later – the leadership of Josip Broz, who called himself Tito.

For, until then, Tito had been one of the few Yugoslav Communists on whom Moscow could safely rely. Indeed, his record as a political organizer had been impeccable ever since the Revolution. As a POW in Russia in 1917 he had managed to make his way to Petrograd to demonstrate against the Provisional Government and had subsequently fought in the Bolshevik Red Guards in the early years of the civil war. Returning to Yugoslavia in 1920, he was to serve the CPY, which was about to be forced underground after two successful years as a parliamentary party, in many different capacities and under a variety of assumed names, of which Tito was only one.

As an activist in the Metal Workers Union, he encouraged strikes and demonstrations, capitalizing on the unrest already manifest in many parts of the country and often leaving a trail of industrial devastation behind him. As a political agitator, he had organized clandestine party cells, and in seven years (five of them spent in jail for his political activities) he had risen from branch secretary in Zagreb to membership of the CPY'S Politburo, helping to reinvigorate a party demoralized by police pressure and the effects of a weak, disputatious, and largely absentee leadership. As a paid Comintern official, he had worked as rapporteur for Yugoslavia in the Balkan Secretariat in Moscow, lectured at the Leninist School and served as Secretary of the Yugoslav delegation for the Comintern's seventh congress in 1935. By this time, he had duly switched from supporting nationalist secessionism in Yugoslavia to a strategy involving a common struggle to preserve the country's integrity against the 'imperialist' designs of Italian, German, Hungarian and Bulgarian Fascism. A year later he was recruiting Yugoslavs on behalf of the Comintern to fight in Spain – a perilous undertaking in which he had to play hide-and-seek with the police of half a dozen countries. His evident energy, courage, and organizing skills, as well as his political reliability, had clearly impressed Moscow, which is, no doubt, why, rather than dissolve the party, the Kremlin called on Tito to lead it, while liquidating most of his former colleagues (possibly with his connivance) in the purges.

For some four years after Tito's appointment as CPY General Secretary in 1937, the Kremlin could be well satisfied with its choice. For, at a time when Stalin's policies were causing misgivings throughout the Communist world, the CPY, reunified and rapidly expanding in membership under Tito, seemingly approved Moscow's every twist and turn. The purges, for example, evoked no hint of criticism from the CPY's new leadership, which had been a major beneficiary, while Moscow's pact with Berlin and the Red Army's subsequent incursions into neighbouring territory were enthusiastically endorsed by the Yugoslav party. The pact was seen as a prelude to war between Germany and the western powers, which, according to one of Tito's aides, 'would create an ideal opportunity for the Soviet Union to spread socialism at the expense of the two warring sides'.[2]

And, while the British and French parties had initially supported their governments in prosecuting hostilities against Nazi Germany, the CPY had decided to keep aloof, regarding the conflict as a struggle between imperialists, even before it had received Moscow's word on the subject. According to Milovan Djilas, the CPY was 'the only party to take this position from the very start of the war, and we maintained it, with certain modifications, until the German attack on the Soviet Union'. As for the partition of Poland, Djilas recalls his fellow Communists as being 'thrilled' by the news. They believed the Soviet Union was liberating Ukrainians and Byelorussians from Polish oppression and 'broadening the territory of socialism' – and their faith was reaffirmed by Moscow's later territorial acquisitions.[3]

It was not until early April 1941 when, with bewildering rapidity, Yugoslavia was herself attacked, divided into a number of 'satellite' states by the Axis powers, and partitioned among Germany, Italy, Hungary and Bulgaria that the CPY began a review of its political strategy that was eventually to put it once again on a collision course with Moscow.

At a party conference in May, Tito called on Communists throughout what had been Yugoslavia to take possession of the large stock of weapons strewn across the country in the wake of the collapse of the Yugoslav army, in preparation for an armed uprising. However, since Moscow was still on tolerable terms with the countries which had just dismembered Yugoslavia, the projected insurrection was to be directed not so much at the occupiers, as against the groups of national secessionists whose struggle against the Yugoslav state the CPY had once backed. The primary target was the Ustaše, Fascists whose 'independent state of Croatia', under Hitler's auspices, was already committing the most brutal atrocities against Communists, as well as Serbs, Jews, and gypsies. The Serbian 'Četniks', who were beginning to mobilize in defence of a country they hoped to control by the end of the war, were another potential target.

What was significant about Tito's tactics is that they had been arrived at without consulting Moscow.[4] Perhaps even more significantly, they were placed in an ideological context at variance with the prevailing Communist orthodoxy. For, whereas the Comintern held that the Communist road to power lay through a preceding 'bourgeois democratic' revolution, Tito postulated an immediate Communist takeover on the defeat of Germany.[5] Though the difference in approach appeared, at the time, to be no more than tactical, the practical implications were extremely far reaching, as was to become clear after the Soviet Union itself became a victim of Nazi aggression. What Stalin wanted was the broadest possible resistance coalition in the countries under Axis

occupation and a curb on Communist manifestations which might alien-
ate the peasantry and alarm Moscow's western allies. For Tito, however, collaboration with those aiming to restore what his partisans were
trying to destroy was anathema, and the only guerrilla groups with
which he would willingly cooperate where those prepared to accept a
new order at the end of hostilities. Before long, his partisans were
having to resist not only the Axis powers, but also the rival Četnik
guerrillas, as well as the censorious messages that were flooding in from
Moscow.[6]

In the first three months of the partisan struggle, all seemed well
between Tito and Stalin. Though Communist-led guerrillas were fighting more or less on their own throughout most of Yugoslavia, in Serbia
they agreed, on instructions by radio from Moscow, to joint operation
with the Četniks. Militarily, this combined effort was a considerable
success, since within weeks the resistance forces had freed most of
Serbia from German control, capturing in the process large quantities
of arms and ammunition. At the same time, their collaboration served
Stalin's aim of maintaining friendly ties with his western allies who,
like the Royal Yugoslav government-in-exile in London, gave military
and financial backing to the Četniks. But relations between the two
guerrilla groups were never easy, and, by the end of October 1941,
they had broken down altogether, to the advantage, as Stalin had
feared, of the Germans, who were beginning to counterattack. Both
politically and militarily, the situation in Yugoslavia was starting to
bear an uncanny resemblance to that of China, where no matter how
bravely the Communists fought, internecine strife sapped the war effort
against the common enemy.

Precipitating the drift into civil war had been Tito's blatant disregard
of Moscow's advice on maintaining a low political profile. In fact, Tito
remained, throughout the campaign, all too open about his revolutionary ambitions.[7] His partisans fought with the Red Star as their emblem,
had political commissars attached to each unit, called their elite troops
Proletarian Brigades, and, in liberated areas, set up National Liberation
Councils under Communist control to take over the functions of local
government. If Tito's high-profile political approach alarmed the Četniks, his bold military tactics were scarcely less worrying. For, the
fearless and daring exploits of the partisans often resulted in the most
terrible retribution on the civilians who got caught in the crossfire, and,
in Četnik eyes, the price of even partial victory was becoming too high.
Increasingly their leader, General Draža Mihailović, came to regard
Tito's partisans as an even greater threat to Yugoslavia than the Axis
powers, whose occupation might be only temporary.[8]

Whether Moscow's failure to answer Tito's repeated requests for aid was for logistical or political reasons is still not clear. What is certain, however, is that having built up an effective guerrilla force of some 150,000 Serbs, Croats, Slovenes, and other nationalities in two years, with little but carping criticism from Moscow, Tito was never going to relinquish control of his country's affairs to Stalin.

At first, Tito shrugged off Moscow's initial criticisms regarding the overtly Communist and anti-Četnik character of his movement. But when the Kremlin reproved the partisans for agreeing to a limited exchange of prisoners of war with the Germans, Tito was clearly hurt, and signalled in return: 'If you can't understand what a hard time we are having and if you can't help us, then at least don't hinder us'.[9] There was worse to come. When Tito formed a National Liberation Committee in November 1942, the Kremlin had counselled him to give it 'an all-party anti-Fascist character' and warned: 'Do not look upon the Committee as a sort of government. Do not put it in opposition to the Yugoslav government in London. . . . Do not make any mention of a republic'.[10] Yet, one year later, Tito had turned the committee into a provisional government with himself, with the rank of marshal, as Prime Minister and Minister of Defence, and charged it with superseding both the monarchy and the government-in-exile.

To Stalin, who had just had an amicable meeting with Churchill and Roosevelt in Teheran, this was an act of gross indiscipline. As Dimitrov told the CPY's representative in Moscow: 'The Boss is quite exceptionally angry. He says that it is a stab in the back for the Soviet Union and for the Teheran decisions [relating to material help to the partisans from Britain and the USA as well as the Soviet Union].[11] In the event, the partisans were to receive more aid in the coming months from the western powers (which were about to abandon Mihailović amid reports of Četnik collaboration with the occupying powers) than from the Soviet Union – a fact which only widened Tito's rift with Moscow.[12]

In the following year, however, there were hopes on both sides that Soviet–Yugoslav disagreements might be laid to rest amid the rapidly changing kaleidoscope of military and political affairs. In the first place, Britain's heavy pressure on Tito to accept a Royalist share in a postwar government, in return for Allied recognition, infuriated him, reinforcing his Communist distrust of 'bourgeois' politicians. More importantly, the Soviet Union was now, for the first time, able to offer the partisans more than homilies and tokens. By the end of August 1944, the Red Army, now sweeping through Romania, was rapidly approaching the Yugoslav frontier, and, in September, Tito flew to Moscow to make his peace with Stalin and the final arrangements for the Soviet entry into his country.

Their meeting was not an unqualified success. Though Stalin was evidently pleased to see the man who had once been one of his keenest disciples, he found the Yugoslav inordinately arrogant. For, Tito insisted in imposing conditions on the entry of Soviet troops. They were to stay on Yugoslav soil only in connection with their military duties, were not to exercise any civil or administrative authority while in the country and were to withdraw as soon as they had completed their military mission. Furthermore, there could be no question of the partisans being placed under Soviet command.[13] To these conditions, Stalin reluctantly agreed, and then saw his hopes of a Soviet-influenced approach to Yugoslav Socialism jeopardized as Tito contemptuously dismissed his suggested list of bourgeois politicians with whom to share power. Having met his match in Marshal Tito, it is doubtful that the Soviet leader could ever have seriously supposed that the Yugoslav would tamely accept the Stalin–Churchill accord of the following month giving Moscow and London an equal claim to influence in the country. In the event, news of the percentages agreement made Tito intensely angry with both signatories, even if he was to some extent in their debt.[14]

That his indebtedness to Moscow increased still further during the closing stages of the war brought little sign of gratitude. For, instead of praising the Red Army's role, Tito found cause for complaint about the conduct of many Soviet soldiers, whom he accused, much to Stalin's annoyance, of bullying, raping, and killing innocent civilians.[15] The precise role of the Red Army in Yugoslavia was another bone of contention. The Soviet leader held that his troops had been crucial to the country's liberation, whereas, to Tito, their significance was as an adjunct to the partisans, who were the real liberators. And the Yugoslav resented the Red Army's failure to assist his quest for *irredenta* at the expense of Austria and Italy.[16] On the other hand, Tito realized that, whatever his differences with Stalin, he would need Soviet and eastern European assistance in the reconstruction of his battered country and, to this end, went to Moscow in April 1945 to sign a treaty of friendship and mutual assistance, thereby appearing to put his country in the Soviet orbit.

Indeed, for some three years after the war, Yugoslavia seemed to be Stalin's most loyal satellite.[17] Its domestic policy appeared to stem from a Soviet Socialist blueprint. The few non-Communists Tito had agreed to take into his government in return for Allied recognition were never given a chance of exercising effective power. Most had been placed under house arrest before the elections of November 1945, and, given the efficiency of the UDBA (the Yugoslav equivalent of the KGB), and the fact that the poll was on the Stalinist model, with one Communist or Communist-approved candidate per constituency, the result was a foregone conclusion. Moreover, as in Russia, a somewhat brutal, though inefficient monarchy was replaced by a Soviet-style federation so constituted as to give the party leader almost unlimited control. Like Stalin, moreover, Tito suppressed freedom of speech, the press and worship, and staged a series of arrests, show trials and executions of opponents, real and imagined, rivalling in their scope and brutality, the worst excesses in the countries under Soviet control.

By the end of 1946, after Belgrade had launched an ambitious five-year plan and nationalized all industry, trade, commerce, banking, transport and communications, Yugoslavia had, to all intents and purposes, become a carbon copy of the Soviet Union. Though the process had been charted in Belgrade and not, as was widely supposed in the West, in Moscow, it produced a critical spiral of East–West hostility that resulted in the shooting down of two 'stray' US planes over Yugoslav territory and the reinforcement of the country's borders in the autumn of 1946. During this period, moreover, Yugoslav propaganda did not echo so much as exceed Moscow in its diatribes against the West, in part, perhaps, because the western powers were a barrier to Tito's foreign political ambitions.[18] British troops backed the opponents of his Communist allies in Greece and forced him to relinquish Trieste and modify some of his other claims on Italian and Austrian territory. They were also on the alert lest he incorporate Albania, already, in effect, a Yugoslav satellite, into the Yugoslav federation.

Yet, despite Tito's cold war attitudes, admiration for Soviet-style Socialism, and entanglements with Moscow, his relations with Stalin were far from easy. Though the Soviet leader clearly respected him more than any other party chief – allowing him a triumphal tour of the USSR in 1945 and a place of honour by his side at a state funeral in 1946[19] – he also distrusted him. For, while the western political establishment had come to view Tito as one of Stalin's satraps, Stalin regarded Tito as a nationalist dangerously premature in his domestic introduction of Soviet-style Socialism, and not easily influenced or controlled. For his part, the Yugoslav leader, who had tended to shrug off Soviet criticisms in the past, was beginning to resent what he regarded as Moscow's unwarranted interference in Yugoslav affairs.

Having already complained about the behaviour of Soviet troops in his country, Tito then had cause to object to the conduct of Soviet officialdom. As in other eastern European countries (though with different results), Soviet intelligence was trying to recruit Yugoslav party and state functionaries, army officers, and even former opponents of the regime for purposes that could only be guessed at. Furthermore, Soviet envoys took what Tito regarded as a disdainful attitude to his regime, offering unsolicited 'advice' and flooding the Yugoslav press with stories about the Soviet homeland, for which there was but a limited appeal. Not surprisingly, when Moscow 'offered' to man Yugoslav airports with Soviet staff (i.e. security police), the offer was refused.[20]

As regards the economic ties on which Tito had set great hopes, these grew from bad to worse. Even though Stalin was himself the inspiration for Tito's development plans, the Soviet leader had reservations about their timing and scope and was reluctant to finance them. To the extent that he felt them overambitious as well as premature, he was probably right. For, Yugoslavia was woefully short of the industrial specialists, trained technicians, able administrators, and skilled workmen on which success would depend. The planned investment targets, moreover, seemed far too high to come from Yugoslavia's own limited resources, even if living standards were kept abysmally low and productivity raised to unprecedented heights. It was doubtful, too, that Yugoslavia could generate sufficient agricultural exports to pay for the machines that would need to be imported before any appreciable rise in industrial exports.[21]

But Stalin's objections were not primarily based on technicalities. In essence they were political. Stalin wanted eastern Europe as an economic reservoir to service Soviet reconstruction, and Tito's plans – especially if emulated by other countries in the area – were detrimental to his purposes. In the Stalinist scheme of things, Yugoslavia was to remain underdeveloped and provide unprocessed metals and minerals in return for industrial products from countries such as Czechoslovakia, Poland and the Soviet Union itself.[22] Though Stalin eventually agreed, albeit reluctantly, to provide the loans, credits and technical help to start Belgrade's five-year plan, Tito soon found that the 'fraternal aid' was likely to cost Yugoslavia considerably more than if it had been obtained from profit-seeking capitalists. That such economic exploitation was no accident seemed confirmed by the way in which Moscow used the joint-stock companies in Yugoslavia to exercise control and make a handsome profit.[23]

If Belgrade's economic relations with the Socialist countries were disappointing, its military relations were even more so. For Tito's plan for an independent defence system was no less anathema to Moscow than his plan for economic self-sufficiency, and the Soviet Union repeatedly stalled on its pledges to supply arms and ammunition. What Moscow was prepared to provide in abundance were military personnel, but it soon became clear why, in this particular respect, Stalin was being so generous. According to Alex Bebler, who was to become Yugoslav representative at the UN: 'On Stalin's orders Russian officers penetrated deeper and deeper into the organization of our army. . . . There were amongst us hundreds of Russian officers who acted as instructors in our army. They were placed all over the country. Russian officers started behaving as if they were the masters and wanted to command our unit' – not the kind of behaviour that would commend itself to Tito.[24]

Ironically, it was Tito's foreign policy, which had so antagonized the West, that also brought relations between Belgrade and Moscow to the brink of rupture. Like the Soviet leader himself, Tito tended to identify his own foreign political ambitions with the interests of world Communism, but, ultimately, this proved no more attractive to Stalin than to Truman or Attlee. It was in the showdown over Trieste that Moscow first distanced itself from Belgrade's aspirations, refusing to back Tito's peremptory claims on a country – Italy – regarded, in any case, as within the western 'sphere of influence'. However, Moscow's failure to support a Communist ally caused considerable ill-feeling in the Yugoslav capital, leading Tito to exclaim, 'Never again will we be dependent on anyone'; and the Soviet ambassador to protest in reply, 'We regard Comrade Tito's speech as unfriendly'.[25] Stalin was again to refuse his support in the row following Tito's order to shoot down two American planes which had 'strayed' into Yugoslav airspace, and Tito was left to apologize and pay compensation.

But it was the Yugoslav leader's plan for a Balkan federation that brought relations with Moscow to crisis point.[26] As originally conceived, it had found favour in Moscow. After all, what was envisaged was that Yugoslavia and Bulgaria (whose leader, Dimitrov, claimed joint parentage of the project), together with Albania and, possibly, Greece (should the Communist rebellion succeed), would be at the hub of a federal process which would gradually lead to the inclusion of eastern Europe's 'Peoples' Democracies' in the Soviet state. However, what seemed promising to Stalin in 1945 soon became far less attractive as Tito turned the federal idea into a personal crusade, conducting discussions on the subject in various east European capitals, sometimes without giving Moscow advance notice. Given, moreover, that Tito appeared to have plans for annexing parts of Italy, Austria, Bulgaria, Greece and the whole of Albania, it began to look as if the federation was designed to serve not international Communism, but Tito's personal ambition. At the same time, it risked plunging the European continent into a new war.

It was a speech by Dimitrov in Sofia, in January 1948, commending a federation to include southern and northern Slavs (other than those in the Soviet Union), together with Romanians, Hungarians, Albanians, and, possibly, the Greeks, that brought matters to a head. What seemed to be in prospect was a rival Communist alignment, and to Stalin, this appeared to present almost as grave a potential threat as an alliance of western powers. At this point, *Pravda* published a critique that left no doubt where the Kremlin now stood on the matter, and both Tito and Dimitrov were hastily summoned to Moscow. Significantly, Tito, who had recently been much in evidence in eastern Europe, absented himself from the Soviet capital, dispatching instead three of his aides to join Dimitrov in Moscow. Before their arrival, however, the Yugoslavs, who had already been told that it would be pointless to give any more assistance to the Communist rebels in Greece, were ordered by Moscow to cancel a recent agreement to send two divisions into Albania, supposedly to help the Communists there to defend their southern border. But however unwelcome such intrusions into Yugoslav affairs, it was nothing compared with what was to follow.

In Moscow, on 10 February, the Yugoslav and Bulgarian leaders were accused of conduct 'inadmissible both from a Party and from a state point of view'[27] and told to drop the whole idea of a single eastern Europe federation. Instead, Stalin proposed three federations: Hungary and Romania; Poland and Czechoslovakia; and Yugoslavia and Bulgaria, and recommended that this latter should be immediately effected.[28] Then the delegations were forced to sign an agreement providing for mutual consultations with the Kremlin on all foreign political questions. The exact implications of the Moscow meeting became clear immediately after the return of the Yugoslav delegation. For, the Soviet foreign trade ministry abruptly broke off negotiations on a new trade agreement, thereby putting Tito's economic plans in jeopardy.[29] In the light of Moscow's recent behaviour, it began to look as if the proposed union with Bulgaria might be a stratagem for controlling Yugoslavia, and, on 1 March, the Yugoslav Central Committee decided to resist it, at the same time placing under surveillance those Yugoslavs recruited to Soviet intelligence.[30] Moscow responded by stepping up sanctions, withdrawing its military and civilian technicians. From then on, even though Belgrade appeared anxious to avoid a breach, its exclusion from the Cominform was only a matter of time.

In the polemics prior to Belgrade's expulsion Moscow reverted to the kind of language it had used in the course of the purges in the previous decade. Tito stood accused of anti-Sovietism, of being undemocratic, of lacking class-consciousness, of being out of touch with the rank and file, of boundless arrogance, of conceit about his war record, and of having secret links with British intelligence. Eventually, the whole party was branded, somewhat incongruously, as Menshevist, Bukharinist, and Trotskyist, the accusation carrying with it a veiled threat to Tito's life: 'We imagine that the career of Trotsky is sufficiently instructive'[31] – a career which ended in Mexico, several thousand miles from Moscow, when a Stalinist agent put an ice pick in his brain. If Stalin had hoped to drive a wedge between Tito and the rest of the party, he would have been disappointed. With one or two notable exceptions, the CPY stood firm in support of its leader's pained response to Moscow's allegations, and applauded the sentiment that was to reverberate throughout the history of international Communism: 'However much each of us loves the Soviet Union, he can in no way love his own country less.'[32]

But the die was cast. Throughout April and May, Stalin mobilized his political divisions for a special meeting of the Cominform, which Tito refused to attend, knowing that the result was a foregone conclusion. On 28 June, a date already resonant with history for the south Slavs,[33] a brief message from the Cominform meeting in Bucharest announced that the CPY had, in effect, seceded from the 'family of fraternal Communist parties' and 'taken the road of nationalism'. Thus, what was effectively the first excommunication of a Communist ruled state was presented as a 'defection'. More ominously, the Cominform looked to 'healthy elements' in the party's rank and file to rid themselves of their 'nationalist' leaders and return the country to 'internationalism'.[34] The implication was clear. Pro-Soviet Yugoslavs were to overthrow Tito and make the country more amenable to Moscow's control. In effect, the Kremlin had issued orders to kill the man who had fought for Communism almost all his adult life and introduced in his country the most Stalinist system outside the Soviet Union.

Though Stalin never doubted that he would prove as successful in obtaining his objectives in Yugoslavia as in other eastern European countries (Khrushchev quotes him as saying 'I will shake my little finger and there will be no more Tito')[35] he was not a man to rely on exhortation alone. As the Cominform resolution implied, he had nominees within Yugoslavia primed for power. In addition, he was able to get his Communist allies in the vicinity to exert constant pressure, directing a stream of hostile propaganda against the CPY and its leaders, withdrawing ambassadors, closing frontiers, and holding military manœuvres on Yugoslavia's borders. Additionally, he coordinated through COMECON an almost total economic boycott of Yugoslavia, thereby presenting a grave threat to a country already in economic difficulties, heavily dependent on Russia and eastern Europe, and on bad terms with the West.[36] Yet, ultimately, Moscow-induced sanctions against Yugoslavia proved no more effective than Washington's strategic embargo against Moscow, and to Stalin's acute embarrassment the Tito regime survived.

What Stalin had overlooked was that his antagonist was no run-of-the-mill apparatchik ready to abandon principle at a signal from Moscow. Tito was a cunning and courageous fighter who had lost none of the qualities which had made him into a Bolshevik in 1917, landed him in jail in the '20s and '30s, served him well in the 'killing fields' of Spain and Yugoslavia, and given him absolute control of a country notorious for its divisions. He could count, moreover, on the loyalty of the most tightly organized Communist apparatus outside the Soviet Union itself – the party, army and security police having been steeled in battle and with no compunction about crushing the 'Cominformists' in their midst as they had liquidated the anti-Communist opposition in the purges preceding the break with Stalin.

Increasingly, too, he could count on the support of the majority of non-Communists who saw him as a patriot, standing up to Stalin as he had faced up to Hitler and Mussolini. After all, whereas most of the other European Communist leaders had spent more time in the Soviet Union than in their own countries, Tito could at least claim to have genuinely national roots. He had also geography on his side, Yugoslavia being a considerable distance from the Soviet Union and having no common frontier with it. Moreover, its mountainous terrain gave those skilled in partisan warfare an advantage over any potential foe. Finally, Stalin had failed to foresee that his disciple might be as adept as himself at making accommodations with the 'class enemy' if it served the interests of the 'revolution'. In fact, by the end of 1949, Tito had closed the frontier with Greece (thereby condemning to death the Communist rebellion), had begun to mend fences with Italy and Austria as well as Greece, and, most important of all, had sought and received from Britain and the USA the trade credits that were to be crucial in helping him to beat the Soviet-imposed blockade.[37]

The ability of Tito's regime to persist in face of Soviet threats and pressures was a watershed in the history of international Communism, for it demonstrated for the first time that it was possible for a state to be under Communist rule, yet independent of, even hostile to Moscow. Yet, for some time, the political impact of the Yugoslav 'defection' was limited. No other Communist country or party sought to escape Moscow's tutelage during Stalin's lifetime. Nor did Belgrade attract the kind of Communist following that Peking and Tirana did in subsequent years. Part of the reason stems from the fact that at the time of the break with Moscow, Yugoslavia had no alternative Socialist model to offer. The quarrel had not been about ideology but about who was to control Yugoslavia, and in the immediate aftermath of his excommunication, Tito tried to underline his Communist credentials by stepping up the pace of collectivization and the persecution of 'reactionaries' in the Catholic Church, the universities, and elsewhere. No distinctive 'Titoist' approach to Socialism materialized until later. In any case, since, for most Communists – even those like the Albanians and Chinese who, like the Yugoslavs, had achieved power largely through their own efforts – the Soviet Union was still the base of world revolution and a political prop on which to depend, there was psychological resistance to the notion of a breach with the Socialist homeland. Moreover, Stalin had ensured in the wave of heresy hunts, show trials and executions throughout eastern Europe that the contagion of 'Titoism' would be kept at bay. Clearly, there was now no place in international Communism for those not falling in line with Moscow.[38]

On the other hand, the Tito–Stalin rupture had long-term implications. In the face of domestic difficulties and its rapidly changing international circumstances, Yugoslavia eventually spawned a distinctly 'Titoist' approach. By 1954, when it had joined Greece and Turkey (both NATO members) in the Balkan Pact, it had developed the first independent and viable Marxist–Leninist alternative to the Soviet model. In place of bureaucratic centralism it began to devolve much more power to the six republics of the federation. Instead of the centrally-planned command economy, forced industrialization and collectivization, it was gradually moving to a decentralized, socialist market economy. As against Stalin's monolithic conception of Communism, Tito was arguing for the independence of each Communist country and party, and invoking the names of Marx, Engels, and even Lenin to back his case. In effect, Tito was giving a new dimension to the old Marxist heresy of 'revisionism', and introducing, in fact if not in name, a new concept into the vocabulary of politics: polycentrism, implying the dispersion of Communist power and authority. Thus, ironically, at the very time when international Communism was perceived by both friend and foe to be on the rise, Tito was putting a nationalist time bomb under the movement that would eventually explode the myth of monolithic Communism.

NOTES

1. For the early history of the Yugoslav Communists and of Tito, see P. Auty, *Tito* (London, 1974).
2. M. Djilas, *Memoirs of a Revolutionary*, trans. Drenka Willen (New York, 1973), p. 330.
3. Ibid, p. 333.
4. F. Maclean, *The Heretic: The Life and Times of Josip Broz-Tito* (New York, 1957), ch. 6.
5. Djilas, p. 388.
6. Maclean, pp. 140–8.
7. Ibid., ch. 6.
8. Ibid., pp. 119–21.
9. Ibid.
10. Ibid., p. 158.
11. Ibid., p. 207.
12. Ibid.
13. Ibid., p. 244.
14. Auty, p. 244.
15. Maclean, p. 267.
16. E. Kardelj, *Reminiscences*, trans. David Norris (London, 1982), pp. 80–7.
17. See Paul Winterton, *Inquest on an Ally* (London, 1948).
18. For a characteristic anti-Western diatribe of the period, see E. Kardelj, *The Communist Party of Yugoslavia in the Struggle for New Yugoslavia* (Belgrade, 1948).
19. Maclean, p. 279.
20. Hugh Thomas, *Armed Truce* (London, 1986), p. 306.
21. P. Auty, *Building a New Yugoslavia* (Fabian Research Pamphlets, London, 1954), p. 6.
22. Ibid., p. 7.
23. V. Dedijer, *The Battle Stalin Lost* (London, 1978), ch. 3.
24. Quoted in N. Beloff, *Tito's Flawed Legacy* (London, 1985), p. 144.
25. M. Djilas, *Rise and Fall* (New York, 1985), p. 92.
26. For an analysis of the Balkan Federation issue, see, for example, A. Werth, *Russia, the Post-War Years* (London, 1971), pp. 400–3, and M. Djilas, *Conversations with Stalin* (New York, 1962), pp. 173–81.
27. F. Maclean, *Josip Broz Tito: A Pictorial Biography* (London, 1980), p. 91.
28. Dedijer, p. 101.
29. Maclean, p. 91.
30. Ibid. p. 92.
31. Cited by F. Claudin, *The Communist Movement* (London, 1975), p. 497.
32. Maclean, p. 92.
33. A day of national mourning in Serbia ever since the Turks extinguished Serbian independence in 1389. It was also on 28 June that a Serbian youth fired the shots that killed the Austrian Archduke Franz Ferdinand, precipitating the First World War.
34. For the text of the Cominform Resolution and the Yugoslav reply, see R. V. Daniels, *A Documentary History of Communism* (London, 1985), vol. ii, pp. 156–8.
35. *Khrushchev Remembers* (London, 1971), p. 544.
36. Maclean, pp. 94–5.
37. John C. Campbell, *Tito's Separate Road* (New York, 1967), pp. 16–27.
38. See B. Morris, *Communism, Revolution and American Policy* (Durham, 1987), pp. 47–52.

7. The East is Red

Nineteen forty-nine had been an especially depressing year for the Communists in Europe. Stalin's failure to force Yugoslavia into line and his crackdown on the countries in the Soviet sphere contributed to yet another haemorrhage of western European Communists, and in Greece the guerrilla group known by its initials ELAS finally had to give up its struggle for power.[1] In the cold-war conditions then obtaining, moreover, a Cominform-instigated wave of strikes in western Europe failed to impede the process of western recovery and reconstruction under the Marshall Plan. At the same time, the countries of western Europe, having combined in an airlift to beat the Soviet-imposed blockade of Berlin and to restore sovereign status to West Germany, were now being organized into an alliance aimed at containing 'Soviet expansionism' and the spread of Communism by force of arms. In fact, the creation of NATO had constituted a European threshold which the Soviet Union and its allies could cross only at their peril.

But, if Europe was now no longer a fruitful field for Communist advance, the same could not be said of Asia. Here the problems of economic backwardness, technological inferiority, political and ethnic diversity, and the general desire to be rid of colonial and neocolonial ties had created a fertile soil for both Soviet penetration and indigenous Communist advance. And in October 1949, only two months after Moscow had been able to add atomic weapons to its formidable arsenal, it had received into the bloc the most populous nation on earth – China. It was international Communism's greatest triumph since the Bolshevik revolution and represented an especial accomplishment for Mao Tse-tung, and for a party which had been given up for dead twice in a decade.

One of the ironies of the Communist success in China is that it owed little to the Soviet Union. Admittedly, when Soviet expectations of European-wide revolution were dashed in the early 1920s, hopes of an early Communist victory had shifted somewhat to Asia. And, of all the countries of Asia, none had seemed to offer better revolutionary prospects than China. For, it was rent by civil war, had been weakened by the breakdown of religious custom and traditional authority in the wake of its encounter with the West, and was strongly anti-imperialist

– the legacy of gunboats, expeditionary forces, opium traders, 'unequal treaties' and 'concessions'.

On the other hand, after Chiang Kai-shek's Nationalist forces had effectively ended the United Front policy by their massacre of Chinese Communists in 1927, the Soviet leader became less sanguine about the revolutionary prospects of a country so different from his own. The industrial proletariat was even smaller than in Russia, and the potential revolutionaries appeared to include landlords and businessmen, while the 'exploiting' classes included categories – warlords, for example – entirely unfamiliar in Russia. In addition, the most potent revolutionary force in the country seemed to be neither Communism nor Socialism, but Nationalism – a political sentiment distrusted by the USSR's former Commissar of Nationalities. Moreover, like Marx before him, Stalin had come to fear that a revolutionary seizure of power almost anywhere in Asia would degenerate into a military dictatorship hostile to the creation of a socialist society.[2] Baffled by the abject failure of the United Front and lacking any clear conception of China's revolutionary potential, Stalin gave its Communists little material or moral assistance during the next 20 years or so, and from the end of the '20s the CCP was left largely to its own devices to work out a strategy for capturing power. This was probably the party's salvation.

The evident failure of the urban uprisings of the '20s led Mao, who had always tended to be more impressed by Leninist practice than by Marxist theory, to question the traditional Marxist–Leninist approach to revolution.[3] He argued that in a vast country like China, with its many villages and comparatively few towns, the peasantry had to be allotted more than a mere subsidiary role in the revolutionary process. Instead, the CCP must learn from the KMT how to win the support of the peasant masses, whose deep and abiding grievances against warlords, landlords and moneylenders could be channelled in a socialist direction. This did not mean abandoning Marx or Engels, but, rather applying their theories, as Lenin had done, in a context somewhat remote from the experience of the founders of Communism.

From Mao's retreat, first to the mountains of Kiangsi and then to the caves of Yenan, following the epic Long March, emerged a technique of revolutionary warfare that was to become a further distinguishing characteristic of Chinese Communism. Drawing as much on his understanding of Chinese history and classical literature as on his appreciation of the current situation, he came to prize political consciousness over technology and, accordingly, organized and indoctrinated groups of discontented peasants into guerrilla units which were to become the vanguard of the Chinese revolution. As he worked out what he was himself to call 'Sinified Marxism,' the newly indoctrinated peasants developed a clearer idea of their part in the revolutionary process. The immediate aim was a secure base in the countryside from which to encircle and harass the cities. The ultimate objective of capturing the towns would depend on the ability to outnumber the enemy by a ratio of some 10 to one. In a famous passage, Mao summarized these tactics as follows:

> The enemy advances, we retreat;
> The enemy camps, we harass;
> The enemy tires, we attack;
> The enemy retreats, we pursue.[4]

Though the strategy of 'encirclement' was dismissed by one CCP leader, Li Li-san, as 'sheer nonsense'[5] (a view which reflected Comintern thinking at the time), it was by means of it that Mao was able to expand his Socialist domain from a base in Yenan to most of the Chinese mainland in only 14 years.

Meanwhile, in the border regions of Yenan, Mao developed a socioeconomic model that was to differentiate clearly the Chinese from the Soviet road to socialism.[6] The emphasis was on the self-sufficiency of each region, in whose construction the Chinese Red Army played a major role. It would assist in productive work such as farming, land reclamation and the development of light industry, and help organize raw material, fuel and food distribution, transport facilities and the promotion of intermediate technology in each locality. If its contribution was intended both to raise the Red Army's esteem among the village population as well as counteract the boredom that can sap the energies of the traditional soldier, it probably succeeded.

But the formula for self-sufficiency encompassed far more than economic development. It also involved establishing a comprehensive system of learning in a people more than 90 per cent illiterate. Capitalizing on the rudiments of rural education in Confucian China, the party, under the slogan 'develop production, expand the schools', established a network of educational centres, including part-time, and night and winter schools, many staffed by itinerant teachers themselves only recently literate. So impressive were the results that in one area (Shansi–Chahar–Hopei) 23,300 primary schools, teaching Chinese language, mathematics and 'general knowledge', were established by 1944. By 1945, the Communists had created several institutes of higher learning and a medical school much praised by a UN visiting team.[7] As literacy spread,

Communist newspapers and journals supplemented the intense propaganda work already undertaken in the 'liberated areas'.

Having established a form of socialist organization specifically adapted to Chinese conditions, Mao went on to modify the structure and role of the CCP itself. Committing himself to the creation of a 'New Democracy', he opened up both the party and the representative institutions established in the guerrilla base areas to China's middle and upper classes, which traditionally provided the country's bureaucratic and managerial skills. In order to integrate the new elements into the party, Mao, in 1942, spearheaded a 'rectification campaign' – a technique of reinforcing ideological conformity and discipline that was to be a hallmark of his system of rule.[8] It was directed against tendencies in learning, working and writing that Mao considered harmful, and took the form not of the traditional Soviet purge, but of a kind of self-expurgation at public party forums held throughout the liberated areas.

In a series of documents prepared for the campaign, Mao identified the 'wrong tendencies' in the party as 'subjectivism' i.e. clinging to theory to the detriment of effective action; 'sectarianism', i.e. pursuing personal and sectional interests separate from those of the masses; and 'formalism', i.e. expressing ideas in forms which take no account of the audience to which they are addressed. Behind Mao's 'rectification campaign' lay a hidden agenda: that of indoctrinating the party faithful with an interpretation of Marxism specifically tailored to Chinese conditions. In short, the 'Sinification' of Marxism, which, in a report to the party's sixth plenum in October 1938, he had defined as 'making certain that in all of its manifestations it is imbued with Chinese peculiarities'. As such it was by no means anti-Soviet. It did mean, however, that, henceforth, Marxism–Leninism throughout the country was to be derived from Chinese rather than Soviet experience.

As the CCP took on a policy orientation of its own, so Mao attempted to give it an independent philosophical basis. In 'On Practice', written in 1937, he argued that all theory, including, presumably Marxist–Leninist theory, must be checked and modified in the light of practice. 'Social practice alone is the criterion of truth. . . . If you want to know the theory and method of revolution, you must take part in the revolution'.[9] A year later, he elaborated on this in his report to the sixth plenum of the party's Central Committee. 'There is no such thing as abstract Marxism, but only concrete Marxism', and in Chinese conditions this meant 'Sinification'.[10] In 'On Contradictions', also written in 1937, he gave theoretical justification for the United Front, arguing that while Marxists were right to see a dialectical pattern in all development, they needed to distinguish between different types of contradictions, since these were not equal in importance or intensity. At the time of writing, he identified among the various contradictions the CCP versus the KMT; Japan versus China; China versus all foreign nations; the Chinese proletariat versus the bourgeoisie; and the bourgeoisie against residual feudal elements.

For Mao, China's survival was paramount, and the struggle against the KMT was of secondary importance to the national struggle against Japan. In this sense, a United Front for the purpose of defeating foreign aggression was entirely justified. At the same time, Mao argued that some contradictions can be resolved without conflict, and instanced the relationship between China's working class and its peasantry as a 'nonantagonistic' contradiction – a theory which became the intellectual rationale for his 'New Democracy'.[11]

By 1945, when the war against Japan was in its final stages, Mao had succeeded in creating the world's second-largest Communist party, but one overwhelmingly of peasant origin and committed to a form of government which would initially be different from Lenin's 'dictatorship of the proletariat'. Whereas the Bolsheviks had been harsh in their treatment of those aristocrats, bureaucrats, priests and intellectuals who had served the tsars, the CCP, somewhat in the fashion of some of the eastern European parties, was working for a 'people's democratic dictatorship' which would embrace all 'democratic' parties, groups, and classes willing 'to build a new China'. On the eve of taking power in 1949, Mao made it clear that all workers, peasants, petty bourgeois and 'national bourgeois' elements would be eligible for office as long as they were prepared to accept overall Communist control along 'democratic centralist' lines. Only 'the landlord class, the bureaucratic capitalist class, and the KMT reactionaries and their henchmen' were to be disenfranchised and 'suppressed'. While Mao emphasized that the 'New Democracy' would be but a transitional form of government, even the CCP's opponents realized the propaganda value of his new approach.[12]

But no matter how effective Mao's public relations, it required military as well as political skill to defeat the KMT. For, the Nationalist forces were not only larger and better equipped than their Communist opponents. They also held China's richest agricultural land and industrial centres, and could count on the continued, if increasingly reluctant, support of the USA, which had backed them against the Japanese. But, as China drifted back into civil war, following the failure of American mediation at the end of the conflict with Japan, the experience, organization, discipline and morale of the Communist forces (now renamed the Peoples' Liberation Army) gave them the advantage.[13] Soon their numbers were swollen by KMT defectors no longer prepared to defend Chiang's corrupt and inefficient regime, and faced with the largest peasant army ever seen in Asia, the Nationalists lost their nerve. One after another, their urban strongholds fell to the Communists, and, as the KMT abandoned their newly furnished American equipment, the Communists were able to take cities like Peking largely in American trucks. As the Communists moved towards the south, the Nationalist retreat turned into a rout and, by late September 1949, the rump of Chiang's army had been forced to leave the Chinese mainland to find refuge in the island of Formosa.

The proclamation in October 1949 of the Chinese People's Republic signified not only the vindication of Mao's tactics, but also the birth of a potential Communist rival to the Soviet Union. For, Mao offered his concept of 'peoples' liberation war', involving the mobilization of peasant armies, guerrilla action and large-scale civil war, as a model for the developing countries. As the theorist, Liu Shao-chi, later Head of State, put it: 'The road taken by the Chinese people in defeating imperialism and its lackeys and in founding the People's Republic of China . . . is the way that should be taken by the peoples of colonial and semicolonial countries'.[14] The immediate effect of Mao's success was, indeed, to give a fillip to the sagging fortunes of those revolutionary movements in Indonesia, Burma, the Philippines, Malaya and elsewhere seeking an end to western influence in Asia. Later, Peking's involvement in the conflict in Korea showed that, unlike Moscow, the Chinese People's Republic was prepared to sacrifice lives to assist the spread of socialism in Asia.

Though, like Yugoslavia, China never became a mere 'satellite' of the Soviet Union, Mao, presiding over a country decimated by 20 years of civil strife and war, lacked Tito's impetus to strike out an independent path. Nonetheless, Peking's relations with Moscow were determined more by necessity than trust, for though Stalin's name was later to be revered in Communist China, Mao had ample cause for resentment. In the first place, had his party relied on the CPSU, its victory might have been indefinitely postponed. For, even after the fiasco of the first United Front, Stalin seemed more concerned to bolster the KMT than the CCP, and he chose to aid Chiang's forces rather than the Chinese Red Army during the anti-Japanese campaign.

The aftermath was even more galling, as Mao himself later recalled. 'Stalin wanted to prevent China from making revolution, saying that we should not have civil war and should cooperate with Chiang Kai-shek, otherwise the Chinese nation would perish.' Mao adds: 'We did not do what he said',[15] and though he makes no specific reference in his revelations of 1962, he must have been especially hurt when, as the Communist victory was in sight, Moscow's ambassador followed the retreating Nationalist government to Canton when it abandoned Nanking and closed Soviet consulates in Communist-captured cities. On the other hand, by this time, Mao will have been well used to Soviet disdain. The Long March of the '30s and the Communist successes of the '40s had received less publicity in Moscow than in many a western capital; and, far from encouraging their endeavours, Stalin was constantly questioning the CCP's ideological credentials. In the presence of western statesmen such as Averell Harriman, James Byrnes and Harry Hopkins he had dismissed Mao's party as 'margarine Communists', 'not real Communists', 'radish Communists – red on the outside, white on the inside'.[16]

But if Moscow had given the Chinese Communists little material or moral support in the past, it could hardly fail them in their attempt to create a 'New Democracy'. In return, the CCP felt obliged to effect some degree of deference, for a time ceasing to commend to the developing countries the Maoist way to revolution. Even so, Stalin appeared somewhat grudging in his approach to the new regime, as Mao was later to complain: 'After the victory of the revolution he next suspected China of being a Yugoslavia and that I would become a second Tito. Later when I went to Moscow to sign the Sino-Soviet Treaty of Alliance and Mutual Assistance, we had to go through another struggle. He was not willing to sign a treaty [but] after two months of negotiations he at last signed'.[17]

But Stalin had driven a hard bargain, and the terms of the treaty must have come as a disappointment to Mao's hard-pressed regime. Its annual provision of $60 million for a five-year period was hardly generous, given that the recipient was the most populous nation on earth. Indeed, it was no more than had been accorded Chiang Kai-shek in 1938 and considerably less than a recent Soviet loan to Poland. Moreover, having already seized much of Manchuria's industrial plant as 'war reparations', Stalin had seemed reluctant to relinquish control, and, through his nominees in administration and on the joint-stock companies, he clearly intended to treat both Manchuria and Sinkiang as if under Soviet suzerainty. Nor would the Soviet leader allow the immediate evacuation of the bases of Port Arthur and Dairen, occupied by Soviet troops since the end of the war. And, of course, in insisting on the continued 'independence' of the Mongolian People's Republic, Stalin had ensured that Outer Mongolia remained beyond Mao's grasp.[18]

On the other hand, for all its imperfections, the Sino-Soviet Treaty had conferred certain benefits on the new regime. For, even if some of the advisers dispatched by Moscow had an intelligence function in addition to their nominal expertise, they helped lay the groundwork for a viable socialist industrial sector, and to re-equip and modernize the armed forces. More importantly, having failed in a secret bid to win American backing, and denied legitimacy and recognition by the major non-Communist powers, the Chinese leaders were glad to be able to cite the Treaty – among other things, a 30-year mutual defence pact – as an indication that they had Soviet protection. It was in this sense that Mao proclaimed as the basis of the country's foreign relations what has become known as the 'lean to one side' principle. Announcing his intention 'to unite in a common struggle with those countries of the world who treat us on a basis of equality', he identified the states concerned as the Soviet Union and 'the new democratic countries of Europe'. He concluded: 'One either leans to the side of imperialism or the side of socialism', and he aligned himself with the Cominform view of the time by declaring, 'Neutrality is merely a camouflage; a third way does not exist'.[19]

Yet, ironically, in his domestic policy Mao for a time appeared to be establishing a 'third way'.[20] For, though anti-capitalist, his socialist model was not proceeding entirely along Soviet lines. In the first place, the system of government was different. The Bolsheviks had never even pretended that their regime was broadly representative of the nation. It was purportedly a government for the proletariat, whereas Mao at least made an effort to appeal across class and even political barriers. The founding conference of the People's Republic was attended by representatives of 45 political groups, and several of the government ministers elected in 1949 were non-Communists, including Soong Ching-ling, Sun Yat-sen's widow; the chairman of the western-leaning Democratic League; and the Chairman of the Revolutionary Committee of the Kuomintang, representing that party's left wing.

At the same time, even though, as in the Soviet Union, the commanding heights of the economy were nationalized and the workers assured that they were the most advanced class, the CCP was determined to avoid the major negative lesson of the Russian Revolution – the alienation of the peasantry. Mao had the largest landowners dispossessed and the title deeds to land handed over to the poorer peasants, but the richer and middle peasants were allowed, for the time being at least, to hold on to their land. Moreover, though Mao did not shrink from executing 'counter-revolutionaries' (over one million reportedly liquidated in the first year of the revolution),[21] he relied less on violence than did Lenin or Stalin, perhaps because, in contrast to the Soviet

Union, the civil war was effectively over when the Communists took power. One has only to contrast the fate of the last Manchu emperor, who ended his days as a gardener, with that of the last tsar, who was brutally murdered, together with his family. Moreover, facing the firing squad in People's China was generally the culmination of a Maoist-style process of Communist-sponsored mass meetings with the participants deciding which 'counter-revolutionaries' were to lose their lives and which were sufficiently redeemable to merit 're-education' (the Chinese called it 'brain-washing').[22]

Ultimately, what distinguished the Chinese from other Communist models was the stress laid on the teaching as well as the leadership of Mao, 'foreshadowing the days', as C. P. Fitzgerald has observed, 'when this new sun in the Communist sky would challenge the power of the older one represented by the successors of Stalin'.[23]

But, if Mao was charting his own path domestically, his denial of a 'third way' seemed more comprehensible in the light of the country's national predicament. For, the People's Republic had been founded at the height of the cold war, when in East and West political attitudes were becoming increasingly polarized. Moreover, like the Bolsheviks in 1917, Mao had good reason to feel that the revolution was under threat and that it was the duty of all 'progressive' forces throughout the world to unite in its defence. After all, the KMT had not abandoned its claim to the mainland, and there was no shortage of anti-Communist regimes in the vicinity to give Chiang support and encouragement.

More importantly, the Nationalist leader had the backing of the USA – the power that had defeated and occupied Japan, was in *de facto* control of the Philippines, was backing a colonial regime in Indochina, and had residual interests in South Korea. More seriously, with the world's largest and most active fleet in the Pacific, as well as the funds and facilities to subvert the People's Republic through its agents still within the country and indirectly through its capacity for global news management, the USA could ensure that Peking was effectively denied the legitimacy and recognition it sought. By February 1950, when the People's Republic of China (PRC) committed itself to a 30-year defence pact with the USSR, the hostility between the superpowers made it difficult for their respective allies to establish 'normal' relations across the Great Political Divide. But what was difficult in February became well-nigh impossible the following June when Communist North Korea attacked the non-Communist South, and Washington and Peking became involved on opposite sides in the ensuing conflict.

The reasons for the North Korean thrust into South Korea are unclear. The original US assumption that it had been masterminded in

Moscow, either to secure a wholly Communist Korea in answer to the American military presence in Japan, or to embroil the People's Republic of China in a war which would strengthen its dependence on Moscow, must be treated with caution. For, in the early years of the cold war, more complex explanations of Communist conduct were often sacrificed for the simple view that the Communist world was a monolithic entity controlled from Moscow – a notion gaining increasing currency with the removal of influential American experts on Asian Communism at the behest of the McCarthyites and the right-wing 'China lobby'.

Though the strike is unlikely to have occurred without Soviet foreknowledge, recent scholarship tends to confirm Khruschev's claim that 'it wasn't Stalin's idea, but Kim Il Sung's. Kim was the initiator'.[24] For, it came following at least a year of border clashes and repeated calls by South Korea's President Syngman Rhee for a 'march northward' and within weeks of an election in which the South Korean leader, though heavily defeated, insisted on clinging to power.[25] To Pyongyang, the situation presented both threat and opportunity. The fear was that if the North did not strike first it would itself be attacked as Syngman Rhee searched desperately for a pretext to retain the presidency. But with the South in disarray, and the Korean peninsula apparently excluded from Washington's sphere of interests, it was also clearly a propitious time for Pyongyang to try to unite the country under the Communist flag. Whether or not the war was designed, in addition, to bolster Kim's position against other potential contenders for the leadership of the Democratic People's Republic of Korea (DPRK), it had that effect.[26]

If Mao bore any responsibility for Pyongyang's action, it comes from his sowing the ideological seeds of a protracted civil war for the establishment of socialism. After all, relations between the two parties had always been close. Many Koreans, including Kim Il Sung, had fought alongside the Chinese Communists in Yenan and Manchuria, some staying on to battle for the Chinese People's Republic even after the establishment of the Democratic People's Republic of Korea following the end of Soviet occupation in 1948. And even though Kim was eventually to become the Soviet nominee for the leadership, he was probably closer in ideology to Mao than to Stalin, having emigrated from Korea in the '20s and spent more years in China than in the Soviet Union. For his part, Mao could not allow North Korea, to which China was traditionally tied by culture, history, geography and now ideology, to lose its historical function as a barrier against invasion. After all, the last country to capture Korea – Japan – had used it as a stepping stone to attack China. Hence Mao's decision, after a verbal warning to the US/UN forces, to send 'People's Volunteers' to the battle zone in October 1950 when the fate of North Korea hung in the balance.

With the hostilities in Korea, the comparatively relaxed atmosphere in the People's Republic came to an end.[27] As the last remnants of the KMT outside Formosa were rounded up, and any outstanding Nationalist assets transferred to the state, the party turned its attention to what remained of the landed gentry and to the 'national bourgeoisie'. The former were dispossessed of their property, many to be branded as 'enemies of the people' at 'accusation meetings' and sentenced to death, the latter to be crushed by a campaign against the 'five anti's' – bribery, tax evasion, fraud, theft of state property, and theft of state economic secrets – which had the effect of virtually destroying the private industrial sector. The Communist Party, too, was 'cleansed', as Mao launched one rectification campaign after another. In 1951, the targets were waste, corruption and bureaucracy; two years later, 'commandism'. 'bureaucratism', and 'the violation of laws and discipline' – each campaign taking a heavy toll of membership.

As Mao moved against his domestic enemies, he also took a more assertive line towards the non-Communist world in general.[28] In 1950, he proceeded to seize or destroy the residual non-Soviet foreign interests left in China, including businesses, schools, hospitals and charitable institutions. At the same time, he curbed the activities of foreign journalists and missionaries, and compelled the churches to sever their overseas ties. Moreover, as if to make amends for decades of weakness and humiliation, the People's Republic made good China's historic claim to Tibet, which had freed itself from Chinese tutelage early in the century, but which Mao, no less than Chiang, regarded as one of the country's 'lost territories'. The PRC was also assiduous in defending the rights of the 11 million or more Overseas Chinese scattered throughout Asia. But it was, of course, in Korea that the PRC made its first major impact on the international stage, its 'volunteers' scoring notable successes against the American-led UN force, while in Indochina the People's Republic again made its mark by giving logistical support to the insurgents who were to put an end to French colonial rule.

As China aligned its foreign policy alongside that of the USSR, its domestic policy, too, took on an increasingly Stalinist hue,[29] as free expression was curbed, labour discipline tightened, and the tax burden on peasants raised so as to ensure a regular supply of foodstuffs to the towns and the army camps. As in the Soviet Union, China's NEP was of limited duration. Proclaiming collectivization as a long-term goal, Mao, within two years of the gift of land to the peasants, sponsored the establishment of 'mutual aid' teams of five or more households (which were collective farms in embryo). Then, in 1953, Mao introduced a five-year plan of industrialization largely based on the Soviet model, albeit with a view to spreading industry so as to reduce both military vulnerability and the influence of existing 'bourgeois' centres such as Shanghai and Canton. Heavy industry took priority, and, though in agriculture the title to land still remained largely with the individual peasant family, the 'mutual aid' teams were transformed into semi-socialist agricultural producers' cooperatives, with income distributed according to contributions of labour and land. Paradoxically, at a time when some other Communist countries were contemplating a shift away from Stalinism after the death of the Soviet leader in March 1953, the People's Republic seemed to be drawing somewhat closer.

On the other hand, in the wake of Stalin's death, Mao's independent contribution to revolutionary theory and practice was there for all to see. He had not only achieved power through his own efforts but had been able to consolidate it rapidly and in the most populous and war-ravaged country on earth. Furthermore, he had stabilized a currency which under Chiang had risen to astronomical heights of inflation; he had restored a communications system devastated by hostilities and had attained remarkable results in both industrial and agricultural production. Above all, he had given to a people whose values had been in flux for nearly half a century a sense of national pride. His accomplishments in foreign policy had been equally impressive. He had freed the country from foreign encroachment, reincorporated the largest and most intractable of China's 'lost territories', helped to drive back the UN forces from North Korea, and given both theoretical and practical help to the Vietminh's ultimately successful quest for national independence. Meanwhile, many Communist parties, especially in Asia, were increasingly looking to Peking, rather than Moscow, for ideological inspiration.[30]

Yet, once the Korean and Indochina wars were over and Peking's perception of threat beginning to dissipate, Premier Chou En-lai prepared his country for a momentous change in foreign policy. This meant playing down the CCP's support of militant revolutionary movements and giving conditional support to a 'third way' of looking at international society – 'neutralism', as espoused by many non-Communist countries of Asia anxious to maintain their distance from Washington's anti-China crusade. Its leading exponent was India's prime minister, Jawaharlal Nehru, and, at an historic meeting shortly before the Geneva conference of June 1954, marking the end of the war in Indochina, the two premiers exchanged declarations of 'peaceful coexistence', pledging mutual respect and noninterference in each other's domestic concerns. Thus, Stalin's 'two-camp' image was set aside and for the next three years, leaders travelled to and from the Chinese capital to preach the virtues of neutralism and nonalignment.[31]

If the rise in Peking's prestige, first as a fighting power and then as an earnest 'peacemonger' was a threat to Washington, it was also, potentially, a threat to Moscow, which, like Peking, was attempting to woo the neutrals of Asia in the wake of Stalin's death. Soon it became clear that the Communism by which the Soviet Union, the countries of eastern Europe, Mongolia, China, North Korea and North Vietnam were in theory bound to one another was so infused with national priorities and preoccupations as to seriously undermine its internationalist pretensions. Certainly, by the mid-'50s it was by no means self-evident that the Communists had effected, as they claimed, a system of international relations of an entirely new type. On the other hand, while Stalin lived, the myth of a specifically Socialist form of international relations seemed as persuasive to anti-Communists as to Communists, and, since it gained especial currency in Stalin's latter years, it merits further investigation.

NOTES

1. See Stefanos Sarafis, *Greek Resistance Army: The Story of ELAS* (London, 1951).
2. Guy Wint, *Communist China's Crusade* (London, 1965), p. 6.
3. Ibid., pp. 36–42.
4. Cited by S. Schram, *Mao Tse-tung* (London, 1967), p. 159.
5. Cited by B. Schwartz, *Chinese Communism and the Rise of Mao* (Cambridge, Mass., 1968), p. 139. Chapter 9 elaborates Li Li-san's views.
6. On life in the 'liberated' areas, see E. Snow, *Red Star over China* (London, 1972).
7. Andres D. Onane, *Chairman Mao and the Chinese Communist Party* (Chicago, 1979), pp. 198–9.
8. Schram, pp. 220–2.
9. *Selected Readings from the Works of Mao Tse-tung* (Peking, 1967), pp. 55 and 59.
10. Cited by Schram, p. 220.
11. *Selected Readings*, pp. 70–104.
12. Schram, ch. 9.
13. See J. Gittings, *The Role of the Chinese Army* (London, 1967), ch. 1.
14. H. Carrère d'Encausse and S. Schram (eds.), *Marxism in Asia* (London, 1966), p. 271.
15. S. Schram (ed.), *Mao Tse-tung Unrehearsed* (London, 1974), p. 191.
16. G. Paloczi-Horvath, *Mao Tse-tung* (London, 1962), pp. 206–7.
17. Schram (ed.), p. 191.
18. R. C. North, *Moscow and the Chinese Communists* (Stanford, 1963), pp. 266–9.
19. 'On the People's Democratic Dictatorship' in *Selected Readings*, pp. 302–15.
20. On the early period of Communist rule in China, see F. Schurman and O. Schell (eds.), *Communist China* (London, 1968), Part i.

21. *Current Background* No. 39 (US Consulate General, Hong Kong, 1951).
22. C. P. Fitzgerald, *Mao Tse-tung and China* (London, 1976), p. 80.
23. Ibid., p. 82.
24. *Khrushchev Remembers* (London, 1971), p. 333.
25. Robert R. Simmons 'The Korean Civil War' in F. Baldwin (ed.), *Without Parallel* (New York, 1974), p. 149.
26. For an analysis of the complex interplay between Korean Communist politics and the politics of the wider Communist world, see Robert R. Simmons, *The Strained Alliance: Peking, Pyongyang, Moscow and the Politics of the Korean Civil War* (London, 1975).
27. Schram, pp. 266–74.
28. Paloczi-Horvath, pp. 256–65.
29. See A. Doak Barnett, *Communist China: the Early Years, 1949–1955* (London, 1964).
30. Wint, pp. 47–66.
31. H. Hinton, *Communist China in World Politics* (London, 1966), pp. 248–59.

8.   The End of the Stalinist Era

It may seem odd today that a political movement embracing a Tito and
a Mao as well as a Stalin could be dubbed a monolith. Yet, at the
height of the cold war, this word was commonly used on both sides of
the Great Political Divide to describe both the structure of the Communist Party and the nature of the relationship among the socialist countries. Since, to the Stalinists, the Yugoslav leader was a heretic and no
longer a member of the Communist fraternity, and the Chinese leader
a 'maverick' who would be forced by circumstances to abandon his
idiosyncratic views, the concept of a 'Socialist monolith' retained its
validity. To many in the West, Tito and Mao were too steeped in
Soviet-style practices to represent any serious fracture in the solid
masonry of Stalinism. In both East and West, it was widely assumed
that while Communist parties remained in power throughout eastern
Europe, they were bound to maintain a rock-like devotion to the Kremlin, to which they owed so much. And after the purges of 'Titoists' and
'national Communists' in the late '40s and early '50s, it was difficult for
critics or admirers to see the socialist system as anything other than
monolithic in structure.

Yet, most ruling parties contained members who had recently fought
as much for their homeland as for a socialist transformation, in areas
where nationalist preoccupations had tended to be notoriously explosive. And, as the history of Soviet Russia had itself demonstrated,
Communists could be no more impervious to the legacy of the national
past than could non-Communists. For government by Marxist–Leninists
did not of itself eradicate age-old disputes over Macedonia, Kosovo,
Transylvania, Bessarabia, Teschen, Mongolia or Tibet, or reduce the
significance of the exact location of the frontier between Poland and
its Communist neighbours. Nor could it entirely bridge the broad differences in perspective on such matters between those Communists who
had stayed in their native land to fight for liberation, those who had
gone into exile in London, and the 'Muscovites' who had returned to
their countries of origin having spent the war years in the Soviet Union.
Neither could Communist rule completely root out the sub-loyalties
among those with a shared political experience of, say, the Spanish
Civil War or the concentration camp. Resettling in East Germany in

1945 after years of exile in the USSR, the former Comintern official
Wolfgang Leonhard recalls many behind-the-scenes disagreements, not
least concerning the meaning of Socialism in a German context and the
pace at which it should be advanced.[1]

On the other hand, even if the notion of a Communist monolith
was an over-simplification, the Communist states shared a number of
common characteristics and together may be said to have constituted
a distinct international sub-system by the time of Stalin's death in March
1953.[2] The most obvious indicator was the existence of the Communist-
ruled state itself, with some variant of Marxism–Leninism as its oper-
ational ideology and the Soviet Union as exemplar. In all, even the
most heretical, the stated purpose was the same – the creation of a
classless, stateless world through global socialist revolution spearheaded
by Communist action. In all, even the most nonconformist, the ideology
was used to validate government by a nonelected apparatus which was
neither accountable to the legislature nor subject to censure by the
judiciary. Wherever non-Communist parties were allowed to survive,
they became little more than 'transmission belts' for the party line, and,
because Communists alone were deemed to possess the key to the
transformation of humankind, no other party could be allowed to compete with it for power. Communist rule meant, moreover, that the
party bureaucracy not only established the political, economic and
social norms, but also devised the means of inculcating them and supervised their implementation at all levels. And to discourage dissidence
and discipline 'deviationists', each party had at its disposal a political
police force as powerful as it was pervasive, equipped with the latest
techniques in the apparatus of terror.

Moreover, though insulated from one another by institutional and,
in some cases, physical barriers, the Communist-ruled states tended to
have more frequent and significant contacts with one another than with
the countries beyond what was dubbed the 'Iron Curtain'. They were
interlinked by a network of bilateral treaties of friendship, both with
Moscow and with one another, which provided for regular consultations
on matters of common concern. Their leading officials would confer at
party congresses or at meetings of Communist international organizations, such as the Cominform or COMECON, and, of course, they
would need to meet to up-date their arrangements regarding trade,
cultural exchange and technical cooperation. More importantly, perhaps, they would hold periodic informal discussions on ideological,
political, or defence-related issues – generally in Moscow and behind
closed doors. By the end of the Stalinist era, moreover, the Communist
states, save for Yugoslavia, which faced a system-wide embargo after

1948, were trading far more with one another than with other countries, and engendering significant movements of personnel – trade representatives, negotiators, service engineers, installation men, etc., all of which required a more regular pattern of communications within than outside the system. With political and economic reorientation had come a perceptible cultural shift. Russian had become the lingua franca of the system, and Moscow the educational, scientific, technical and artistic hub of the Communist world.

Though some commentators argue that inter-Communist relations under Stalin were no less governed by national interest than relations among non-Communist states, this is, at the very least, to ignore the powerful impact of myth on reality. For, while objectively it is not difficult to dismiss the claims of Stalinist theorists that relations among the Communist-ruled states were of a new type and based on equality, mutual advantage, non-interference, and respect for sovereignty, subjective perceptions are not always grounded in hard fact. And, since the propaganda proclaiming their 'monolithic solidarity' in the fight for socialism was so relentless, it can hardly have failed to have had an impact. At the same time, the *nomenklatura* system bequeathed to the People's Democracies by Stalin, according to which key appointments were in the gift of a closely knit corps of loyal functionaries, ensured that decisions affecting inter-Communist relations were taken in the context of a shared value system and a common ideological framework.

One consequence of that shared framework of assumptions during this period was the establishment of clear criteria by which states were recognized as members of the international Communist fraternity. Broadly speaking, membership was accorded those with stable governments, organized along Stalinist lines, dedicated to Stalinist economic and political principles and willing to accept the leadership of the CPSU. Since neither the Chinese Soviet Republic of 1931–6 nor the Greek provisional government of 1946–9 was regarded as stable or secure, they failed the test of 'recognition'. For those that passed the test, continued membership depended on conformity to norms of internal and external conduct formulated in Moscow. And, since the rules of behaviour were based on an ideology presupposing a high degree of accord among those speaking in its name, no member could be indifferent to the conduct of its fellows.

As within parties so among them, differences and disagreements tended to be regarded as heresy, so that when one of their number was held to have deviated from the prescribed standards, the party itself ran the same risk as the individual member who fell out of line – isolation and eventual expulsion. Thus, when Yugoslavia refused to accept Moscow's directives in 1948, Belgrade's credentials as a member of the Communist fraternity were withdrawn, and its leaders subjected to the unremitting hostility of every other Communist state and party.

As the system began to be consolidated, it developed a distinctive culture, embodied in an official language heavily infused with Marxist, Leninist and Stalinist concepts. As such, the phraseology employed was designed to engender and reinforce a sense of Communist solidarity and to foster feelings of animosity towards those deemed hostile. In the view of the philosopher Louis Althusser, this use of language was crucial in fostering revolutionary consciousness, since, as a Marxist, he regarded words as more than indicators of meaning. 'In political, ideological and philosophical struggle, words are also weapons, explosives, or tranquillisers or poisons'.[3] Though Althusser lived in France, his phraseology reflects the political vocabulary permeating the Communist countries until comparatively recently. It was the peculiar language of 'class struggle', according centrality to the 'proletariat' (a curiously outmoded notion in contemporary English) and reflecting something of the siege conditions in which the vocabulary originally developed. In it, military metaphors abound. The world is divided into two 'camps' and the workers are 'mobilized' into 'armies' and 'brigades', forming 'united fronts' and 'advancing' against their 'enemies' in the class 'war'. They score 'heroic victories' in the 'struggle', and 'beat', 'defeat', and sometimes 'annihilate' their opponents. Equally, it was a language rich in terms of opprobrium. Those too far to the Left were labelled 'sectarian', 'adventurist', 'pseudo-revolutionary', 'ultra-leftist', or of a 'Trotskyist' mentality. Anyone too far to the Right might be dubbed 'a paid hireling of the Gestapo', 'a Fascist', 'a lackey' or 'running dog of imperialism', or, more simply, 'reactionary', 'opportunist', 'social chauvinist', 'revisionist', or 'Bukharinist'; while terms like 'diehard', 'cretin', and 'phrasemonger' could be used of people of Left or Right who happened to fall out of line with current policy.

As the vocabulary changed, a more general conditioning process was under way – one spawning a plethora of 'consciousness-raising' political meetings and discussion groups, a prolific literature, and a host of displays and demonstrations to convey the regime's approval or disapproval of a particular idea or event. Soon the Communist movement as a whole had its heroes and villains, living symbols, and dead martyrs, both individual and collective, and was encouraging an almost obsessive interest in tractor drivers, steel mills, military science, physical education and fertile motherhood, all of which rated highly in social esteem, whether in Moscow, Belgrade, Pyongyang or Peking.

On the other hand, the postulate of 'monolithic unity' could only strengthen the cohesion of the Communist countries so long as it had some basis in fact. Clearly, mere rhetoric could not of itself produce uniformity, and when inter-state conflicts arose, the bloc had few mechanisms available for mitigating them. That the belief system on which inter-Communist relations was based claimed both 'scientific' objectivity and moral superiority only compounded the problem. For such a system virtually precluded resort to the juridical, mediatory, or fact-finding procedures available to other members of international society and effectively left Moscow as the arbiter in any dispute. This was a position it would use to especial advantage when its own interests were involved, as in its altercation with Poland and Czechoslovakia concerning Marshall Aid, or with Bulgaria and Yugoslavia over the proposed Balkan federation. But then, no matter how inter-Communist relations were portrayed, there was one inescapable fact – the predominance of the Soviet Union in almost every respect, which no amount of semantic subterfuge could conceal.

It soon became apparent that far from pioneering a relationship of a new type, the Communist countries had reverted to one of the oldest political structures in history – that of dominance and dependency. The Communist international system was no less hierarchical than the Communist parties comprising it, and, at its apex, exerting what some Marxists have called 'hegemony', stood the Soviet Union. According to *Pravda*:[4]

> In our time one can be a sincere revolutionary and internationalist only by unconditionally supporting the CPSU and the Soviet Union itself, only by basing one's actions on the principles of Marxism–Leninism and proceeding from the experience of the Russian Communist Party – the leading force in the international Communist movement.

In part, this claim to supremacy was based on the age and intensity of the USSR's own revolutionary experience and the theoretical and practical contribution it had made in the development of international Communism. But, of course, the sheer weight of the Soviet Union's military, political, economic and technological resources gave it an immense advantage in its dealings with weak and impoverished countries emerging from the turmoil of war, under inexperienced and usually unelected Communist leaders.

Though Moscow never clearly defined its rights and duties as 'the leading force' in the movement, in practice they were quasi-feudal. Moscow spoke and acted in the name of the system as a whole, offering its protection in return for political and economic services as well as deference. But towards the end of the Stalin era, the deference demanded and received amounted to sycophancy.[5] In the first place, the cult of Stalin was assiduously fostered throughout the system. Statues, busts and icon-like portraits of him were generously distributed abroad, and almost every town in the Soviet sphere had its Stalin street, boulevard, or square. His *Problems of Leninism* (required reading in the schools and universities) and other books were available at a nominal charge, while a volume on *Stalin, the Liberator of Eastern and South-Eastern European People* to mark his 70th birthday in 1949 was translated into the relevant languages and distributed free.

With the apotheosis of Stalin came the veneration of things Russian (the nation with which Stalin, though not a Russian, identified). Russians were credited with the invention of the lightning conductor, the electric motor, the electric telegraph, the radio, the tank, penicillin, and much more. The Russian language was, in the words of one Czech periodical 'the language of the future', while Russian cultural, economic and scientific achievements were lauded as second to none. Experts as well as party propagandists would testify to Russian superiority in most fields of endeavour. In Prague, biologists pledged themselves 'to follow undeviatingly the teaching of Lysenko', a Stalin favourite whose controversial work on genetics is now thoroughly discredited. In Poland, an exhibition of Russian architecture produced a promise to follow Russian models. In Bulgaria, the party paper reported that Bulgarian clowns would be sent to Moscow to learn how to 'instil the Socialist spirit into the Bulgarian circus'. If some of the bloc's greatest paens of praise were reserved for the 'invincible' Red Army, this is understandable given that throughout this period it remained in occupation of much of eastern Europe and eastern Asia.[6]

No doubt, the fear engendered by Moscow's formidable arsenal of political, economic, and diplomatic, as well as military, weapons and its evident willingness to use them accounts, in part, for the widespread obsequiousness, but this is not a sufficient explanation, since it ignores the effects of political conditioning and Stalinism's emotional appeal. After all, not all the devotees were from the Soviet orbit. Many western scientists, social scientists, and artists also voiced admiration for the Soviet leader and his works, and their adulation can hardly have been the product of intimidation or fear.[7] No one forced Harold Laski, Sidney and Beatrice Webb, or Hewlett Johnson, the former Dean of Canterbury, who all visited Moscow at the height of the purge trials of the '30s, to acclaim what they saw as the New Civilization. No one coerced the distinguished British geneticist, Prof. J. B. S. Haldane, into silence on the fate of the Soviet geneticists displaced by Lysenko, nor was the British physicist, Prof. J. S. Bernal, under any compulsion to laud Stalin's 'deeply scientific approach to all problems'.

For them, as for many others, Stalin was utilizing a 'scientific' theory to construct a 'science'-based society in which the requisite social engineering was in the hands of people who knew how best to tap the human potential. And if Stalin sanctioned policies which appeared arbitrary or even cruel, he was no more culpable than is a natural scientist who dissects animals in the interests of human betterment. It was an approach combining 'scientism', i.e. the belief that science could solve all problems, with a highly 'unscientific' disregard of inconvenient facts, giving to Stalinism – the scourge of organized religion – paradoxically, the status of a surrogate religion. As a former Communist, Charlotte Haldane, put it, there was a close analogy between the Communist 'church' and the Christian Church.

> The former also has an Old Testament – the works of Marx and Engels; a New Testament, the development of Marx–Engels doctrine by Lenin and Stalin. Its hierarchy is not unlike that of the Roman Catholic Church, with Stalin as the Communist Pope; the leaders of other Communist countries as his College of Cardinals; the various secret and internal security organizations as the instruments of their inquisition.[8]

On the other hand, no religion – not even a surrogate one – can command adherence if it does not inspire trust, and, while critics of Stalinism rightly point to the degree of personal insecurity and distrust pervading the system, its supporters were constantly being furnished the 'evidence' they needed to be persuaded of Stalinism's continued validity. First and foremost, Moscow could use statistics to appeal to them as 'historical materialists'. If one takes the figures at face value and disregards the low base, the social costs, the conditions of labour and the quality of production, the USSR's industrial development under Stalin was spectacular.[9]

During the '30s, at a time when the capitalist world faced falling production and mounting unemployment, Soviet industry had been booming. Oil, steel, coal, and electricity output soared and improvements in rail and water transport helped expand industrialization beyond the Urals. Though four years of war devastated the economy, its recovery, aided by exploitative trade agreements and the raw materials and equipment exacted as reparations, was almost as impressive as the industrialization of the '30s. For, the centrally planned, command economy can work well in a country in the early stages of industrialization, feeling itself under siege, and blessed with a pliant and obedient work force – and Stalin's USSR fulfilled all three conditions.

Furthermore, Stalin's Soviet Union could claim to have conquered inflation as well as unemployment and, at the same time, to have developed an extensive range of social services, contributing to a vast improvement in the health and education of the nation.

Further 'evidence' of the validity of Stalinism lay in the outcome of the war itself. Despite the loss during the purges of some of the Soviet Union's best army officers, Stalin's unpreparedness for the Nazi onslaught and the massive war tally, the country had emerged victorious against the world's most formidable military machine. Moreover, the Red Army had succeeded in 'liberating' not just the Soviet Union but also many other countries as well, imprinting the Soviet system on most of them. In addition, millions of new citizens had been incorporated into the Soviet system – in part, the product of Red Army successes in Latvia, Lithuania, Estonia, eastern Poland, Bessarabia, northern Bukovina, East Prussia, Carpatho-Ukraine, Karelia, Petsamo, Tannu Tuva, the Kurile Islands and southern Sakhalin. To the credulous, the fact that the USSR was virtually the only country to have made sizeable gains at the end of the war, was 'proof' of its 'invincibility'. The fact that many of the Soviet Union's new recruits were conscripts, rather than volunteers, and did not wish to be Soviet citizens was easily dismissed. The disaffected were as much the product of 'outdated thinking' as the voters who had rejected Bolshevism in 1917, only to discover later the 'error of their ways'. In the meantime, under Stalin's leadership, a comparatively backward and despised nation had been elevated to superpower status – one of the two strongest and most feared countries in the world.

But perhaps Stalinism's greatest attraction was the fear and hostility it engendered in others. That it was anathema to Fascists, Catholics, conservatives, liberals, Social Democrats, Trotskyists and non-Communist Marxists, among others, testified to its power. That the political systems espoused by such critics of the Soviet system had failed to produce anything resembling 'proletarian rule' Stalin-style, or 'the end of exploitation', merely underlined for the Stalinist their inadequacy. Like the Hyde Park orator who thrives on heckling, the Stalinist tended to regard the censure of opponents as a commendation, and as the cold war intensified, so did the sense of conviction – on both sides of the Great Political Divide.

Today, as the Soviet journals begin to fill in some of the 'blank spaces' of the country's history, and western scholars learn to detach themselves from cold war preconceptions and prejudices, it is possible to make a more informed assessment of the differences, theoretical and practical, as well of as the similarities, between Leninism and Stalinism.

Though, doubtless, the debate will long continue as to whether or not the latter was but a logical outcome of the former (as both Stalin and his anti-Communist critics alleged), their starting point was identical.

Both Lenin and Stalin inherited from Marx certain convictions about history, politics and economics in which unproven and often unprovable assertions about the thinking, behaviour patterns and destinies of social groups were accorded the status of 'scientific' laws, as if this rendered them beyond dispute. At the same time, they acquired from both Marx and the Russian revolutionary tradition an unshakeable belief in their own infallibility as interpreters of the 'laws of history', a corresponding intolerance of criticism and dissent, and a lack of scruple in their treatment of those they perceived as impeding the development or consolidation of the 'revolution'. From the Russian revolutionary tradition they also derived a penchant for political organization along military lines, in which loyalty, discipline, and deference to central authority were regarded as cardinal virtues. In other respects, however, the similarities may well have been more apparent than real.

It is, of course, undeniable that even during Lenin's years of effective office, power became increasingly concentrated. Rival parties and periodicals were suppressed, the trade unions and soviets, which had begun as decision-makers in their own right, became mere 'transmission belts' for the party line, and dissident naval ratings were gunned down by the Red Army, while the independent voice in the party was undermined by the ban on 'fractionalism'.

For theorists such as Leonard Schapiro, Zbigniew Brzezinski and Carl Friedrich, these are symptoms of the 'totalitarianism' implicit in both Marxism and Leninism.[10] In their view, the Marxist prospectus – involving the abolition of private property, the eradication of class conflict, and the elevation of society above self – is so far removed from human nature that any attempt at its implementation can only be through coercion and oppression. Further, in the hands of a man like Lenin – in their view, an authoritarian personality – all the negative features implicit in the Marxist perspective were likely to be accentuated. For, in his writings on party organization, 'democratic centralism', and the 'dictatorship of the proletariat', as well as in his dealings with fellow revolutionaries both before and after 1917, he had demonstrated (at least, to the satisfaction of such theorists) that he would brook no opposition, and that his idea of socialism must mean suppressing independent thought at home and expansion abroad as a justification for authoritarian rule.

There is, of course, another way of looking at Lenin's record. After all, the author of *What is to be done?*, with its elitist and undemocratic overtones, had, only four years later, espoused accountability and the election and recall of party functionaries, as the tsarist dictatorship was relaxed. On the eve of the Revolution, he had seen the soviets (in which several parties participated) as the instrument of 'proletarian democracy', and in *The State and Revolution* he had anticipated mass participation in the formulation and execution of policy.

If the reality fell far short of Lenin's professed ideal, it may have had far more to do with the unfavourable circumstances in which he took and held power – his country largely isolated and ravaged by the effects not just of war, but of civil war, anti-Bolshevik terrorism, intervention and blockade – rather than any defect of personality or programme. Moreover, far from rejoicing in the degree of bureaucratic control his regime came to acquire, he seems to have been appalled by it and continued to maintain to the end that 'the proletariat' should be able to hold to account the government acting in its name. Writing in December 1920, he deemed it 'essential' for the trade unions (which included large numbers of non-Communists) to combat 'bureaucratic distortions' in administration, and in subsequent years was at pains to reconcile his belief in central control with inner-party debate and other 'proletarian' checks on arbitrary power.[11] Sadly, as hundreds of thousands of ex-Red Army cadres, helped to swell a state and party machine already burgeoning with former tsarist officials, he found the requisite balance increasingly elusive. That his approach to administration was essentially different from Stalin's surfaced during Lenin's lifetime, as he reflected from his sick-bed on the failings of the Soviet state.

It appeared that in each of the areas troubling Lenin, Stalin was playing a pivotal role.[12] As Commissar of Nationalities, he had employed considerable brutality in the annexation of his native Georgia and towards the succeeding Bolshevik administration, and Lenin found this no less disturbing than Stalin's proposal that the Russian Federation become the government of all the Soviet republics. To Lenin, this was akin to 'imperialism' or at least 'Great Russian chauvinism', and he feared that any constitution which did not guarantee 'equal rights' to each republic might become a potential source of friction. Though Stalin reluctantly conceded to what he dismissed as Lenin's 'national liberalism', he yielded on little else. As Commissar for the Workers' and Peasants' Inspectorate, Stalin did not prune, but expanded, the vast bureaucracy, and when elevated to party General Secretary, he increased it still further.

Indeed, Lenin was himself to encounter bureaucratic obstructionism as his repeated requests for a copy of a report on the number of civil servants in large cities were ignored, according to his chief secretary, on Stalin's instructions. He was also increasingly concerned at other manifestations of the General Secretary's officiousness, and demanded an apology for Stalin's threat to have his (Lenin's) wife, Krupskaya, investigated for taking dictation from her sick husband contrary to doctor's orders. By the time of Lenin's final 'testament', in which he proposed that a 'more tolerant, more loyal, more courteous and more considerate' person be appointed as General Secretary in Stalin's stead, his power had been almost totally eclipsed and his request went unheeded. Within two years of his death, Krupskaya confided to a group of Left Oppositionists her fears for a Stalinist future: 'If Volodya [Lenin] were alive, he would now be in prison'.[13]

What the former French Communist, Roger Garaudy, called the 'turning point'[14] seems to have come at the end of 1929 when the Stalinist impact was already being felt in the Soviet Union and throughout international Communism. In the first place, the nature and style of leadership had changed. Despite Lenin's immense prestige and persuasive power, his 'mastery of Russia' had been neither uncontested nor uncontestable. In the case of the Brest-Litovsk negotiations with Germany or the decision to carry the Russo-Polish war to the gates of Warsaw, for example, he met considerable opposition from his querulous colleagues. Nor could he count on automatic support in the international Communist arena – witness M. N. Roy's rival text to Lenin's *National and Colonial Theses* and the cool reception many European Communists accorded the United Front. As Robert Tucker has pointed out: 'The Leninist system was basically oligarchical rather than autocratic. Soviet politics in the Lenin period were, in their way, a continuing drama of persuasion of the ruling minority by its own acknowledged supreme leader'.[15] In this sense, his rule was consultative, not arbitrary, and his ultimate sanction in securing compliance was the threat of resignation. Stalin, on the other hand, sought the kind of untrammelled authority Lenin had tried to restrain. Having crushed the Left Opposition and then routed his former allies on the Right, he transformed the system from oligarchy to autocracy, complete with a 'personality cult' scarcely equalled even under the tsars.

If Lenin's ban on 'fractionalism' provided a pretext, Stalin's rise to supremacy was facilitated by the existence of a sizeable body of officials owing their positions and their manifold privileges directly or indirectly to him. At the same time, however, the sheer enormity of his economic agenda seemed to call for a style of leadership that could only reinforce his authoritarian instincts. For, his plan to accomplish in roughly a decade an industrial revolution taking other countries a century or more could hardly have been successfully implemented without considerable bloodshed. For, it involved a radical transformation in the lives of some of the country's most conservative people – the peasants – and he was determined that neither they nor their sympathizers in the party should force him to the kind of retreat they had imposed on Lenin a decade earlier.

In the event, in what the Marxist scholar, Leszek Kolakowski, calls 'probably the most massive warlike operation ever conducted by a state against its own citizens',[16] the kulaks as a class were 'liquidated' (Stalin's own term), . . . and the rest of the peasants were herded into collectives, with deportation, forced labour, or even execution for those overtly resisting. As Stalin confessed to Churchill, some 'ten millions' of peasants were 'dealt with' by one or other of these methods,[17] and, in the meantime, the rest were prevented from fleeing to the towns by a system of internal passports used to control movement. Nor was there much respite for the urban workers, subject, as they were, to the strictest factory discipline and direction of labour, though their conditions were idyllic in comparison with those of the forced labourers who constructed the country's roads, railways, canals and airports, working up to 16 hours a day, often in temperatures 50 degrees celsius below zero for virtually nothing but their keep.

Yet, notwithstanding the pervasive atmosphere of fear, there was considerable defiance, particularly in the countryside, as millions of peasants chose to starve to death rather than work under the new system. Their passive resistance in slaughtering or else neglecting their livestock led to a drastic fall in the total between 1929 and 1933 – with serious knock-on effects throughout the economy. According to Soviet sources, the number of horses fell from 34 to 16 million; of cattle from 68 to 38 million; of pigs by more than a third; and of sheep by over a quarter.[18] Nor had Stalin's right-wing critics in the leadership been effectively silenced. For, though they paid lip service to a policy Bukharin had originally condemned as 'military-feudal exploitation of the peasants', Stalin had reason to suspect that their support was more apparent than real. In 1933, he had peacefully defused an anti-Stalin plot by a group of Old Bolsheviks,[19] and though his colleagues generally fell into line, in January 1934, at the party's 17th congress, for many it would be their last. For, Stalin now had to hand a police force brutalized by five years of punitive raids against recalcitrant peasants, and he intended to use it against the instrument that had been the original source of his and Lenin's power – the Party.

The murder of Sergei Kirov, sent to Leningrad to 'clean up' Zinoviev's supporters there, provided the pretext, while the refusal of the Central Committee to back Stalin's proposal to have Zinoviev,

Kamenev and other 'Old Bolsheviks' tried as accomplices, merely strengthened the Soviet leader's determination on a thoroughgoing purge. In fact, he was about to act out a scenario he had outlined to Kamenev and Dzerzhinsky one summer night in 1923: 'To choose one's victim, to prepare one's plans minutely, to slake an implacable vengeance, and then to go to bed'.[20]

From 1936 to 1938, the main 'victim' of Stalin's 'vengeance' was to be the party itself.[21] In those two years, he unleashed against it the apparatus of terror Lenin had used sparingly against known opponents of the regime.[22] He had most of the surviving leaders of the Bolshevik old guard, and many former people's commissars, former ambassadors, and Comintern officials arrested, interrogated, exhibited at 'show trials' before the public prosecutor, and sentenced to either death or a lengthy sojourn in a labour camp after their 'confession' to crimes of which they were frequently innocent. But the party purge did not stop there. It encompassed upwards of a third of the membership, from the Central Committee to the smallest local branch. Any hint of association with opposition groups, or of remarks critical of Stalin or his policies was sufficient to warrant arrest. And, of course, it reached well beyond the confines of the Soviet state, sucking into its cruel vortex thousands of foreign Communists who had hoped to find refuge in the 'Socialist motherland'. In fact, Stalin needed no lessons from Hitler – whose bloody purge of the Nazi Brown Shirts had impressed him[23] – on how to be rid of insubordinate or overambitious party officials.

In the course of breaking the back of the ruling party, Stalin refashioned the secret police, modelling the NKVD quite consciously on the *oprichnina*, which Ivan the Terrible had used in the bloody suppression of the powerful landed aristocracy of his day. Having effectively neutralized the political instrument that had made possible the Russian Revolution, Stalin then turned against the other pillar of the Revolution – the Red Army, which, apart from the NKVD itself, was the only powerful institution capable of toppling him. Here discontent was rife, among both the peasant conscripts, whose way of life had been transformed by collectivization, and the general staff, which entertained serious doubts about Stalin's capacity for leadership. But a mass of fabricated documents was all that was required to secure the execution of the distinguished army Chief of Staff, Marshal Tukhachevsky, and most of his colleagues. According to Soviet figures now available, the scale of the massacre of the high command was even greater than western scholars had originally estimated. Historian Yuri Perechnev, attached to the Soviet defence ministry reveals: 'Out of our five marshals three were killed, out of our 15 army commanders – 13, out of the 57 corps commanders – 50, out of the 186 division commanders only 32 survived' – all of which had a disastrous effect on the country's fighting capacity in the years that followed.[24]

Ironically, among the last of the prominent 'victims' of the period was the principal assassin, N. I. Yezhov, who, as head of the NKVD, had carried through the purges at Stalin's behest. By the time his successor, Lavrenti Beria, took charge of the security services, the whole country had been remoulded according to a Stalinist blueprint – the Soviet leader maintaining his supremacy by 'holding the ring' among a number of competing and conflicting bureaucracies, each fighting for a share of power.[25]

With Stalin as supreme arbiter in all matters, the arts and sciences, which had flourished under Lenin, went into decline. The dictates of 'Socialist Realism' put an end to expressionism and abstract art, which had blossomed in the early '20s, and composers like Shostakovich and Khachaturian were forced to change their style. Soviet science, once so promising, languished because, in the words of a contemporary Soviet scientist, 'the plurality of opinions and approaches' on which scientific investigation is based contradicted Stalin's aim of suppressing 'every form of independent thinking or activity'.[26] Mendelian genetics, Einsteinian physics, cybernetics, psychoanalysis, and structural analysis in linguistics were all dismissed as 'bourgeois pseudo-science', and hundreds of eminent scholars found themselves in jail or labour camps.[27] Today, Soviet scientists recall with bitterness that it was as convicts that aircraft designers Andrei Tupelov and Vladimir Petlyakov and the future space scientist, Sergei Koralyov, made their first contributions to the war effort, devising their blueprints in NKVD establishments and viewing their prototypes in the May Day parade of 1940 from a vantage point behind bars.[28]

Surrounded by sycophants and with virtually unfettered power, Stalin felt free to take measures any other Soviet leader, including Lenin, might have shrunk from pursuing. The Non-aggression Pact with Nazi Germany of August 1939 is a case in point. Though Lenin did not hesitate to sign accords with notorious anti-Communists, this pact was different. For, Stalin's virtual ban on the expression of anti-Nazi sentiment, which followed, appeared to make nonsense of all those years of anti-Fascism, while the pact's secret protocols, for which there is no Leninist precedent, made a mockery of Lenin's strictures against 'imperialism'.

Another instance of Stalin's absence of constraint was his deportation to remote and inhospitable areas of whole national communities, regardless of whether such action was justified by military necessity.

Such ethnic groups as the Crimean Tartars, the Volga Germans, and the Chechen, Ingush, and Kalmyk peoples were removed from the lands they had inhabited for generations, and there were massive transfers of population following the entry of the Red Army into eastern Poland and the Baltic States. Though the precise numbers are disputed, it is generally agreed that well over a million men, women, and children were involved in the four mass deportations between February 1940 and June 1941.[29] Others suffered an even worse fate. Though the Soviet authorities have been slow in admitting responsibility for the thousands of Polish officers discovered in mass graves in Katyń, near Smolensk, in 1943, they have recently been much more forthcoming on the repression in the Baltic States. Soviet sources testify that in June 1941 alone, 12,562 Lithuanians were accused of conspiracy and 'subjected to reprisals' by the Soviet secret police. Further, they reveal that in consequence of the unrest following the reimposition of Soviet rule in Lithuania after the Nazi defeat, 'a new wave of reprisals carried away 108,362 people, affecting 29,923 families' in the years 1945–52.[30]

Though Stalin's apologists might plead some kind of strategic rationale for such ruthlessness, there can surely be no similar defence for his treatment of many of the returned POW's after the war. While it is understandable that he should have sought punishment for those who had collaborated with the enemy during the hostilities, there was no rational warrant for detaining in Soviet camps men who had already spent time as prisoners in Germany or the other Axis countries. Yet, as Solzhenitsyn has detailed, the majority of returnees merely exchanged one prison camp for another, to be branded as 'traitors' or 'spies', either 'because they had allowed themselves to be captured', or because 'they had seen a little more of the West than a German death camp'.[31] But by this time, as one Soviet author bitterly recalls, Stalin was likening his citizens to 'little screws', i.e. 'small cogs in a machine'[32] fashioned entirely to his specification. It was a far cry from Lenin's popular crusade for socialism!

The cold war and the developing rift with Yugoslavia formed the background to yet another wave of repression, as Stalin struck out against those he suspected of being infected with the contagion of Titoism. Once again, it was the party which had to bear the brunt, but with Socialism now in process of being established in one zone, Stalin insisted that in this, as in everything else, the countries of the bloc emulate the Soviet pattern. And there were enough NKVD men in the area to ensure that they did. Within the USSR itself, the party apparatus of Leningrad seems to have been singled out for especially harsh treatment. After his conspicuous failure to bring Yugoslavia into line, Stalin's ideological 'watchdog', Zhdanov, 'died' in mysterious circumstances, and soon Zhdanov's associates, including the country's top economic planner, N. A. Voznesensky (once regarded as Stalin's heir apparent), found themselves facing a firing squad.[33] Though Beria and his close associate, Georgi Malenkov, who prepared the indictments, may have had a personal interest in the disappearance of the Leningrad hierarchy, the removal of yet another stratum of leading Communists enabled Stalin to dispense with even the formality of Politburo meetings.

By mid-1952, however, Stalin seemed to be contemplating a shift in political direction in both domestic and foreign policy. Within the Soviet Union itself, he played host to the first CPSU congress since 1939, presaging a number of significant changes. First, the central institutions of the, by now, moribund party structure were refurbished. The Central Committee and the Secretariat were enlarged, and both Politburo and Orgburo were replaced by a Central Committee presidium, also with expanded membership – the effect being to bring new faces into the hierarchy.

As for the doctrinal tone of the congress, whose keynote speech was read by Malenkov (by now Stalin's latest heir apparent), it followed the logic of Stalin's recently published *Economic Problems of Socialism in the USSR*.[34] On the one hand, there were hints of a yet heavier burden on the peasantry, with the miniscule but highly productive private plots on the collectives being wiped out as all farms become 'public property'. On the other hand, there were also suggestions of a more relaxed attitude in foreign policy, as the contradictions between capitalist and Socialist camps were held to be potentially less lethal (the Korean War, notwithstanding) than the contradictions among the capitalist states themselves. Such a formulation seemed to hold out the possibility of some future détente and was in keeping with a perceived shift in policy, as Stalinist officials for the first time appeared to acknowledge the existence, hitherto denied, of a Third World of underdeveloped but independent states.

Yet, whatever changes were in prospect, Stalin held fast to what Robert Tucker calls that 'paranoid logic' which turned 'friends' into 'enemies' and led to the labour camp, the torture chamber and the execution squad.[35] In his final months, Stalin seems to have been preparing for yet another massive political bloodbath, with the announcement in January 1953 of the arrest of nine doctors attached to the Kremlin on charges of having murdered several prominent figures, including Zhdanov. As in a number of other cases involving Soviet and eastern European Communists, there were anti-Semitic overtones, since six of the accused were of Jewish origin.[36] What made this case different, however, was the fact that the security police stood accused of a lack of vigilance in its failure to 'detect' the 'Doctors' Plot' – a sure sign that Beria and his close associates were in danger of being exterminated by the terror machine they controlled.

Though the death of Stalin, in March 1953, saved the country from yet another round of blood-letting, it came too late for the millions starved, corrupted, brutalized or butchered by a quarter of a century of Stalinism. The irony is that a man now reviled in his own country as probably the most vicious of its many despots should have inspired such affection and admiration during his lifetime that many of his victims died with his name on their lips. 'We thought', says the writer Ilya Ehrenburg, 'that Stalin knew nothing about the senseless violence committed against the Communists'.[37] Even more paradoxical, perhaps, is the fact that this arch proponent of state power should have been regarded as the leading exponent of a theory concerned with the 'withering away of the state'. With hindsight, it is perfectly clear that Lenin's apprehensions of the General Secretary were amply justified, which makes it all the more ironic that during the latter years of Stalinism, the international Communist movement should have been at its zenith. From 1953 onwards, however, as revelations about Stalin began to appear in the Communist press, the situation changed, and the incubus of national Communism, which had surfaced in Yugoslavia and, to a lesser extent, in China in the '40s, began to infect the whole movement. Thereafter, though the number of Communist parties may have grown, as a cohesive, potentially universal and internationally organized movement, Communism went into a slow, but perceptible decline.

NOTES

1. W. Leonhard, *Child of the Revolution* (London, 1957).
2. The systemic characteristics are analysed in George Modelski, *The Communist International System* (Princeton, 1961).
3. *New Left Review*, 64 (December 1970), 10.
4. 12 January 1949; cited in Geoffrey Stern 'The Foreign Policy of the Soviet Union' in F. S. Northedge (ed.), *The Foreign Policies of the Powers* (London, 1974), p. 95.
5. See I. Ratiu, *Moscow Challenges the World* (London, 1986), pp. 285–7.
6. For more on Russification, see L. Schapiro, *The Communist Party of the Soviet Union* (London, 1960), chapter 29, and R. Medvedev, *Let History Judge* (New York, 1971), ch. 13–14.
7. On fellow travellers, see D. Caute, *The Fellow Travellers* (London, 1973), and N. Wood, *Communism and British Intellectuals* (London, 1959).
8. *Truth Will Out* (London, 1949), p. 306.

9. See A. Nove, *An Economic History of the USSR* (London, 1969) and J. P. Nettl, *The Soviet Achievement* (London, 1967).
10. See C. Friedrich and Z. Brzezinski, *Totalitarian Dictatorship and Autocracy* (London, 1963), and L. Schapiro (ed.), *Political Opposition in One-Party States* (London, 1972).
11. For an elaboration of this view, see M. Johnstone, 'Socialism, Democracy and the One-Party System', *Marxism Today*, Vol. 14, Nos. 8, 9 and 11 (August, September, and November 1970).
12. See, for example, M. Lewin, *Lenin's Last Struggle* (London, 1973).
13. Cited in L. Trotsky, *Stalin* (London, 1969), vol. 2, p. 122.
14. *The Turning Point of Socialism* (London, 1969).
15. *The Soviet Political Mind* (London, 1972), p. 212.
16. Cited in Paul Johnson, *A History of the Modern World* (London, 1983), p. 271.
17. *The Second World War* (London, 1951), vol. IV p. 447.
18. *History of the Communist Party of the Soviet Union* (London, 1963), p. 443.
19. A. Kassof (ed.), *Prospects for Soviet Society* (London, 1968), pp. 80–1.
20. Quoted in Tucker, p. 57.
21. Ibid., pp. 49–86.
22. On the purges, see R. Conquest, *The Great Terror* (London, 1971). For recent Soviet estimates, see R. Medvedev, 'The Bitter Truth', vol. 3, No. 4, *Pravda International*, (April 1989). 6.
23. G. Kennan, *Russia and the West under Lenin and Stalin* (New York, 1961), pp. 284–5.
24. 'Ten Volumes about the War', *Moscow News*, 38 (1987), 10.
25. See I. Deutscher, *Stalin: A Political Biography* (Oxford, 1961), esp. ch. 7–9.
26. Prof. D. Dubrowsky as reported in 'Scientists restore truth to Soviet history', *Moscow News*, 51 (1987) 10.
27. See Z. Medvedev, *Soviet Science* (New York, 1978). See also D. Joravsky, *The Lysenko Affair* (Cambridge., Mass., 1970).
28. See the reminiscences of Leonid Kerber, as reported in 'Performance of Duty' *Moscow News*, 48 (1987), 13.
29. See R. Conquest, *The Nation Killers* (London, 1970) ch. 4.
30. Olaf Kuuli, 'On Deportations', *Soviet Weekly* No. 2429 (3 September 1988) 5.
31. *The Gulag Archipelago* (London, 1974), p. 82.
32. 'When the soldiers return home', V. Kondratyev in *Moscow News*, 35 (1987), 12.
33. On the Leningrad purge, see M. Heller and A. Nekrich, *Utopia in Power* (London, 1986), pp. 488–501.
34. The implications are spelled out in Tucker, pp. 87–102.
35. Ibid., p. 70.
36. Heler and Nekrich, pp. 502–3.
37. Cited in Tucker, pp. 52–3.

PART III

The Decline of International Communism

9. The Limits of the 'Thaw'

Stalin's demise on 5 March 1953 posed for his newly orphaned heirs a number of serious questions whose answers could not long be delayed. Could or should Stalinism survive its creator, either as a mode of rule or as a pattern of ideas? If it could, who was to fill the political vacuum? If it could not, how was the Stalinist structure to be modified, and in respect of what – Soviet society, Moscow's relations with the Communist world, or both?

To supporters and detractors alike, the system appeared secure. Throughout the USSR, the centralized bureaucratic apparatus charged with planning and administration was still in place, and its privileged functionaries had a vested interest in ensuring that it was retained intact. The fact, moreover, that authoritarian rule and a sense of global mission had at least as much of a basis in Russian history as in the Bolshevik tradition appeared to give the system staying power. In addition, it seemed to have some of the trappings of success. Under Stalin, the country had risen from an economic and technological backwater to become a potential superpower, with a heavy industrial base, powerful standing army, atomic weapons, a host of allies in eastern Europe and east Asia, and a vast network of party members and sympathizers throughout the world, for whom there was no valid left-wing alternative – Trotskyism being too 'wild', Social Democracy too 'tame', and Titoism too 'treacherous'. In any case, Stalin's departure in no way affected Communist loyalties, since it was to the CPSU as the incarnation of revolution, rather than to Stalin, to which Communists gave their allegiance, even though his death occasioned displays of public grief throughout the Communist world.

On the other hand, the apparent strength of international Communism and its seeming solidarity in face of first Fascism, then war, and finally cold war was something of an optical illusion. For, beneath the façade of unity, assiduously fostered by propagandists, were rifts and divisions. Perhaps F. Claudin goes too far when he suggests that a state of 'de-composition' had set in as early as the dissolution of the Comintern.[1] Nonetheless, it is undeniable that the character of the movement was affected by the end of Moscow's isolation and the advent of a bloc of Communist-ruled states, some owing little or nothing to the Red Army. For, it was one thing for Moscow to determine strategy when most of the world's Communists were concentrated in generally small and weak opposition parties fighting for their political lives; quite another for it to lay down the law to ruling parties trying to construct socialism in societies very different from that of the USSR. That their leaders had originally looked to the Kremlin for guidance and support may have encouraged the belief in Moscow that it was possible to continue organizing the movement as if little or nothing had changed. If so, this was a costly misconception since as soon as the leaders of the Communist states gained in confidence, like Tito (who had, of course, once been an international apparatchik), many began to acquire the kind of national perspective on issues, which the Kremlin regarded as incompatible with its conception of world Communism.

It is in this context that the purges of 'Titoists' and 'national deviationists' must be understood. But there were several other indicators of dissension. That the number of Soviet citizens deserting to the enemy during wartime or fleeing immediately afterwards was proportionately higher than that of any other Allied country[2] says something of the reality behind the 'agitprop' image, while the low productivity and high incidence of alcoholism, juvenile delinquency and clandestine religious activity involving the young of most of the Socialist countries, also testify to disaffection.[3] Moreover, the officially encouraged displays of anti-Semitism throughout eastern Europe can be interpreted as both symptom and cause of disaffection. Had it not been for the West's strategic embargo on the countries of the Soviet orbit and its backing for West Germany, Japan, South Korea, and others with territorial demands on the countries of Socialism, the discord masked by the profession of 'solidarity' might have been more transparent.

Among those probably best informed about the cracks at the base of the Stalinist 'monolith' were, of course, those now at the top of it. They knew that for every Communist shedding tears in the streets of Moscow, Prague or Budapest on the demise of 'the leader of progressive mankind', others rejoiced, and that the Stalinist edifice was unlikely to hold without its chief architect. Nor does any of them appear to have wanted it to survive intact. Having just been spared, by Stalin's departure (which, conceivably, some of them may have hastened), the fate of some of their former colleagues, they had an interest in a system with safeguards against arbitrary power – which only a collective leadership could provide.

In any case, it was now clear that personal rule was as inefficient as it was distasteful. Crucial decisions requiring urgent attention had often been either delayed or mishandled, because the man at the top had insufficient information or else did not understand the basic issues.[4] As for Stalin's widespread use of terror, his successors found this, if not morally objectionable, then at least detrimental to economic progress. Forced labour might be profitably employed in the construction of roads, railways and canals, but it had no economic rationale in a complex chemical plant or in the manufacture and processing of atomic fuels. In fact, brutal administrative methods, coupled with excessive centralization and bureaucratism, were slowly strangling the economy. Initiative was stifled, and people had become afraid of taking responsibility. Few factory managers would dare to initiate a new scheme for fear that if it were unsuccessful they might end up in Siberia or headless.

On the other hand, whilst the men in the Kremlin were agreed that some of the Stalinist superstructure should go, they faced an uncomfortable dilemma. If they made only minor adjustments and continued to honour the name of the dead dictator, there was the danger that the system might atrophy and then fall apart as its weaknesses became manifest. Conversely, if they tried to dismantle it and disparage its creator, they would undermine their own political legitimacy, which was wholly derived from the system. They were, after all, Stalin's appointees. From their predicament a range of alternative solutions emerged.

At one end of the spectrum were Malenkov, the man once expected to inherit Stalin's mantle, and Beria, the secret-police chief. Though the pair had shared in some of the more unedifying chapters in the history of the purges,[5] they did, it seems, a remarkable turnabout. They began advocating far-reaching measures for a more equitable relationship with the Communist countries, a more constructive approach towards the non-Communist world, and a more tolerant and relaxed system of government within the Soviet Union itself. But to the former foreign minister, Molotov, once described by Lenin as 'the best filing clerk in all Russia',[6] their radical approach was far too risky, and, though he granted that the Stalinist system required certain modifications, he wanted these strictly limited. In between these extremes, the former party boss in the Ukraine, now running the Moscow organization, Nikita Khrushchev, held that though de-Stalinization should proceed apace, nothing should be done to weaken party control. As in the '20s, however, so in the '50s, policy differences interfused with personal rivalries, and the political line of the day became dependent on the outcome of the political tug-of-war in Moscow.

For a brief time after Stalin's death, Malenkov appeared to take charge. He combined the post of party chief and head of government, cut Stalin's enlarged party Presidium and Secretariat back to something like their original size, and allowed his name and picture (suitably retouched) to dominate the Soviet press.

Yet, in little more than a week he had relinquished (whether voluntarily or not is still an open question) the leading party position to an old antagonist, Khrushchev, and the 'collective leadership' took immediate steps to curb the apparatus of terror. Alterations in the penal code combined with a wide-ranging amnesty led to the release of first thousands and then millions from the labour camps. Among the freed detainees were the nine Kremlin doctors, whose 'plot' was discovered to have been a complete fabrication. Then the secret police was cut down to size, the Soviet people being given to understand that, henceforth, there would be no further violations of 'socialist legality'. The return to 'the rule of socialist law' did, however, entail a brief, final round of blood-letting as some of those responsible for administering Stalin's terror, including Beria himself, were arranged on a variety of charges, some more plausible than others, and executed, after a secret trial. Paradoxically, the leadership 'collective' in Moscow had made one final reversion to Stalinist methods in order to deter any possible reversion to Stalinist terror in the future.

As the apparatus of terror was being slowly dismantled, Stalin's successors embarked on a 'New Course' to try to improve living and working conditions in both town and country. The penalties for unpunctuality and other breaches of labour discipline were substantially reduced, and soon workers were again relatively free to change their jobs. In the larger towns, the real wages of the lower paid were raised, and such consumer durables as refrigerators and television sets began to be made available for those who could afford them. In the countryside – the Achilles heel of the Stalinist system – urgent steps were taken to try to reverse the catastrophic effects of doctrinaire administration, underinvestment, high taxes, and low procurement prices, which had led to a sizeable drop in per capita output in the 25 years since collectivization. Under the new dispensation, the burden of tax on the household plot was considerably reduced, and the state agreed to increase payments for farm produce while lowering compulsory delivery quotas. That it could raise by more than 500 per cent its purchasing price for compulsory deliveries of meat and poultry merely underlined how inadequate were the payments in Stalin's time. As working conditions improved, there was a perceptible loosening of bureaucratic controls all round. Censorship was relaxed, and the word 'thaw' (emanating from the writings of Ilya Ehrenburg) began to be used to depict the change of atmosphere. It was as if the 'winter' of despotism were giving way to a 'spring' of liberalization.

There were, however, storm clouds on the horizon, and these crystallized in the form of a barely concealed power struggle between Prime Minister Malenkov and Party First Secretary Khrushchev.[7] At first it was expressed as a conflict over investment priorities. The Prime Minister challenged the traditional emphasis on heavy industry and argued for a better balance between light and heavy industry, to the benefit of the Soviet consumer. To strengthen his case, he brought into the government bureaucracy industrial managers and technicians who shared his enthusiasm for a radical restructuring of the Soviet budget. Khrushchev countered with a proposal of his own to help the Soviet consumer – to plough up 13 million hectares of virgin lands in Kazakhstan and Siberia to increase production of foodstuffs. On the other hand, he was firmly against any radical departure from traditional investment priorities, and sought to mobilize support among the party apparatus and the army for a restoration of the more familiar Soviet budget.

The defence and foreign policy implications of the debate over resource allocations brought further altercations between Malenkov and Khrushchev. Following on from his report to the 19th congress of the CPSU, Malenkov used the theory of the erosion of the immediate threat from capitalism to justify a freeze in defence-related appropriations. To accord with his view that 'there is no disputed or unresolved question that cannot be settled peacefully by mutual agreement of the interested countries',[8] he launched a series of initiatives to lessen international hostility and make any rise in defence spending unnecessary. His administration granted Soviet citizens married to foreigners the right to leave the country, re-established diplomatic relations with Greece, renounced claims to Turkish territory, withdrew earlier objections to the proposed new UN Secretary General, began giving economic aid to a number of developing countries, and – most importantly – helped to end the Korean War. Moreover, had not the Western Powers incorporated West Germany into NATO, the Red Army might have withdrawn from the GDR.[9] Whilst there is no evidence that Khrushchev opposed any of these measures (indeed, he made similar initiatives after Malenkov's fall from power), he strongly objected to the strategic assumptions underlying them, and the announcement, on 8 August 1953, that the USSR had acquired the hydrogen bomb brought matters to a head.

For Malenkov, nuclear war could now threaten 'the destruction of world civilization', and was, therefore, unthinkable. It followed that

East and West could accommodate many of their differences, secure in the knowledge that they could not eliminate one another by military means. For Khrushchev, such reasoning, which seemed at variance with Lenin's theory of 'inevitable war', to say nothing of Marxist notions of Communist victory, was wholly misconceived. Though he was later to change his view, the party leader then held that a thermonuclear conflict would mean the destruction only of 'imperialism', and he backed the service chiefs in their demand for a strategy not merely to deter, but, if necessary, to wage nuclear war successfully. To this end, he fiercely opposed Malenkov's unilateral freeze on the budgetary outlays for defence, and may well have had a hand in the veiled attack on 'weak-nerved and unstable people' who might yield to western 'dictation and ultimatums', which appeared in the theoretical journal *Kommunist* shortly after Malenkov's 'resignation' from the premiership in February 1955.[10]

Such momentous changes in Soviet political, economic and cultural life in the aftermath of Stalin's death could not but have serious repercussions throughout the movement of which Moscow still claimed to be the head. In eastern Europe, with its especially close ties to the Soviet Union, the effects were particularly dramatic. For the leaders – all Stalin appointees and survivors of the purges most had helped to introduce – the outlook was uncertain, not least since the power struggle in the Kremlin made it unclear where they should look for patronage. What was clear was that they would have to make substantial changes in their *modus operandi*. At various meetings, both before and after Beria's arrest, the Soviet leaders called upon their somewhat apprehensive allies to introduce 'collective leadership', to correct the violation of party norms occurring during the 'cult of personality' and consider making reforms along Soviet lines.[11] In return, the Soviet Union was willing to reconsider its more exploitive economic arrangements with its eastern European allies, to withdraw the bulk of its security forces, and to concede a measure of diversity to the region. The response from the 'little Stalins' in eastern Europe, reassured by the continued presence in the Kremlin of 'hardliners' like Molotov and Kaganovich, was for the most part grudging – too grudging, indeed, for their long-suffering citizens, many of whom took to the streets, in June 1953, on a wave of rising expectations.

In view of the country's democratic traditions, perhaps it is not altogether surprising that Czechoslovakia was the first to experience the convulsion of mass violent protest, and that it should have been spearheaded by elite workers at the Lenin (formerly Škoda) industrial complex at Plzeň.[12] Touched off by a currency reform, which effectively wiped out the savings of those forced to put money in the bank because of a shortage of consumer goods, it spread from one industrial centre to another. In Plzeň, where the rioting began, some 5000 workers took possession of the town hall and called for the overthrow of the government, after trampling on portraits of Stalin and Gottwald (who had died shortly after returning from Stalin's funeral), ripping up the Soviet flag and hoisting a large portrait of Beneš, Czechoslovakia's last democratically elected president. Within two days, the riots in Plzeň and elsewhere had been suppressed, but their short history made a deep impression on the country's neighbours.

In the GDR, to the north of Czechoslovakia, the situation was even more precarious.[13] Here party leader Ulbricht, trying to cope with a serious food crisis made worse by his doctrinaire policies for agriculture, tried to ease the lot of the peasants while making even greater demands on the urban workers. But the decision to raise work norms by 10 per cent (in effect, reducing real wages) roused the people of East Berlin to fury, and on 16 June, a strike of building workers rapidly turned into a general strike, with economic demands giving way to demands for the resignation of the government and free elections. By 17 June, the strike had turned into an insurrection, with several thousand demonstrators trying to occupy government buildings. As in Czechoslovakia two weeks earlier, the demonstrations in one part of the country led rapidly to demonstrations elsewhere – fanned in this instance by Western broadcasts from Berlin. As German security forces failed to suppress the mounting disorder, Moscow felt obliged to act to contain a perceived threat to its interests in the capital of a country so often a danger in the past. As at Kronstadt in 1921, Soviet forces were called into action against workers demanding the right to be 'free'.

The use of Soviet troops in East Berlin and the repression which followed (42 executed, 25,000 arrests) had indicated the limits of Moscow's tolerance. But there were contradictory theories as to the cause of the uprising that had led to the Red Army intervention. The more reform-minded attributed it to the folly of disregarding widely felt grievances – especially those of the working class. The more conservative traced it to the corrosive effect on national discipline and morale of the perceived lack of unity in the East German and Soviet capitals. Whatever the reason, the Red Army's action saved Ulbricht from the political fate planned for him by reformers in Moscow and East Berlin, and under his continuing iron grip, the GDR made the fewest possible concessions towards the 'New Course'.

On the other hand, while Moscow could not countenance disorder in a state of such strategic importance as the GDR, neither would it tolerate the kinds of Stalinist practices it considered economically and politically damaging. At a meeting in the Kremlin immediately prior to the upheaval in East Berlin, the Soviet leaders instructed Hungary's strong man, Mátyás Rákosi, to give up the premiership to the deputy premier, Imre Nagy (a founder member of the party, whom they knew well from his years of exile in Moscow), in the hope that Nagy might arrest the policies of overindustrialization and forced collectivization which were 'driving the country to the verge of catastrophe'.[14] Though Rákosi conceded, his successor soon went further along the road of reform than Moscow had anticipated and began exploring the potential for independent action within the bloc. For, not only did Nagy give priority to light industry and food production and increase agricultural investments, he also allowed for the dissolution of a collective farm and its replacement by a small-scale commercial enterprise of peasants. In addition, he curbed police powers, freed some 150,000 political prisoners, relaxed censorship and permitted much more freedom of movement, as legal procedure began to replace police despotism.

Under Soviet pressure, the other eastern European countries also made adjustments, albeit half-hearted and belated, as regard forms of leadership, investment priorities, policing and punishment, and the degree of central control. More modest than the Hungarian reforms, these were not at risk with the fall in Moscow of the chief architect of the 'New Course' – Georgi Malenkov.

In Hungary, however, it was different.[15] After nearly two years of reform, the First Secretary, Rákosi, having instructed party officials, in effect, to sabotage many of Nagy's measures, secured Soviet backing for his claim that the economy was in worse shape than before. By this time, however, the hapless Nagy was becoming a casualty of Kremlin in-fighting. For, to stack the 'evidence' against Malenkov, Khrushchev, now aligned with the hardliners Molotov and Kaganovich, needed, as scapegoat, a foreign Communist leader whose 'failure' could be attributed to Malenkov's baleful influence. In Nagy, he found the ideal subject, and within a month of the Soviet prime minister's fall, the Hungarian premier was out, too – the victim of a plot hatched jointly in Moscow and in Communist Party headquarters in Budapest. Refusing to follow his Soviet mentor into exercising self-criticism, Nagy was expelled from the Central Committee and by November, when he lost his party membership, his reforms had been put largely into reverse. In the meantime Rákosi's authority had been fully restored.

Imre Nagy's first premiership had demonstrated both the possibilities and the limitations of self-rule within the post-Stalinist Soviet bloc. Moscow still established the basic framework of policy and could exercise the power of veto. The rest was up to the individual member country – and, clearly some leaders were more eager for radical change than others.[16] If, under Nagy, Hungary had been more reformist than the Soviet Union, after his fall the roles were to be reversed. For, while Rákosi was trying to put the clock back in Budapest, in Moscow, Khrushchev, now emerging as the strongest figure in the Soviet hierarchy, was beginning to demonstrate that he was far from being the Stalinist many had taken him to be. Having dispatched the USSR's former premier to a minor ministry, Khrushchev appeared to appropriate some of Malenkov's ideas – for example, those regarding the satisfaction of consumer demand (possibly to gain popular support at a time when his position was by no means secure), the need to break down cold-war barriers, and the catastrophic implications of a nuclear exchange.

On the other hand, both Khrushchev's policies and his style of leadership were soon to land him in trouble. In particular, his diplomatic offensives of 1955 turned Foreign Minister Molotov from a reluctant accomplice to a firm opponent.[17] Still steeped in the Stalinist imagery of a world divided into two hostile camps, Molotov had misgivings about the offer of aid to non-Communist India, Burma and Afghanistan during Khrushchev's high-profile tour of those countries with Marshal Bulganin, the new Prime Minister. His reservations about selling arms to Syria and Egypt either directly, or indirectly through third parties such as Czechoslovakia, were even stronger, since Moscow might be drawn into conflicts in which it had little interest. Though Molotov appreciated that developments in military technology necessitated some alteration in policy towards the West, he thought Khrushchev even more rash in his concessions than Malenkov. After all, the First Secretary had consented to a pull-out of Soviet troops from Austria, under the Vienna Treaty which provided for that country's neutralization, and had abandoned the Soviet base at Porkkala in Finland – thereby yielding to 'capitalism' positions hard won for 'Socialism'. That this *rapprochement* was preceded by the Warsaw Treaty of 14 May 1955, which incorporated all the European People's Democracies, save Yugoslavia, in a military alliance under a unified (Soviet) command, only marginally mitigated Khrushchev's policy 'errors'. For, it was followed by what Molotov and his conservative supporters perceived as the First Secretary's most dangerous initiative to date – the attempt at reconciliation with Belgrade.

Khrushchev's decision to mend fences with Tito followed logically from an agreement he and Bulganin had concluded with Mao on a visit to Peking in October 1954. For, in it, they conceded to China many of the claims for equal treatment denied Yugoslavia in 1948.[18] But it was Tito's recent conclusion of the Balkan Pact with Greece and Turkey, both members of NATO, that gave urgency to Khrushchev's quest for reconciliation. For, if the Yugoslav leader were to be prised from the western orbit, possibly to return to the Soviet fold, he would clearly need to be reassured that the days of Stalinist hegemony were over. Khrushchev reasoned that the best way to dramatize Moscow's change of heart would be a personal visit to Belgrade expressly to repudiate and apologize for his country's past treatment of Yugoslavia. At the end of May 1955, much to Molotov's chagrin, this was duly accomplished, and as Khrushchev and Tito exchanged bear hugs in Belgrade, the late Lavrenti Beria was made a convenient scapegoat for the original anti-Titoist policy.[19]

The end result, however, of the Soviet leader's trip to the Yugoslav capital was perhaps even worse than Molotov had feared. For the final document of 3 June declared 'matters of internal organization' to be 'exclusively the concern' of each country, thereby opening the way to political pluralism within the Communist movement.[20] As if to underscore the point, the Soviet ideological journal *Kommunist* (No. 14, 1955) advanced the concept of a 'Commonwealth (*sodruzhestvo*) of Socialist states'.[21] For the first time, Moscow had explicitly admitted the legitimacy of different forms of socialism, and the repercussions throughout the movement were bound to be far-reaching. At the very least, such an admission undermined the authority of all those eastern European leaders who had secured their positions in an orgy of anti-Titoist blood-letting and gave the man regarded until recently as posing the gravest threat to the cohesion of international Communism an ideological foothold in the Soviet orbit. More seriously still, it appeared to presage an unholy alliance between men whose commitment to socialism Molotov believed to be highly suspect. All the Foreign Minister's worst suspicions seemed confirmed when Khrushchev took the floor for the CPSU's 20th congress in Moscow, in February 1956, and issued the two reports which were to make this assembly an ideological and political watershed in Communist history.

In the first place, Khrushchev spelled out what had been implicit in his resumption of ties with Yugoslavia – that there could be different ways of attaining socialism, implying thereby that other Communist-ruled countries might be permitted to chart their own Socialist paths. Later, in the same report, Khrushchev modified a key Leninist tenet by declaring that the creation of a strong Stalinist system had strengthened the anti-war forces to such an extent that war with the capitalist states was no longer 'fatalistically inevitable'.[22] Henceforth, the ideological struggle between 'Socialism' and 'capitalism' could be waged in nonviolent ways, with economic competition as a means of determining the final victory between the two systems, and with the developing countries as the major 'battleground' on which the struggle was to be fought. In this sense, 'peaceful coexistence' was no longer, as it had been for Lenin, a mere interlude between wars, but a multifaceted strategy to secure socialism through a dialectic of competition and collaboration with existing governments. While national liberation wars and violent revolutions were still legitimate forms of struggle, Khrushchev held there could be a peaceful, parliamentary transition to communism, and that in a thermonuclear age the 'peaceful path' might be preferable.

Having provoked the conservatives to fury by his far-reaching revisions of accepted orthodoxy, Khrushchev then struck his hammer blow against them. In a bid to secure Tito's loyalty, regenerate the Soviet party, and strengthen his own role within it, he launched into a bitter attack against the man he and his colleagues had faithfully served for decades – Josef Stalin. Presumably to avoid public discussion of the legitimacy of the Soviet regime, as such, and of the role played by people like himself in the Stalinist era, he delivered his four-hour tirade to a closed session of congress, from which all foreign delegates were excluded; but within days the text (which was not published in the Soviet Union until more than 30 years later) was 'leaked' to the outside world.

In fact, his 'secret speech' was not an unrestrained onslaught on Stalin and all his works.[23] The bureaucratic, centralized system, the destruction of the non-Communist opposition, the command economy, collectivization, and the infallibility of the party were left unscathed. It was rather Stalin's paranoia ('He could look at a man and say: "Why are your eyes so shifty today?" . . . Everywhere and in everything he saw "enemies", "two-facers", and "spies" '), his contempt for the party ('Everything was decided by him alone without any consideration for anyone or anything. . . . The importance of the Political Bureau was reduced and its work disorganized'), and the methods by which he operated ('Of the 139 members and candidates of the party's Central Committee who were elected at the 17th party congress, 98 persons, i.e. 70 per cent, were arrested and shot') that earned Khrushchev's especial censure.

By implication, Khrushchev's indictment of Stalin was also an attack on those Soviet leaders closer to Stalin than he had been and, not surprisingly, it had the effect of uniting Molotov, Kaganovich, and Malenkov in opposition to him. Within the wider movement, it put the

Soviet leader sharply at odds with the 'little Stalins' still in charge of the various Communist parties, and gave encouragement to their critics. But what seems to have been intended as an exercise in damage limitation began to slip rapidly out of control. For, throughout international Communism his speech, confirming the truth of many of the things that party members had hitherto refused to believe, had a shattering effect on morale, causing a ferment of doubt and soul-searching. For many, Khrushchev's attack on Stalin and Stalinism was the moment of truth, not least since it put in question the Leninist system that had made Stalinism possible. Though some of the doubters resisted the temptation to tear up their party cards, others could not, and as a result there occurred, in 1956, the most significant exodus from Communism since 1939.

It was, however, in eastern Europe that Khrushchev's 'secret speech' had its most serious repercussions. It was not simply that the very people who had carried out the purges of 'national deviationists' and 'Titoists' on Stalin's behalf a few years earlier were still in power. It was also the fact that many of the survivors were still languishing in jail or under some other form of restriction. For Stalin's eastern European heirs to have to repudiate earlier actions and rehabilitate some of their victims could not but create a crisis of confidence in their leadership, in the system in whose name they had acted, and in the country from whom they received their instructions and inspiration. In the event, the sense of disillusionment permeating all the eastern European parties and societies threatened the stability of the recently created Warsaw Pact and the cohesion of the bloc.

Amid the turmoil, fundamental questions about the origins and nature of Communist rule, hitherto confined to its critics, began to surface in the Communist forums of eastern Europe. Was the fate of Poland sealed by the Nazi–Soviet Pact? Why, 10 years after the establishment of Communist rule in Romania, were Bessarabia and northern Bukovina still in Soviet hands? Had there been a popular mandate for Soviet-style socialism anywhere in the region? Was Communist rule merely a disguised form of Soviet imperialism? Even in Yugoslavia, Communists were putting the regime under scrutiny, many challenging the decision to jail Milovan Djilas, once Tito's close associate, for exposing the persistence of privilege and patronage in the party.[24] If frankness was now to be *de rigueur* in the countries of the Soviet bloc, why should Yugoslavia, which, since the early '50s had allowed more freedom of expression than any other Communist-ruled state, appear to be moving in the opposite direction?

Though few eastern European leaders could provide satisfactory answers, most tried to defuse popular discontent and prevent a slide to 'counter-revolution' by making, at least, token gestures in the direction of de-Stalinization, while keeping a tight rein on critics and party dissidents. With one notable exception, they attempted a *rapprochement* with Belgrade, finding scapegoats to demote for their 'abuse of power during the period of the cult of personality', freeing some political prisoners, and rehabilitating some of the better-known Communist victims of the purge trials. Only Tito's arch enemy, Albania's Enver Hoxha, stood aloof. Far from rehabilitating the executed pro-Yugoslav, Koçi Xoxe, Hoxha held him responsible for the 'personality cult' and the break with Belgrade, and then proceeded to a fresh purge of elements in the party favouring better ties with Tito.[25] In the event, while a combination of 'carrot' and 'stick' tactics enabled most of the parties to ride out the storm, two of them – Poland and Hungary – were unable to cope. Both were to experience a serious breakdown in law and order, and in the latter, the Communist system, as understood throughout the bloc, was virtually overthrown.

In Poland, even before Khrushchev's 'secret speech', the party – never very popular in such a Catholic, nationalist, and traditionally anti-Russian country – seemed to be in disarray.[26] What had prompted the display of disunity were the revelations, concerning the private lives and political methods of the party leaders, from documents smuggled out to the USA by a defecting security-police official – Colonel Swiatło – and broadcast back to Poland on Radio Free Europe. But the divisions and the disaffection grew to crisis proportions after Khrushchev's denunciation of Stalin, the sudden death in Moscow, in March 1956, of the Polish leader, Beirut, and the vain attempt by the Soviet leader to influence the Polish succession. Bowing to popular pressure and disregarding the residual Stalinists in the leadership, the new party chief, the veteran Communist, Edward Ochab, propelled the party in the direction of radical reform. He released some 30,000 political prisoners – among them former officers of the Home Army (AK) and officials of the Socialist and Peasant parties – and lifted the remaining restrictions on Władysław Gomułka, the popular, former party First Secretary who had served a four-year jail sentence for 'national deviationism'. At the same time, he allowed Communism's critics access to the press and encouraged Poland's economists to debate the reconstruction of the ailing economy.

But, as in Czechoslovakia and the GDR three years before, unfulfilled expectations generated by a change in political atmosphere had explosive results. In June 1956, in full view of foreign visitors attending a trade fair, workers staging a strike in Poznań for better pay and conditions, went on an anti-Communist rampage, attacking a police headquarters, the courthouse, the prison and the radio building. Though it took more than a day for the armed security forces, backed by tanks, to restore order (amid a tally of 54 dead and some 300 wounded), Ochab ensured that the trial of the ringleaders was open to western journalists and conducted with scrupulous fairness. Each of the accused had an able defence lawyer, and most, even those involved in bloodshed, were either acquitted or given light sentences.

Both Moscow and the hard-line factions in Warsaw greeted these developments with alarm. De-Stalinization was one thing: showing weakness in the face of anti-Communist rebellion was another. If the Polish party failed to keep proper control, worker unrest could spread, with incalculable consequences. As reformers and Stalinists held their inquest on the Poznań rising at a Central Committee meeting in Warsaw in July, Khrushchev, now under fire from his domestic critics for sowing the seeds of confusion and chaos in the bloc, decided to intervene. In dispatching two marshals – Zhukov and Bulganin – to Warsaw, he was hoping to boost the fortunes of the more hard-line, pro-Soviet elements in the leadership and to ensure that Gomulka, whom Moscow still regarded as more of a nationalist than a Communist, never returned to power. As Bulganin put it in a speech ostensibly to mark Poland's national day: 'We cannot idly bypass attempts that aim at weakening the tier of the Socialist camp under the slogans of so-called national peculiarities'.[27]

The appearance of the marshals was counter-productive. It merely intensified resentment among the reformers, leading to demands for a redefinition of the country's relations with the Soviet Union (still buying coal from Poland at a tenth of the world price), for the repatriation of Poles held in the USSR since the war, and for the reinstatement of the one man whose leadership might conceivably unite the nation and restore the party's self-respect – Władysław Gomułka. Buoyed by statements of support from Tito and Mao, both of whom advocated the independence of each party, Ochab put the security forces under the control of a Gomułka supporter, dismissed the minister who had charted Poland's economic policy since 1949, proposed the dismissal of the defence minister, Rokossowski, a marshal in the Soviet armed forces, and finally agreed to Gomułka's return to the leadership.[28]

At this stage, the hard-line 'Natolin' faction planned a coup, having previously alerted Moscow and drawn up a list of 700 reformers to be arrested. But with pro-Gomułka security forces controlling key posts and the Polish Army's reliability in doubt, only Soviet troops could be trusted to march on Warsaw – an enterprise which would have risked a possible war between Poland and the Soviet Union. As the forces stood on the alert, Khrushchev, on 19 October, arrived in Warsaw with Molotov, Kaganovich, Mikoyan, and several Soviet generals to try to re-establish Moscow's authority and keep Poland's reforms within bounds. But the Poles, now led by Gomułka, refused to retreat, and issued counter-threats, following reports of Soviet troop movements in and around the country. In the end, their firmness, combined with a pledge to maintain Communist control and allegiance to the Warsaw Pact, on which they depended for protection of the Oder-Neisse territories, led to a Soviet climbdown. Moscow accepted Gomułka's leadership and his reform programme, and agreed to the repatriation of Rokossowski. It was another turning point in eastern European history. Henceforth, Moscow could no longer expect total subservience from its Communist clients.

Yet, within two weeks of Gomułka's victory, Khrushchev was to demonstrate the limits of eastern European autonomy. The test was to come in Hungary, which had been seething with discontent since Rákosi had ousted Nagy from the premiership, restoring a degree of authoritarianism inconsistent with the Moscow 'thaw'. By June 1956 the Hungarians, both within and outside the party, had become so antagonistic to Rákosi that he was being openly attacked in the party press and could no longer count on the loyalty of even the security police. To try to defuse the crisis and as a further concession to Tito, who had long despised Rákosi, the Soviet leaders agreed to his removal in July. But, in replacing him with the almost equally discredited Ernö Gerő, Rákosi's deputy and a man totally lacking the political sensitivity of an Ochab, they merely intensified the degree of national frustration. In the months that followed, the pattern of Communist rule began to disintegrate, amid demonstrations of solidarity with the Poles and demands for a free and independent Hungary and the return of Nagy.[29]

On 23 October, what started as a student demonstration in support of Gomułka soon took on the character of an insurrection, as massive crowds in Budapest toppled a mammoth Stalin statue, laid siege to the radio building, and, finding themselves under fire from the AVH (security forces), started to strike back with weapons supplied by rebellious Hungarian soldiers. When Gerő, after fanning an already inflammatory situation with an ill-judged broadcast, called on Soviet troops to aid the AVH in suppressing the uprising, there was a critical spiral of violence which Nagy, restored to the premiership as the Soviet tanks made their appearance, was powerless to stop. Nor could he resist, even had he wanted to, the popular demands for the removal of Soviet forces, Hungary's neutralization on the Austrian model and the reintroduction of the multiparty system. Though Moscow led Nagy to believe that he had its support when he announced on 30 October the abolition of the 'one-party system', his statement seems to have been a critical factor in hardening Kremlin attitudes, despite a lull in the fighting in Budapest. For, coming so soon after Moscow's capitulation in Warsaw, it was perceived as posing a grave ideological and political threat to the bloc at a time of apparent western military superiority. Moreover, as the leading proponent of de-Stalinization, Khrushchev's own political credibility was on the line, and on a visit to Yugoslavia just prior to the suppression of the Nagy regime, he tried to enlist Tito's support for a Soviet clampdown in Hungary: 'If we let things take their course, the West would say we are either stupid or weak, and . . . we can't possibly permit it'.[30]

On this occasion, Tito was sympathetic. After all, despite his many differences with the Soviet leadership, he was as dedicated as Khrushchev to the principle of one-party rule, and, like most Communist leaders, considered that Hungary was in a state of 'counter-revolution', with potentially disastrous consequences for the international movement. Hence, when after initial hesitation, Soviet tanks were ordered to crush the 'counter-revolution' on 4 November (while much of the world's attention was focused on the fighting in connection with the Suez crisis), reinstating party rule under János Kádár, a reform-minded Communist who had recently deserted Nagy, virtually every party leadership (including the Chinese), voiced approval. Only the Poles openly expressed reservations, dissociating themselves from the rest of the bloc when the Soviet intervention was discussed at the UN.[31]

On the other hand, though the intervention was excessively bloody and resulted in the execution of Nagy and his closest supporters and the arrest of thousands more, the repression was of limited duration and did not presage a return to Stalin-style Soviet hegemony over the bloc. For the Soviet role in international society had considerably enlarged since Stalin's day, and most Soviet leaders accepted that without some overhaul of its relations with eastern Europe, Moscow would be handicapped in its bid to convince the peoples of the developing countries of the superiority of the Socialist system. In any case, with the nuclear stalemate and the steady development of East–West economic ties, eastern Europe no longer had the same importance for Soviet policy as in the Stalinist era. Furthermore, the daunting political and economic costs of the use of force in eastern Europe made it an increasingly unattractive option for Moscow. Nonetheless, the Kremlin could not be indifferent to developments in an area so closely bound up with its security, welfare and prestige – hence, its periodic and forceful reminders since 1956 of its determination to arrest the process of 'decomposition'.

For tens of thousands of Communists throughout the world, however, the Soviet intervention in Hungary, coming so soon after the revelations about Stalin, was the last straw. But unlike earlier mass defections, many former Communists chose to remain within the Marxist tradition. Both 'capitalism' and 'Communism' seemed to them equally flawed, and by rediscovering the ideas of heretical Communists like Rosa Luxemburg, Paul Levi and Antonio Gramsci, as well as the writings of Imre Nagy, and by exploring non-Marxist critiques of society as expressed in the feminist, ecological, anti-colonial, and peace movements, they felt they could make a contribution to the creation of a new, democratically inclined socialist society.

While the New Left was finding its identity, the old Left in Moscow remained unconvinced that Khrushchev would be able to maintain the leadership and cohesion of international Communism, despite the virtual accord over his tough handling of the Hungarian 'counter-revolution'. Clearly, the events in eastern Europe in the autumn of 1956 had diminished his stature in the Soviet hierarchy and within the wider Communist movement, and in the following year he found himself having to do battle on two fronts – for political survival at home and against carping criticism from Peking. In June 1957, in Moscow, he only defeated a challenge against him as party leader by having his case transferred from the party Presidium, in which he had been voted out of office, to the Central Committee, which was packed with supporters flown in for the crucial meeting in planes provided by the sympathetic defence minister, Marshal Zhukov. Though the support of the Central Committee enabled him finally to expel from the top policy-making body Molotov, Kaganovich, Malenkov, and others for their 'antiparty' conspiracy,[32] Khrushchev seems to have found a much more formidable antagonist in the Chinese leader, Mao Tse-tung. For his insensitive handling of relations with Peking from the time of the 20th CPSU congress onwards opened up all the CCP's latent resentments and helped precipitate a rift between the Communist giants that some commentators were to call 'the new cold war'.

NOTES

1. *The Communist Movement* (London, 1975), *passim*.
2. According to Martin Gilbert, some 1,850,000 Russians, Balts, and Ukrainians fled westwards in the Soviet Union's first two years of war. See his *Soviet History Atlas* (London, 1979), p. 56.

3. Robert Tucker, *The Soviet Political Mind* (London, 1972), p. 188.
4. This is one of the conclusions of Roy Medvedev, *Let History Judge* (London, 1972).
5. See, for example, M. Heller and A. Nekrich, *Utopia in Power* (London, 1986), pp. 488–501.
6. Cited in E. Crankshaw, *Khrushchev* (London, 1966), p. 130.
7. The details are traced in R. Pethybridge, *A Key to Soviet Politics* (London, 1962).
8. Cited in M. Rush (ed.), *The International Situation and Soviet Foreign Policy* (Columbus, Ohio, 1970), p. 162.
9. See I. Deutscher, *Russia, China and the West* (Oxford, 1970), pp. 46–51.
10. Cited in S. Ploss (ed.), *The Soviet Political Process* (Washington, 1971), p. 133.
11. F. Fejtö, *A History of the People's Democracies* (London, 1971), pp. 17–20.
12. Ibid., pp. 26–8.
13. Ibid., pp. 20–3.
14. Cited in Z. Brzezinski, *The Soviet Bloc* (New York, 1961), p. 159.
15. See Charles Gati, 'Imre Nagy and Moscow', *Problems of Communism* Vol. 35. No. 3 (May–June 1986), pp. 32–49.
16. See Fejtö, ch. 4, 5, and 6; J. Steele (ed.), *Eastern Europe since Stalin* (London, 1974), ch. 8–11; and C. Harman, *Bureaucracy and Revolution in Eastern Europe* (London, 1974), ch. 4–5.
17. Pethybridge, pp. 61–72.
18. Fejtö, pp. 32–3.
19. Ibid., pp. 34–8. See also, *Khrushchev Remembers* (London, 1971), pp. 503–56.
20. P. Zinner (ed.), *National Communism and Popular Revolt in Eastern Europe* (New York, 1956), p. 6.
21. R. H. McNeal (ed.), *International Relations Among Socialists* (Englewood Cliffs, New Jersey, 1967), p. 73.
22. For relevant extracts see R. V. Daniels (ed.), *A Documentary History of Communism* (London, 1985), vol. 2, pp. 223–7.
23. The secret speech is reproduced in *Khrushchev Remembers*, pp. 503–56.
24. Fejtö, pp. 36–7.
25. Ibid., p. 50.
26. On events in Poland, see Fejtö, pp. 62–3, and N. Bethell, *Gomułka* (London, 1969), ch. 13.
27. Zinner, p. 144.
28. Bethell, ch. 14, and Fejtö, pp. 66–72.
29. On events in Hungary, see M. Molnar, *Budapest 1956* (London, 1971); G. Mikes, *The Hungarian Revolution* (London, 1957); and B. Lomax, *Hungary 1956* (London, 1976). For an orthodox Communist view, see H. Aptheker, *The Truth about Hungary* (New York, 1957).
30. C. Gati, p. 49.
31. See Richard Hiscocks, *Poland: Bridge for the Abyss?* (Oxford, 1963), p. 231.
32. See R. and Z. Medvedev, *Khrushchev: The Years in Power* (London, 1977). See also R. Medvedev, *All Stalin's Men* (London, 1983), pp. 104–6.

·10. The New Cold War

If 1956 was a critical year in Moscow's relations with eastern Europe, revealing the centrifugal tendencies beneath the facade of 'monolithic Communism', it seems to have been no less momentous in the Kremlin's ties with Peking. Certainly, the Chinese in their subsequent polemics tended to date the rift with Moscow from the 20th CPSU congress, though whether or not they found Khrushchev's 'revisionism' quite as offensive as they later claimed is debatable. After all, until the mid-'50s there had been more than a hint of 'revisionism' in China's own domestic policies, while the concept of 'peaceful coexistence', which dates back to Lenin, had already been enshrined in an agreement of 1954 between China and India.

What is clear, however, is that the Chinese leaders felt aggrieved that neither they nor anyone else had been taken into Khrushchev's confidence before the Soviet congress. For, his brand of 'revisionism', with its emphasis on Soviet economic development and great power status, would have had grave implications for every Communist party, including the Chinese, irrespective of whether or not he expected the 'Socialist Commonwealth' to follow suit. That he did count on their compliance only made it worse. Moreover, though China's leaders could have had little affection for Stalin, who had so often treated the CCP with disdain, Mao had admired him as one of history's great men and was profoundly apprehensive about the effects (not least in China itself) of a sustained attack against the 'personality cult'. In the Hungarian turmoil of 1956, his worst fears seemed confirmed.

Ironically, by the time of the 20th party congress of the CPSU, Peking had cause for satisfaction at the state of relations with Moscow. The Soviet residual hold on Manchuria and Sinkiang had been relinquished, the joint-stock companies that had facilitated its economic and political penetration wound up, and the Soviet bases in Port Arthur and Dairen evacuated and returned to full Chinese control. Moreover, the Kremlin was being much more generous with its trade credits, while Soviet technicians were doing invaluable service in industrializing the country and modernizing its army.

Moreover, now that Stalin was dead and discredited, Moscow was treating Mao with much greater respect. In the autumn of 1954, the

Soviet Union's top leaders paid court to Mao in Peking, crediting the People's Republic with 'fighting successfully for the building of the foundations of socialism'. In 1955, the Soviet Foreign Minister, Molotov, had bracketed China with the Soviet Union as joint leaders of the Socialist camp.[1] And, in the very speech which apparently caused Peking so much offence, Khrushchev was attempting to make amends for Stalin's display of 'lack of faith . . . in our Chinese comrades' which had the effect of 'retarding . . . the establishment of a government of Popular Democracy'.[2] If there were strains in Sino-Soviet relations arising out of their disputed frontier, the status of Mongolia, their rival bids for influence in Asia, and Khrushchev's call for 'volunteers' to settle in the borderlands of eastern Siberia, they were not so serious as to cause any major rift. As far as may be judged, the People's Republic had given guarded approval to Moscow's attempt to heal the breach with Tito, was reasonably satisfied with Moscow's concessions to its material well-being and self-esteem and had no qualms about accepting the Soviet Union as head of the Socialist Commonwealth.

Nor is there much evidence to suggest a sudden deterioration of Sino-Soviet relations as a result of the proceedings of the 20th congress. Though a *People's Daily* editorial of 5 April 1956 expressed reservations about the attack on Stalin (possibly to protect Mao against similar accusations), it, nonetheless, praised the Soviet party's 'courageous self-criticism of its past errors' and endorsed the charges of self-aggrandizement, lack of vigilance prior to the anti-Fascist war, indifference to the peasantry, and lack of judgement on the Yugoslav question levelled against Stalin by Khrushchev.[3] Soon Mao was presaging a degree of de-Stalinization in his own country, calling for a nationwide debate on policy under the slogan: 'Let a hundred flowers bloom – let diverse thoughts contend'! At the same time, he voiced support for the aspirations of the Polish party for greater autonomy, thereby strengthening the resolve of those who sought to accelerate the pace of reform in that country.

On the other hand, China's earlier reservations about Khrushchev's attack on Stalin and resentment over his unilateral 'revisions' of accepted doctrine resurfaced as the Hungarian events began to unfold. In the collapse of the Marxist–Leninist system in Budapest, Mao saw the perils of unrestrained 'revisionism' and the unacceptable face of untrammelled anti-Stalinism, and drew his conclusions. A *People's Daily* article of 29 December 1956 reflected his views.[4] Firstly, it recognized the Soviet Union as 'the centre', rather than the leader, 'of the international Communist movement', and by virtue of its material resources and seniority, not its superior knowledge of Marxism–Leninism. Secondly, it insisted that unity of the Socialist Commonwealth be on the basis of common understandings through 'genuine exchanges of view', not unilateral impositions or interference. Thirdly, it warned against adopting a 'negative attitude towards everything connected with Stalin', and castigated Tito for a speech that was a virtual declaration of war against Stalinist tendencies, wherever and in whichever party they existed. Here, then, was the CCP's justification for supporting both Polish autonomy and the suppression of the Hungarian revolt, but it also contained the first indications of the kinds of arguments China would later deploy to devastating effect against the Soviet Union and much of the Communist world.

If the Russians were uneasy about China's new-found interest in the traditional Soviet preserve of eastern Europe, underlined by Premier Chou's excursion to Warsaw and Budapest, as well as to Moscow, in the spring of 1957, they did not show it. But domestic developments in both countries later in the year were soon to put them on a collision course. In the Soviet Union, after a brief period in which Khrushchev's Stalinist opponents seemed to be gaining ground, the Soviet leader staged his counter-coup, and by the end of June had established his personal and political ascendancy. In China, the political outlook was clouded by the fate of Mao's 'Hundred Flowers' experiment, which gave rise to far more severe and deep-rooted criticisms of the Communist system and of its leaders than he had bargained for.[5] To make matters worse, this manifest discontent coincided with a serious economic crisis, as rapid industrialization and collectivization engendered severe imbalances, bottlenecks, and shortages of the kinds experienced earlier by the Soviet Union. In effect, Mao, who had hoped to win over the country's non-Communist intellectuals through the 'Hundred Flowers' process, took fright, and with the aid of another 'rectification campaign' along the lines of the 'Five Anti's' of 1952, turned against the leading 'rightists'.[6] Effectively, Moscow was moving to the right while Peking lurched to the left.

Nevertheless, alarmed by the prospect of a growing rift in Sino-Soviet relations, Moscow made a last major effort in the latter half of the year to repair the breach. With the confidence of a country which had just successfully tested an intercontinental ballistic missile and launched the world's first artificial satellite into space, the Soviet Union agreed to help China become a nuclear power. According to a Chinese statement published six years later, Moscow promised to hand over to Peking a sample atomic bomb, together with technical data on its manufacture.[7] At the same time, it formed a Soviet–Chinese Friendship Association to try to foster good feeling towards its eastern neighbour. Finally, at the Moscow Conference of Communist parties to commemorate the 40th anniversary of the Russian Revolution, the Kremlin made a number of concessions to the Chinese delegation, led by Mao, to reach an accord on a final 5000 word declaration.[8] Though the document reaffirmed the non-inevitability of war, the possibility of peaceful transition, and the different roads to Socialism, it represented a much more militant statement than Khrushchev's report to the 20th CPSU congress. There was, for instance, more than a hint of subsequent Chinese rhetoric in its searing attack on 'modern revisionism' (which made the document unacceptable to the Yugoslavs), in its attitude of uncompromising hostility to the western powers, and in the stress laid on the revolutionary dynamic of national liberation movements. And, though the declaration reasserted Moscow's 'leadership' of international Communism, it was in the context of a joint struggle against 'imperialism' for the spread of socialism worldwide. As such, the document left open the possibility of a Chinese share in the formulation of a programme to guide the Communist movement, now lacking any formal world organization.

Yet, despite the semblance of accord between Moscow and Peking, anyone hearing Mao's address to the Moscow Conference – the first forum of world Communist leaders he had ever attended – will have had some idea of the yawning gulf separating the two Communist giants. For in his diatribes on war, peace and the balance of power, he used the kind of imagery which might well have appealed to an audience of Chinese Communists hardened to suffering and accustomed to victory against overwhelming odds, but which sounded disturbingly incongruous to many European Communist ears.[9] Referring to what he saw as a rising tide of revolutionary sentiment throughout the world, as well as to the impact of the Soviet Union's recent advances in military-related technology, Mao called for a tough and uncompromising policy towards 'imperialism', which he referred to as a 'paper tiger'. Using a meteorological analogy which became famous almost overnight, he contended, 'The east wind prevails over the west wind', and though he indicated that it was meant to suggest a decisive shift in the global balance in favour of Socialism, not a few of his listeners thought they detected geographical and even racial overtones in this conception. Yet, even taken at face value, it caused consternation in Moscow since it suggested that Mao's recommended strategy for the world movement was based on a gross underestimation of the military and economic strength at the disposal of 'imperialism' and a corresponding overestimation of the resources available to Socialism.

Still more ominous were Mao's interjections on the subject of thermonuclear war. While emphasizing that the Socialist countries would never be the aggressor in a world conflagration, he concluded, nevertheless, that Communists should not shrink from nuclear warfare since it would bring further victories for Socialism, even if it killed half the world's population. Such a sentiment could hardly have sounded reassuring to those now committed to helping China become a nuclear power.

Yet, for nearly a year, Moscow shrank from the consequences of a breach, and, by September 1958, had helped the Chinese to construct a nuclear reactor and a 20 million electron-volt cyclotron in the suburbs of Peking.[10] Moreover, assuming a more militant posture itself, the Soviet Union had joined China in denouncing the Yugoslav League of Communists for a programme which seemed to place it outside the Communist orbit as hitherto understood. For, from its 7th congress of April 1958, the Yugoslav party held that Communists 'should no longer be concerned primarily with questions relating to the overthrow of capitalism', that it was possible to achieve socialism without a revolution and that Communist parties need not enjoy a power monopoly in pursuit of socialism. More seriously, the Yugoslav programme drew no distinction between the Warsaw Pact and the western alliance systems, and in a clear bid for support among Asian, Arab, and African neutralists, condemned both blocs as equally militaristic.[11] In response, Khrushchev, to Peking's satisfaction, held up the credits and grain supplies he had earlier pledged to Belgrade, ordered the execution of Imre Nagy, who had for a time taken refuge in the Yugoslav Embassy in Budapest, and made no attempt to discourage Bulgarian and Albanian irredentist claims against Yugoslavia.[12]

By the end of 1958, however, Moscow found it increasingly difficult to maintain even verbal solidarity with Peking, as Mao's militancy was translated from the rhetoric of 1957 to the realm of politics. Domestically, having announced his intention to restructure the lives of China's 600 million 'poor' and 'blank' people, Mao introduced, under the slogan of 'The Great Leap Forward', an organizational revolution of a scope and magnitude unprecedented. Designed to exploit the one resource the country had in abundance – unskilled manpower – it sought to mobilize the masses into 'people's communes' – each with an average of about 5000 households – in which virtually everything would be shared equally and everyone give freely of his labour. At its extreme, it meant the abolition of private property, save for personal possessions and small tools, the free distribution of food and other goods, the segregation of men and women in separate dormitories, and a system of militarized labour, with people waking up to the sound of bugles, eating in communal mess halls, and often marching to work 'at the double'. Though the communes were based in the countryside, their members engaged in manufacturing, mining, and military service, as well as in farming. Particular emphasis was laid on the construction in every backyard of small iron and steel furnaces to supplement production from the modern metallurgical combines built with Soviet help.

Though originally designed to deal with the country's critical shortage of capital, the system was increasingly presented as a short cut to a communist society. But the party's claim that the communes would 'accelerate socialist construction, complete the building of socialism ahead of time, and carry out the gradual transition to communism', whose realization was 'not something distant', was one which Moscow found as subversive as it was arrogant.[13] For, in purporting to be within sight of communism, the Chinese were issuing a serious challenge to Soviet political and ideological primacy, as well as establishing a model that some of the less developed Communist-ruled countries, such as Albania, Bulgaria and North Korea might want to emulate.

But Mao's external policy was, if anything, even more worrying to the Kremlin. For, in one international crisis after another, China took up a belligerent posture that carried the danger of dragging Moscow into a war that was none of its choosing.[14] During the Middle Eastern crisis of summer 1958, when American and British forces landed in Lebanon and Jordan following the overthrow of the pro-western government in Iraq, there was a major row between Mao and Khrushchev on the Communist response. The Chinese seemed to favour a military riposte. The Soviet leader favoured an East–West 'summit' on the issue, but was persuaded to drop the idea after an unscheduled secret visit to Peking at the end of July. He continued, however, to display a more conciliatory attitude than the Chinese, and the British and Americans agreed to refrain from hostilities against the new regime in Iraq. A few weeks later, when China began to shell the Nationalist-held offshore islands of Quemoy and Matsu, it found Moscow less than enthusiastic. Though Khrushchev sent a letter to Washington warning that a nuclear attack on mainland China (a most unlikely contingency, as the Chinese were later to point out) would precipitate general war, he refused to furnish China with the air power essential for any confrontation with the US Seventh Fleet.

On the other hand, whatever Moscow's misgivings, it had never hitherto refused to give at least token backing to Peking in its various squabbles with non-Communist states. In 1959, however, this was to change as China got embroiled in a series of border skirmishes with its Indian neighbour. The first round of frontier clashes occurred in March, following China's brutal suppression of a revolt in Tibet which forced thousands, including Tibet's spiritual leader, the Dalai Lama, to flee over the border. As a wave of anti-Chinese sentiment swept throughout India, Moscow maintained a discreet silence, refusing to support Peking's allegation of an Indian hand in the Tibetan rising. Later in the year, as China sought to make good its claim to two border areas the Indians regarded as theirs, the Soviet news agency TASS issued a statement deploring the frontier incidents, thereby, as Peking was later to allege, making 'no distinction between right and wrong'.

To Mao, Moscow's neutrality in the face of a conflict involving a 'fraternal' ally was a betrayal of 'proletarian internationalism'.[15] As the Chinese press was to bitterly recall: 'Here is the first instance in history in which a Socialist country, instead of condemning the armed provocations of the reactionaries of a capitalist country, condemned another fraternal Socialist country when it was confronted with such armed provocation'.[16] That Khrushchev had gone to Washington for a 'summit' with President Eisenhower at the height of the Sino-Indian border dispute only compounded the injury to Mao's pride. And though he had agreed to report to Peking after his trip to Washington, he merely added insult to injury with a barely disguised public rebuke to his hosts. 'Such a noble and progressive system as socialism cannot be imposed by force of arms against the will of the people'.[17]

It was to be Khrushchev's last meeting with Mao, but by this time – October 1959 – relations between the two Communist giants were already near breaking point. For, Khrushchev was then engaged in a multifaceted strategy to puncture Mao's pretensions and possibly unseat him. Though the CCP claim that in 1958 the CPSU had plans to bring China under Soviet military control has never been substantiated, Khrushchev does seem to have given encouragement to those, like Defence Minister P'eng Teh-huai, opposed to the Great Leap Forward policy. He was also going out of his way to belittle Mao's latest blueprint for a communist society. In answer to Peking's boast that China was within sight of communism, Khrushchev at the CPSU's 21st congress, in January 1959, had declared that there could be no skipping of stages in the progression from capitalism to communism, that the transition would inevitably be lengthy, and that the only sure way of speeding the process would be to increase the production of material goods, as Russia had done.[18] Later, in a speech in Poland, he described China's communes as an exercise in 'primitive communism', and castigated those advocating them as people with a 'poor idea of what communism is and how it is to be built'.[19]

In the meantime, having failed to moderate Peking's ideological assertiveness in return for increased economic assistance, Khrushchev decided to oppose Mao's call for an all-out Communist offensive in countries like Iraq, Egypt, Algeria, and, of course, India, and, most serious of all, to renege on his earlier decision to share Russia's nuclear secrets.[20] After all, with China already deploying Soviet resources to the detriment of Soviet interests, he no longer wished to speed the military and economic advance of a potential rival with a population over three times that of the Soviet Union. By mid-1960, as Soviet largesse was gradually withdrawn, the Sino-Soviet alliance was effectively dead, and within a further decade the two countries seemed to be on the verge of war.

As in the other major conflicts of our time, the origins of the Sino-Soviet dispute are manifold and complex.[21] No matter how deep the ideological divergencies, they were to some extent derivative of more basic differences, in which incompatible national ambitions, power political rivalry, clashes of personality, disagreements on geographical and strategic priorities, disparities of international esteem and economic and military strength, and differences in political culture, temperament, and outlook were all intertwined. In addition, their antagonism represented a clash between two revolutions at different stages of development – the one having acquired maturity, status, power and possessions, the other just emerging from militant adolescence and still troubled by strategic fears and unfulfilled ambitions.

What made the conflict all the more critical, however, was the fact that it had a significant historical dimension. Russia and China had been traditional enemies sharing 4500 miles of common frontier, much of it disputed, and, while in Moscow there were serious apprehensions regarding China's future technological and political development, in Peking there were the accumulated resentments at China's treatment by successive Russian governments. For, since the seventeenth century, the Russians and Chinese had been continually embroiled in border skirmishes in what used to be known as Outer China – the regions of Manchuria, Mongolia, and Sinkiang. Generally speaking, China had been on the losing end of these conflicts, and by the time of the collapse of the old Chinese Empire in 1911, the Russians had taken the lion's share of the spoils, securing well over 600,000 square miles of Outer China, by 'unequal treaty', and appropriating, without treaty, some 7,500 square miles in addition.[22] The pledges of the early Bolshevik leaders to renounce the territories and privileges wrung by their tsarist predecessors from the Chinese Empire were never honoured, and the Chinese had grounds to complain that the Soviet Union had merely continued the piecemeal absorption of Outer China. It had helped to detach part of Mongolia, had incorporated Tannu Tuva, and, for some time after Mao's advent in power, had retained effective control of Manchuria and Sinkiang.

But history had added a further abrasive in the relations between the two Communist giants – the idea sustained for some 5,000 years that in culture and political organization the Chinese were somehow set apart from other peoples. China was the Chung Kuo (the Central Land) – an island of elegance located in the middle of the world and surrounded by a sea of political inferiors and barbarians, i.e. people as yet untouched by Chinese civilization. So far as the Soviets were concerned, China's sense of cultural superiority had survived the end of Empire, the civil war and the Communist takeover, not least since most of its leaders, unlike the founders of the Soviet state, were unfamiliar with the world outside their own country. Moscow found it in character, for example, that shortly after the launch of the first Sputnik in 1957, an article in *People's Daily* boasted: 'We Chinese have played a glorious role in this field. At the beginning of the 11th century, T'ang Fu and Shih Pu invented the rocket. . . . This was the first step taken by man on the road to satellites. Nine hundred years later a Russian professor studied the problems of interplanetary flight . . .'[23]

In Soviet eyes, China's ethnocentricity had given the Communists an unhealthy preoccupation with national rather than international problems, with Mao speaking openly of the country's need to regain its 'lost territories', insisting on the 'Sinification' of Marxism, and commending to the developing countries, even before the CCP had achieved power, the Chinese road to socialism. In this sense, Peking's claim to have discovered a short cut to communism was only the latest example of Chinese arrogance, and, in dismissing the communes as 'primitive communism' (implying that they were a step backwards into prehistory), Khrushchev, no doubt, chose his words with care.

Moreover, long before there was any formal ideological dispute between the parties, the disparity in their revolutionary experiences had produced significant differences of outlook. Naturally, the Chinese Communists, who had known little peace since the foundation of their party in 1921, had tended to put more stress on struggle and violence as means towards the desired goal than had the Soviets. Understandably, too, there was more enthusiasm for revolutionary ideas in a strategically vulnerable country like China, with much less cause for satisfaction with the status quo. And, not surprisingly, having suffered so many physical and psychological deprivations at the hands of foreigners (many of them Russian), China's anti-imperialist sentiments tended to go even deeper than those of the Soviet Union, leading to the belief that the USA, the dominant power in a traditionally Chinese sphere, should not be bargained with or appeased. Finally, of course, having been given such poor advice by Moscow in the past, it was not to be wondered at that the Chinese should want to chart their own socialist path.

One does not need to be a Marxist to see that the ideological dimension of the Sino-Soviet dispute was grounded in material as well as sociocultural factors. It had, nevertheless, a life of its own, and, because it symbolized the breakdown of a relationship which had aroused high expectations on both sides, it merely exacerbated the tensions already built into the relationship. In view of the tendency of each disputant to shift its ideological ground and to distort the viewpoint of its rival, it is not easy to summarize the points at issue. Nonetheless, their basic disagreements, at least until the early '60s, appeared to centre on a number of interrelated issues: in particular, the 'correct' interpretation of Marxism–Leninism, the prerequisites for a global socialist transformation, and the organization of relations among Socialist states.

Though it was not until 1962 that each made direct accusations against the other – each preferring instead to criticize unspecified 'revisionists' and 'dogmatists' – the Chinese effectively opened up the Sino-Soviet rift to public view with an article published in April 1960 to commemorate the 90th anniversary of Lenin's birth. Entitled 'Long Live Leninism', it was a stinging rebuttal of Soviet policy under Khrushchev, and prompted the Soviets to deliver a withering attack on Mao at the Romanian party's third congress in Bucharest in June.[24] Two months later, the USSR delivered its most telling blow to date against China by withdrawing all aid and technicians from China, leaving a mass of uncompleted projects.[25] By the end of the year, relations had sunk to a new low as another Moscow summit of Communists, attended by 81 of the 87 Communist parties then in existence, became a battleground, with each protagonist lobbying for support. For the first time, the Chinese were laying claim to eventual leadership of international Communism, and receiving some support from among the Albanian, North Korean, and North Vietnamese delegations, as well as from leading Burmese, Indonesian, Japanese, Malayan and Australian Communist officials.[26]

Until the early '60s the Chinese position seems to have been basically as follows:[27] The USSR's recent space triumphs had indicated that, provided the Communist world remained united and strong, the 'east wind' of Socialist revolution would prevail over the 'west wind' of capitalism and imperialism. What was required was a united Communist front against imperialism, and it was the Soviet Union's international proletarian duty, as the most powerful Socialist state, to strengthen cohesion by furnishing generous economic assistance to members of the bloc in need.

But the wealthier Socialist states had a further obligation, namely, to give every support, regardless of risk, to national liberation movements in Africa, Asia and Latin America. These had become the 'storm centres of the world revolution', the developed countries having abandoned the revolutionary torch. Indeed, the test of a revolutionary lay in his attitude to these national liberation struggles against unpopular, generally western-orientated regimes. Prompt and effective action in support of these revolutionary movements would not necessarily entail the risk of wider conflict since the imperialists, whose strength and morale were already being sapped by their failure to suppress the revolutionary tide, were likely to be constrained in the face of overwhelming opposition. On the other hand, while imperialism still existed, war was inevitable and would be a permanent feature of international life if the militant movements in the developing countries went unaided.

Nuclear war, however, was unlikely, but fear of global nuclear conflict was not to be allowed to blow the Communist powers off their revolutionary course. For, world war had been of considerable service to revolution. 'The First World War was followed by the birth of the Soviet Union with a population of 200 million; the Second World War led to the emergence of a Socialist camp with a population of 900 million. In the event of a Third World War, it is certain that several million more would turn to socialism'.[28]

As regards the ultimate revolutionary transformation of the world, the PRC held that although there might be several roads to that end, the 'parliamentary road' was not one of them. To expect communism to come through a form of 'peaceful transition' was mere 'parliamentary cretinism'. 'Political power grows from the barrel of a gun'.[29] It did not result from parliamentary elections or structural reform of the capitalist system. Nor was the attainment of a socialist stage of development any necessary guarantee that a society would progress towards communism. For there were always cynical politicians who would betray Marxism–Leninism by agreeing to 'peacefully co-exist' with imperialism and to introduce material incentives, the profit criterion and other devices associated with the capitalist mentality, instead of advancing towards the ideal of a disciplined, self-reliant, unselfish and classless community. Such politicians, moreover, seriously endangered the revolutionary movement, since by their 'revisionism' they blunted the revolutionary drive both at home and abroad. Unfortunately the Soviet Union had become the leader of 'revisionism' and an accomplice of imperialism, and could no longer, therefore, be regarded as the hub of world revolution.

As against this, Moscow held that though communism would prevail in the long run, its cause would not best be served by Soviet willingness to make crippling economic sacrifices on behalf of the poorer Communist states, or by precipitate action in support of national liberation movements. The Soviet Union's main hope for strengthening world Communism lay in improving its own capacity for catching up with the West in economic terms – the ultimate proof of the relevance for the world of its political and economic model. It was not that Moscow had ceased to believe in the national liberation struggle, but that to assist it might be more hazardous than the Chinese were prepared to admit. It could provoke counter-revolution or Western intervention, and, even if world war was no longer inevitable, there was always the possibility of a serious escalation of a local conflict. As against the Chinese, the Russians held that global conflict would be a catastrophe from which neither capitalism nor socialism would recover.

In the Soviet view, the establishment of relations with all states on the basis of 'peaceful coexistence' was no betrayal of Communism's revolutionary mission. The concept, after all, dated back to Lenin. Nor did détente mean *rapprochement*. East–West cooperation facilitated the transmission of socialist ideas, since capitalist countries were always more divided and less on their guard against Communist advances in a relaxed international atmosphere. So far as the parliamentary road to socialism was concerned, this had received the explicit approval of Marx in his latter years and seemed an appropriate means to power in developed societies such as Italy, France and Finland, where there were already sizeable Communist parties with considerable influence in the legislature.

Moscow granted that domestic and international policies are interconnected, but drew inferences different from those of the Chinese. Intelligent economic reform, allowing enterprise managers greater freedom than hitherto to produce in accord with local demands and conditions, helped to increase output and created a better impression abroad. Moreover, it facilitated the process of catching up with the USA in economic terms, the attainment of which would vindicate the Soviet model of economic development and encourage its imitation abroad. In short, the ultimate success of communism depended on the material success of Soviet society. The global transformation could not flow, as Khrushchev once jibed, 'from a table with empty plates at which are sitting "highly politically conscious" and "completely equal" people'.[30]

As Sino-Soviet tensions grew, they had serious repercussions throughout the Communist movement and beyond. One of the first countries to be affected was Albania, whose Communist system, like that of China, had been moulded by guerrilla struggle, not by Soviet imposition, and whose tough and uncompromising leader, Enver Hoxha, feared the impact of 'revisionism' on a country prey to foreign intervention and internal disintegration in times of weakness. Having also been involved in a long-standing feud with Tito, who had once had plans for incorporating Albania into the Yugoslav federation, Hoxha had noted with alarm the trend of Soviet policy since the mid-'50s and had not been afraid to say so. At the Bucharest and Moscow Conferences of 1960, he had lined up firmly behind the Chinese, risking thereby not simply the abuse, but also the active hostility of the Soviet Union and its closest allies. Soon, Albania found itself being treated by its European allies in much the same way as its old enemy Yugoslavia in the late '40s, and within a year it had become the first Communist country to sever diplomatic ties with Moscow, following an abortive, possibly Soviet-inspired coup and a COMECON-wide trade embargo, which left a grain-hungry Albania close to starvation.

What saved it was the unexpected airlift of grain from China's own meagre stocks – an act of generosity which marked the beginning of a Peking–Tirana axis that was to last nearly two decades. By means of it, Albania had a much-needed source of economic and technical assistance, and China a valuable base from which to counter Soviet 'revisionism', now fortified by the proclamation of the end of the 'dictatorship of the proletariat', as well as by a 'Soviet-first' ideology, as enshrined in a party document envisaging the USSR's attainment of communist abundance by the 1980s.[31]

Two critical international events of October 1962 strengthened the Peking–Tirana axis while straining Sino-Soviet relations almost to breaking point – the Sino-Indian border war and the Cuban missile crisis. Facing the threat of an Indian offensive to drive them out of the frontier areas they had held since the border skirmishes of 1959, the Chinese launched a swift counteroffensive over the Himalayas, driving the Indians almost to the plains of Assam and taking thousands of prisoners before withdrawing as swiftly as they had advanced. China's thrust produced a fateful response from Moscow. Angered at not having been consulted beforehand and fearing that Peking's action would negate all its efforts to bring Delhi into the 'Socialist Commonwealth', the Kremlin, after initial hesitation, continued its economic and military aid programme to India.[32] Given that China had received no Soviet assistance for two years, Moscow had, in effect, demonstrated a prefer-

ence for a non-Communist friend over a Communist opponent, and the
Chinese drew their own conclusions.

> The stand and policy of the Soviet leaders on the Sino-Indian boundary
> question amply prove that they have betrayed the Chinese people, the Soviet
> people, the people of all the countries in the Socialist camp, the Indian
> people, and all the oppressed peoples and nations. It is becoming clearer
> and clearer that the Soviet leaders no longer consider the imperialists . . . to
> be their enemy. It is the Marxist–Leninists, the revolutionary people and
> China in particular who are their enemy.[33]

It was, however, the Cuban missile crisis, occurring almost simultaneously with the Sino-Indian border conflict, which gave Mao the
opportunity to make official the quarrel with Moscow. For the whole
history of the Kremlin's relations with Havana since Fidel Castro's
advent in power, in January 1959, was an indictment of the Kremlin's
cavalier approach to revolutionary nationalism.[34] In the first place,
neither Moscow nor the Cuban Communist Party had originally supported Castro's bid for power, and for some 16 months after his installation, the Kremlin had hesitated to give him recognition, let alone
trade credits or military assistance. After all, historically, Latin America
was far from the Soviet orbit, and Moscow had no wish to antagonize
Washington in an area regarded as America's 'backyard'. In any case,
it had learned to be suspicious of the revolutionary Left in Latin America and had no guarantee that Castro's regime would prove any more
durable than any other in the area.

What had led Moscow and Havana to close ranks was not an action
precipitated by Khrushchev, but one sanctioned by President Kennedy
– the abortive Bay of Pigs invasion, in April 1961, by some 1,400 anti-
Castro exiles equipped by the CIA, after two years of mounting hostility. That act, together with Castro's claim to Soviet support on the
basis of his (recently invented) Marxist–Leninist past and his decision
to merge his revolutionary coterie with the Communist Party into a
single organization, more or less forced Khrushchev to think seriously
about a military as well as an economic presence on the island. But
Khrushchev's real object, in positioning missiles on Cuba, in autumn
1962, the evidence suggests, was less to protect the island, which is
only 90 miles off the coast of Florida, than to alter the global balance
in the USSR's favour. Certainly, the Cubans were never consulted
about either the stationing of the missiles or their withdrawal after the
'eyeball to eyeball' confrontation between the Soviet and US fleets in
the island's vicinity. But the whole issue enabled the Chinese to
denounce Khrushchev as both an 'adventurist' for emplacing the miss-

iles to begin with, and a 'capitulationist' for taking them out at Washington's behest, as well as a 'great power chauvinist' for treating the Cubans as mere pawns in an essentially superpower chess game.

Any hope of a reconciliation between the two Communist giants, as they met for ideological talks on 5 July 1963, was doomed to failure, as the talks came only days before the Soviet Union was due to conclude with the USA and Britain a treaty to ban nuclear tests from the atmosphere, under water and in outer space. To Peking, such a treaty, with its consequent ban on giving nuclear know-how to non-nuclear powers, was an assertion of the identity of interests between the superpowers at the expense of countries like China, and a move incompatible with Moscow's treaty obligations to its Communist neighbour. 'The policy pursued by the Soviet government is one of allying with the forces of war to oppose the forces of peace, allying with imperialism to oppose socialism, allying with the United States to oppose China, and allying with the reactionaries of all countries to oppose the peoples of the world'.[35] The vehemence of the Chinese response provoked an exchange of vituperative articles in which Moscow accused Peking of warmongering, nationalism and racism; and Peking seemed to be pitting itself against the white-skinned, comfortably off and industrialized Europeans and North Americans.

Then, on 16 October 1964, the Chinese displayed the hand they had concealed during the previous acrimonious years – they tested their first nuclear device. No 'paper tiger' this; in Peking there was a double cause for celebration. For, it came, as if in answer to Mao's recent call to 'leading comrades' of the Soviet party to 'liquidate Khrushchev's revisionism', the day after Khrushchev's dismissal as premier and Soviet party leader.

In fact, Peking's rejoicing was premature. For, Khrushchev's fall was due not to his 'revisionism' so much as to his capricious and often abrasive political style, which alienated many of the country's powerful interest groups – the army, the KGB, the government bureaucracy, and the party itself. What such vested interests had objected to was his interference in their affairs, his 'hare-brained schemes', and, above all, his tendency to make far-reaching commitments without adequate consultation. His successor, Leonid Brezhnev, though more tentative and less theatrical in approach, inherited many of his predecessor's advisers on foreign policy and was to be hardly better disposed towards Peking, and within a year the Chinese were to indicate, by means of Defence Minister Lin Piao's *Long Live the Victory of the People's War*, that they still regarded Moscow as an adversary.[36] In this treatise, the world balance was depicted as triangular: the camp of the true revolutionary followers of 'Mao Tse-tung's thought'; the camp of imperialist reaction, led by the USA; and the camp of 'revisionism' and 'social imperialism' (i.e. professing socialism, but practising imperialism), headed by Moscow. Furthermore, the enemy was on the advance. US forces were again within striking distance of southern China as they sent troops to bolster the anti-Communists in South Vietnam. In addition, Washington was believed to have played a role in the downfall of China's radical nationalist ally – President Sukarno of Indonesia. At the same time, Moscow was trying to prevent Peking from profiting from the armed conflict between India and Pakistan in September 1965.

It was, however, largely as a consequence of China's domestic upheaval in the wake of Mao's Great Proletarian Cultural Revolution, proclaimed in August 1966 and designed to remould the Chinese people into a society of efficient and selfless individuals bristling with revolutionary fervour, that Peking made its definitive ideological and political break with Moscow. With all the fury of a people believing itself to have been betrayed, Chinese mobs staged violent demonstrations outside Soviet bloc embassies and manhandled the diplomats. In early 1967, the Soviet Embassy in Peking was virtually under siege as thousands of young Red Guards converged on its gates shouting quotations from Mao's writings, burning effigies of Soviet leaders and calling for them to be hanged or roasted alive for their 'Fascist' and 'revisionist' policies. For a time, the diplomats could neither leave nor enter the embassy, and supplies had to be delivered by their Communist allies through a side door.

So embittered were Sino-Soviet relations that, by May, the Soviet government had withdrawn most of its embassy staff after a warning from China's Foreign Ministry that the safety of Soviet diplomats venturing outside the embassy compound could no longer be guaranteed. As the 150 or so officials departed, all but two of Moscow's foreign correspondents in Peking were expelled. Such tensions inevitably had repercussions on the frontiers, and as both sides strengthened their border defences, the Chinese repeated accusations they had already made a few years before: that the Soviets were intriguing with dissident minorities in Sinkiang, luring Chinese citizens over the frontier, and conducting provocative military manœuvres in Soviet and Mongolian territory adjacent to the PRC. In response, the Soviets charged that the Chinese were interfering with their shipping along the Amur river on the frontier between Manchuria (Heilungkiang) and the Soviet Far East. They also complained that the Chinese were obstructing the passage of aid to the Vietnamese Communist war effort, possibly creaming off Soviet supplies for their own benefit.[37]

The Soviet-led intervention in Czechoslovakia, in August 1968, unleashed a fresh torrent of abuse from Peking. Though, in Chinese terms, the Dubček regime was no less 'revisionist' than the Soviet, the intervention had unpleasant implications for other Communist powers that happened to fall foul of Moscow, and in a speech shortly after, Premier Chou En-lai compared the Soviet action with Hitler's invasion of Czechoslovakia and America's 'aggression' against Vietnam. Later, Peking's propagandists were to denounce, as 'an outright doctrine of hegemony', the 'Brezhnev doctrine' of 'the limited sovereignty' of the members of the 'Socialist Commonwealth', by which intervention was justified.[38] And, when Soviet propagandists insisted that the 'doctrine' could apply as much to China as to Czechoslovakia,[39] Mao began an 'agonizing reappraisal' of foreign policy that was to result in a shift no less dramatic than that of the mid-'50s.

Some Soviet sabre-rattling directed against China's infant nuclear capacity in Sinkiang, combined with five months of Sino-Soviet skirmishing on the Damansky/Chenpao island on the Ussuri river and also in the Ili-Kazakh central Asian frontier region, finally convinced Mao that of the two superpowers, the USSR was the more threatening. For, while Moscow seemed on the advance in Asia, Washington, after the failure of Tet offensive in Vietnam, seemed on the retreat, and under its new President, Richard Nixon, and National Security Adviser, Henry Kissinger, appeared ready to take a more pragmatic approach towards the People's Republic. By December 1971, when both Washington and Peking were trying to preserve Pakistan's integrity in face of a Bangladeshi national liberation struggle, a Sino-American *rapprochement* was already in the making, which Mao could justify in much the same terms as his alignment with Washington against Tokyo during the Second World War.

For, the Chinese leader had already taken a critical step to make possible Kissinger's first visit to Peking, in July 1971 – he had virtually suspended the Cultural Revolution at the CCP's ninth congress two years before. Moreover, the Cultural Revolution's chief ideologue, Lin Piao, was to be literally 'brought down' in a flight, allegedly to the Soviet Union, in September 1971, after what appears to have been an attempted coup against Mao.[40] There followed, in February 1972, President Nixon's visit to Peking, concluding with the Shanghai communiqué, putting in doubt Washington's continued support of Taiwan. Though full normalization of Sino-American relations was not to come until December 1978 – long after the enforced resignation of Nixon, the end of the Vietnam War, the deaths of Chou and Mao, and the arrival of 'Jimmy' Carter in the White House – they were close enough to strengthen Peking's resolve to resist Soviet attempts at reconciliation.

If China's shift from revolutionary moralism to more traditional power political calculations began to blunt the force of the ideological differences between Moscow and Peking, the territorial and border disputes remained unresolved. In addition, three other major factors served to frustrate any attempt to bridge the political chasm between them. In the first place, each was acutely concerned at the diplomatic activities of the other in the world at large. The Chinese, of course, had long resented Moscow's ties with Washington, and their apprehensions increased after the first Treaty on Strategic Arms Limitation (SALT I) of 1972 and the Helsinki agreements concluding the Conference on Security and Cooperation in Europe of 1975, which they perceived as western appeasement of Moscow, reminiscent of the appeasement of the Nazis in the '30s.

In addition, Chinese suspicions of Soviet designs on Asia were deepened by several developments: Moscow's accord with India shortly before the conflagration on the sub-continent that led to the dismemberment of Pakistan; the attempt to create a manifestly anti-Chinese 'collective security' system in the region; the coups in Afghanistan in 1973 and 1978, which Peking interpreted (probably wrongly) as Soviet-inspired, and as a potential vehicle for the encirclement of Pakistan; Moscow's periodic overtures to the technologically advanced countries, including Japan, to develop the resources of Siberia, strategically close to the Chinese frontier; and the Soviet acquisition of bases in Vietnam and its support of Hanoi's virtual colonization of Laos after the Vietnam War. From Peking, it looked as if Moscow had tilted the Asian balance of power significantly in its favour.

As regards Soviet fears, these had grown as Peking had gained in international respectability after its dramatic political somersault of the early '70s. Clearly, Moscow was perplexed by Peking's sudden switch from revolutionary to diplomatic offensive and dismayed by its scale and apparent success. After all, by the mid-'70s, the People's Republic had already established a working relationship with most of the technologically advanced countries, while its new-found admiration for NATO, the EEC, and even the American Seventh Fleet in and around the Indian Ocean suggested alarming congruities of interest between China and the West. Worse still, many of Peking's newly acquired western friends were prepared to revise COCOM's embargo list to provide sophisticated military-related equipment they would never have agreed to sell the People's Republic before.[41] And when, in August 1978, Japan concluded with China a treaty of peace and friendship

Tokyo had refused to make with Moscow, it could only fuel the Kremlin's anxieties about encirclement. Scarcely less disturbing was the powerful impact of Peking's new diplomatic and trade offensive on the governments of such developing countries as Zaïre, Sudan, Sri Lanka, or the members of the Association of South East Asian Nations (ASEAN), which were clearly willing to forgive Peking's earlier insistence on their revolutionary overthrow.[42]

A second major impediment to an improvement in Sino-Soviet relations was each nation's fear of losing support in the international Communist movement to the advantage of the other. The Soviet leaders had been somewhat perturbed by Peking's interests in the European Communist orbit ever since its encouragement of a specific Polish road to socialism in 1956. Then had come its backing for a very different Albanian path and its support for Romanian autonomy in the early '60s and '70s, followed by its sudden burst of cordiality towards Belgrade in the mid-'70s, as dramatized by the decision of Hua Kuo-feng, Mao's successor as party Chairman, to include the Yugoslav capital on his itinerary during an eastern European tour in 1978. It was, however, Peking's military assistance to the anti-Vietnamese Khmer Rouge regime in Kampuchea (Cambodia) that occasioned the most anxiety in Moscow since, apart from the regime's notorious record of domestic brutality (it is reported to have liquidated upwards of 1 million of the country's 7 million inhabitants in seeking to fashion a 'classless society'), its repeated incursions into Vietnam meant a continual drain on the resources of a Soviet ally, which had ultimately to be borne by the none-too-healthy Soviet exchequer.[43]

For their part, of course, the Chinese were especially annoyed when the Kremlin undercut their influence in the Communist parties of Asia, Africa, Latin America and Australasia, but the conclusion, in November 1978, of a 25-year Soviet friendship treaty with Vietnam, whom China had accused of multiple border violations, filled Peking with alarm. For, such an alliance between Peking's Communist rivals to the north and south appeared to represent a formidable threat, and may be said to have hastened China's exchange of ambassadors with Washington.[44]

The third, and most important, impediment to a Sino-Soviet accord was the fear of each that the other might drag it into a military confrontation, either by accident or design. China's apprehensions in this respect were perhaps more understandable. After all, in terms of military and industrial technology, trained manpower, and political organization, the Soviet Union was vastly superior. In addition, Moscow, with nearly a million men on the frontier and a heavy concentration of missile power in Mongolia less than 400 miles from Peking, had the means to destroy Peking's major cities and its nascent nuclear capability. Already the Kremlin had tried to construct a *cordon sanitaire* around China, of which the Red Army intervention in Afghanistan, in December 1979, seemed to be the latest example, while, of course, the Chinese knew only too well how Moscow had dealt with the more intractable Communist governments in the past.

On the other hand, each year Moscow's advantages were diminished by China's own military and economic advance, and if the Americans could be disquieted by the presence of three or four thousand troops in Cuba, it is hardly surprising if the Russians were alarmed by the prospect of a billion potentially hostile Chinese beyond their eastern frontier. It was, moreover, difficult for them to forget that of the many invasions against the country, the most devastating had come from the east – the Mongols having destroyed and laid waste the original Russian state.[45] However, the main source of Moscow's more recent concern was the Chinese strike against Vietnam in February 1979, following the Vietnamese overthrow of the Khmer Rouge in Phnom Penh, for Peking implied that 'social imperialism' – its epithet for the Soviet Union – might yet have to learn 'the lesson' China's troops had just 'taught' the Vietnamese. Moreover, the fact that Peking seemed to be at the hub of a global anti-Soviet alignment, including countries even in the USSR's eastern European 'backyard', was profoundly disturbing.[46] For, Moscow's ties with India, Afghanistan, Vietnam, Laos and the new, Vietnamese-backed government of Kampuchea hardly compensated for what Moscow perceived as a significant tilt in the world balance to its disadvantage, with all that that implied.

Ironically, by February 1980, when both sides had agreed to 'kill off' the 30-year-old Sino-Soviet Friendship Treaty, their dispute had just about run its course, and in the two and three-quarter years before the death, in November 1982, of Soviet leader, Leonid Brezhnev, both protagonists made a serious effort to tone down hostilities and unfreeze relations.[47] Though the 'cold war' between Moscow and Peking remained, its intensity was to be scaled down for a combination of reasons, of which the domestic needs of each country were paramount. Each faced a multiplicity of economic, political and strategic difficulties more easily addressed by relieving themselves of a further problem – their mutual hostility. In any case, they were beginning to recognize the complementarity of their economies, so that there was economic as well as political mileage in an improvement of their trade and financial relations.

Moreover, the ideological differences, so crucial in the early years of the dispute, were now of much less significance, as Peking had itself moved, in its post-Maoist phase, towards 'revisionism'. A further factor in helping to unfreeze Sino-Soviet relations was the change in the balance between Washington, Moscow and Peking. In the '70s, Washington's ability to be on reasonable terms with both Communist giants merely fuelled their animosities, as each suspected the other of doing deals with the Americans at its expense. However, in the early '80s, President Reagan succeeded in alienating Moscow and Peking simultaneously, thereby encouraging a reassessment of relations in both Communist capitals.

By the time of President Gorbachev's visit to Peking, in May 1989, following the Red Army withdrawal from Afghanistan, significant Soviet troop reductions on the Chinese frontier and a scaling down of the Vietnamese presence in Kampuchea, the cold war between the two Communist giants was virtually over. It had, nonetheless, left an indelible imprint on the political movement both had claimed to serve. Indeed, of all the factors precipitating the decline of international Communism, few can have been more damaging than the Sino-Soviet dispute. In the first place, it had called in question the moral and political credentials of the Marxist–Leninist state, as each 'Marxist–Leninist' disputant provided convincing evidence of the 'imperialistic', 'anti-democratic' and 'chauvinist' proclivities of the other. In the process, it had generated a series of inter- and intra-Communist rifts, weakening Communist alliance structures and the effectiveness of Communism as an international political movement.

At the same time, it had reduced the overall pressure on the West, since each disputant had to concentrate part of its military and economic potential against its Communist rival; and, in drawing first one and then the other Communist power into a closer relationship with the USA in an effort to strengthen its hand against its Communist antagonist, the rift had helped to create a favourable climate for 'peaceful engagement' between Communist and non-Communist and the modification of ideological stereotypes. Certainly, it had eliminated the possibility that, in the event of an international crisis, the Communist movement as a whole would always be placed at the service of the Soviet state. What was more debatable, after such a prolonged dispute which had subsumed nationalist preoccupations under the heading of ideological differences, was whether the international Communist movement had been damaged beyond repair. Communist optimists thought that it might be possible to refit the pieces (like a jigsaw) into a coherent whole. Others, generally non-Communist, wondered whether an international Communist movement in any meaningful sense could be said any longer to exist at all. Though the debate continues, Peking's reversion to arbitrary rule after the massacre of pro-Democracy activists in June 1989 can hardly have furthered the cause of Communist reconciliation or unity.

NOTES

1. D. Floyd, *Mao against Khrushchev* (London, 1964), p. 221.
2. See B. Wolfe, *Khrushchev and Stalin's Ghost* (London, 1957).
3. J. Gittings (ed.), *Survey of the Sino-Soviet Dispute* (London, 1968), app. C.
4. Ibid., app. D.
5. Stuart Schram, *Mao Tse-tung* (London, 1967) p. 289.
6. Ibid.
7. Gittings (ed.), doc. 44.
8. Floyd, chapter 5.
9. Gittings (ed.), docs. 32–4.
10. Harry Schwartz, *Tsars, Mandarins and Commissars* (London, 1964), p. 166.
11. Cited in V. Benes, R. F. Byrnes, and N. Spulber (eds.), *The Second Soviet–Yugoslav Dispute* (Bloomington, Indiana, 1959), pp. 75–7.
12. F. Fejtö, *A History of the People's Democracies* (London, 1971), pp. 95–6.
13. Floyd, p. 63.
14. See Gittings (ed.), docs. 37–8 and app. I.
15. Gittings (ed.), docs. 49–50 and app. J.
16. Ibid., p. 111, n. 3.
17. Ibid., p. 332.
18. Floyd, p. 65.
19. Ibid.
20. See Geoffrey Stern, 'Sino-Soviet Dispute' in *Marxism, Communism and Western Society, A Comparative Encyclopedia*, Freiburg, 1974, vol. VII, pp. 330–3.
21. For an excellent overview, see Schwartz, op. cit.
22. Schwartz, pp. 50–61 and ch. 4–5.
23. Quoted in Geoffrey Stern, *Fifty Years of Communism* (London, 1967), p. 111.
24. Gittings (ed.), app. L and M.
25. Ibid., docs. 60–7.
26. Ibid., docs. 68–71. See also G. F. Hudson *et al.* (eds.), *The Sino-Soviet Dispute* (New York, 1961), ch. 7.
27. Sino-Soviet ideological differences are set out in the relevant sections of A. Dallin (ed.), *Diversity in International Communism: A Documentary Record 1961–1963* (New York, 1963).
28. From 'On the Correct Handling of Contradictions among the People' (February 1957), *Extracts in Quotations from Mao Tse-tung* (Peking, 1972), pp. 67–8.
29. From 'Problems in War and Strategy' (November 1938). Extracts in S. Schram (ed.), *The Political Thought of Mao Tse-tung* (London, 1969), p. 290.
30. Cited in Stern, *Fifty Years*, p. 121.
31. Dallin (ed.), docs. 9–21; J. Steele (ed.), *Eastern Europe since Stalin* (London, 1974), pp. 99–112; and W. Laquer and L. Labedz (eds.), *Polycentrism* (New York, 1962), pp. 107–26.
32. Gittings (ed.), pp. 174–6, doc. 85 and app. T.
33. Ibid., doc. 86.
34. On the Soviet approach to Cuba, see ibid., pp. 87–8 and app. U. See also M. Tatu, *Power in the Kremlin* (London, 1969), part 3.
35. See Gittings (ed.), doc. 89–92.

36. *Peking Review*, no. 35 (1965).
37. Gittings (ed.), pp. 271–7 and A. Westoby, *Communism since World War II* (Brighton, 1981), ch. 11.
38. *Peking Review* 34 (1968), supplement, p. iv.
39. An article by Soviet official Victor Louis in the *London Evening News* (16 September 1969) attributed this view to 'sources close to the Kremlin'.
40. Wang Gungwu, *China and the World since 1949* (London, 1977), pp. 125–8.
41. See for example, *Keesings Contemporary Archives*, vol. 25 (1979), pp. 29,500, 29,502, and 29,503. See also vol. 26 (1980), p. 30,387.
42. See J. Steele, *The Limits of Soviet Power* (London, 1985), ch. 8.
43. See Sheldon Simon, vol. 27, no. 5, 'New Conflict in Indochina', *Problems of Communism* (September–October 1978), pp. 20–36.
44. Steele, pp. 149–53.
45. The continuing relevance of the Mongol invasion is attested to in Harrison Salisbury, *The Coming War between Russia and China* (London, 1969).
46. See Geoffrey Stern, 'The Soviet Union, Afghanistan and East–West Relations', *Millennium: Journal of International Studies*, vol. 9, no. 2 (Autumn 1980), pp. 135–46.
47. See W. Griffith, 'Sino-Soviet *Rapprochement*', *Problems of Communism*, vol. 32, no. 2 (March–April 1983).

11.   The Impact of Nationalism

In strictly ideological terms, the Sino-Soviet dispute was reminiscent of the conflict that tore the Second International apart on the eve of the First World War. Like the German Social Democratic Party of 1914, the CPSU four decades later was beginning to undergo a process of what Robert Tucker calls 'deradicalization',[1] i.e. of adjusting to the very order it is pledged to overthrow and accepting its institutions as a framework for socialist change. Similarly, like the Bolshevik opponents of 'revisionism', Mao and many of his fellow Chinese Communists, fearing that 'deradicalization' might percolate, corrode, and eventually destroy the CCP and its revolutionary élan, sought to wrest control of the international movement from its 'revisionist' leaders.

Yet, in trying to restore the integrity of international Communism, Peking did more than any previous Communist malcontent to undermine it. After all, no rival Communist centre had been created in the wake of Tito's 'defection'. Every party had fallen into line against Belgrade and had purged the 'Titoists' from its ranks. Even the fragmentation immediately after Stalin's death had been contained. Despite the growing aversion in eastern Europe to Soviet hegemony and to doctrinaire Communism, the leaders had found it difficult, in Claudin's words, 'to break the umbilical cord that linked them to Eastern "socialism" '.[2] If they sought change, it tended to be within the framework of the one-party state and in terms of the accepted norms of what was called 'Socialist internationalism' – implying the responsibility of each member for the fate of Socialism throughout the bloc.[3] Imre Nagy, the one leader who sought to move beyond the permitted limits by dismantling the single-party system and proclaiming neutrality in the cold war, was crushed, with the approval of virtually every party.

What made Peking's challenge different was not just that it involved an attempt to set up a rival international Communist centre. It was also that this challenge emanated from a country too large to be invaded, and from a party too influential to be excommunicated. For, neither Peking's small but by no means insignificant band of Communist followers nor the many parties who secured greater leverage for themselves as a consequence of the continuing dispute were prepared to sanction the CCP's expulsion from the Communist 'fraternity'. Yet, the insidious bacillus of Maoism managed to infect, to a greater or lesser degree, most Communist parties, leading several groups to form break-away Marxist–Leninist organizations in opposition to the more orthodox Communist parties, thereby causing even greater fragmentation in the once monolithic movement.

If the fragmentation process within and between the parties – ruling and non-ruling – went further and faster than Moscow anticipated, it was for two major reasons. In the first place, the body of theory on which modern Communism is based leaves room for conflicting interpretations. As already indicated earlier in this volume, there are in Marx, Engels, and Lenin inconsistencies and false prognoses which compound the problems of interpretation in changing conditions. The fact, moreover, that the ideas appeal to peoples of different levels of sophistication, many living in conditions very different from those of the nineteenth-century Europe in which they first took root, is a further complication. As with almost all idea systems, secular or religious, the volume of prescribed texts is far greater than the capacity of most people to master them, and the inevitable need for selection leads to the development of different schools within the broad philosophical tradition.

On one reading, a Communist is entitled to sit back and wait for the revolutionary process to unfold: on another, he is obliged to give history a push. Armed with one set of texts, a Communist can make out a good case for supporting right-wing nationalist regimes in the Third World: but if he chooses a different set, his duty is to struggle resolutely against such regimes. Interpreted in one way, the path to communism lies through the kind of political and economic pluralism characteristic of western 'bourgeois' society: interpreted in another, the centrally planned, command economy under a single party is the only possible way.

On the other hand, while the Soviet Union remained the only state to have effected a thoroughgoing revolution in the name of Marx, it was able to check any tendency to ideological diversity. Stalin proclaimed himself guardian and interpreter of the orthodoxy, and, through the Comintern, was able to lay down the strategy and tactics for the movement as a whole, to isolate those with views inconsistent with his own, to root out opposition among the leaders or the rank and file, and, in some cases, to have entire parties dissolved. And though the objective situation changed after 1945, with the emergence of new Communist-ruled states, several factors served to prolong the Soviet Union's status as fount of Communist orthodoxy – among them, the conditions of the cold war; Moscow's ability to use a combination of pressures against independent-minded Communists like Tito, and the existence of the Cominform, which, though lacking the scope and muscle of the Comintern, gave direction to the movement through its oddly named journal, *For a Lasting Peace, For a People's Democracy!*

Ironically, it was the very success of Communism in broadening its appeal after the Second World War that finally wrecked the monolithic edifice Stalin had tried to preserve. As with the spread of other belief systems with pretensions to universality, the more diverse the ethnic and national cultures attracted to it, the more diverse the interpretations. In practice, the conceptual framework of a Communist tended to be col-oured as much by national and other prerevolutionary aspirations and antipathies as by Marxism–Leninism, and it was only a matter of time before the discrepant views among the various parties stood revealed. After all, the world as seen from Peking, Tirana, or Havana looks different from the world as seen from Moscow, and regardless of how appealing the original idea of the international solidarity of the working class, many, especially in the Third World, had looked to Communism not for world revolution, but as a remedy for injustices often rooted, at least in part, in national conditions.

Yet, if the Kremlin, post-Stalin, was to be increasingly troubled by the nationalist manifestations of its 'fraternal' allies – some, like Peking, far from friendly – it had only itself to blame. For, the Soviet Union itself had acquired a reputation for national self-conceit, despite its commitment to 'internationalism'. Stalin, in particular, would appeal to patriotic and nationalist sentiment,[4] sometimes against minorities such as the Jews, in order to mobilize his citizens in defence of the regime and in support of socialist construction, while, even after the establishment of 'Socialism in One Zone', he appeared to demand greater sacrifices from the international movement than his country was prepared to make for it. Moreover, the Stalinist equation of 'inter-nationalism' with unquestioning support for Moscow, and insistence on the Soviet Socialist model for every Communist-ruled state smacked of national arrogance, while the behaviour of successive Soviet govern-ments towards the country's neighbours revived memories of the 'dzier-zhymorda' – the traditional Russian bully – that Lenin feared might reappear after his death. But, since Moscow was already widely per-ceived to have given 'Communism' a national face, it was hardly in a position to complain, therefore, if other Communist parties felt they could do likewise.

In fact, the role of nationalism in exacerbating the various inter- and intra-Communist conflicts, which reached epidemic proportions in the wake of the Sino-Soviet dispute, is not quite as clear cut as it may seem. For, if 'nationalism' refers to a popularly felt emotion in which the nation in question becomes the highest focus of loyalty and the main repository of values, it did not suddenly reappear. For, the peoples of eastern Europe and east Asia were probably neither more nor less nationalistic after Stalin's death than before it. The relevant changes were occurring at the level of government. Though Mao had not been afraid to 'sinify' Marxism, the leaders of eastern Europe felt obliged to ignore or suppress national sentiment even before Tito had demonstrated its explosive potential in 1948.

However, when Stalin's successors loosened the reins in an effort both to improve the USSR's image and promote in eastern Europe greater stability, economic rationality and support for its anti-Chinese stance, Moscow's Communist allies reassessed the position. Many concluded that the Kremlin was far more reluctant than before to use military or economic coercion against properly constituted Communist governments, and that this effectively gave the ruling parties much greater scope to pursue national objectives. They realized, moreover, that in limited disengagement from Moscow and identification with certain traditional needs and aspirations, they were likely to increase domestic support. It was a recipe for greater diversity, and though the Kremlin would sometimes issue a forceful reminder that it retained the ultimate right of veto, as in Hungary in 1956 and Czechoslovakia in 1968, there was still a steady drift towards a conception the old Bolsheviks would have regarded as a contradiction in terms – national Communism.

In this regard, Yugoslavia, whose leader had once declared, somewhat ironically, 'National Communism doesn't exist. Yugoslav Communists, too, are internationalists',[5] remained the frontrunner. Throughout the '50s and '60s, its economy became increasingly decentralized and market-orientated, and its political system relaxed sufficiently to encompass contested elections and politically effective parliamentary debate, albeit within the one-party framework. For example, more than one Federal budget had to be redrafted because it failed to secure a majority in the Yugoslav parliament. And though the party retained sufficient power to have men like Djilas and the writer Mihajlo Mihajlov jailed for allegedly attempting to organize opposition, it was soon to find itself at the mercy of the kind of regional nationalism that had helped to destroy the first Yugoslav state before the Second World War.[6] But Yugoslavia stayed outside the Soviet orbit – first as a member of the western-orientated Balkan Pact, then as a sponsor of the non-aligned movement of developing countries. Within the Soviet orbit, after the crushing of Nagy's two attempts at reform, it was Poland that led the way.

Ironically, though Khrushchev had originally opposed Gomułka's reinstatement, he soon learned from the Polish leader that 'national Communism' need not be unduly injurious to Soviet interests.[7] For, though within days of his return, in October 1956, Gomułka had initiated a programme of thoroughgoing reform, he was able to strike a balance between national and alliance concerns. Never an enthusiast for collectivization, he conceded, in large measure, to peasant demands for restoring land to private ownership, and secured a degree of economic decentralization and a place for the individual entrepreneur in the trades and professions. He restored to the Church some of the rights of instruction and dissemination lost in the Stalinist era, and he created an environment in which travel to and from the West was eased, information from abroad made more freely available, and all forms of art liberated from the straitjacket of 'Socialist realism'. Under Gomułka, moreover, Poland became the first Communist country to allow a choice of candidates, albeit Communist-approved, in certain constituencies, and a place in parliament for a small but vocal group of independent-minded Catholic deputies, who would take the government to task when the interests of the Church were adversely affected. In foreign affairs, too, Poland made its mark, reorientating its trade westwards; securing (to Moscow's evident dismay) US economic assistance a decade after Stalin had crushed Warsaw's hopes of Marshall Aid; dissociating itself from the rest of the bloc in the UN vote on Hungary, and, for a time, consolidating ties with Peking.

But Gomułka also understood the limits to 'national Communism'. Clearly, Moscow would not have tolerated the abandonment of 'democratic centralism', of the one-party state or of membership of the Warsaw Pact. Nor would it have allowed national deviations from Communist norms to be held up as models for export – and the Polish leader never ventured beyond the permitted boundaries. In any case, by the end of the '50s, Warsaw's growing sense of vulnerability in face of West Germany's rapid military and economic advance, combined with Gomułka's own growing doubts about the wisdom of freeing his volatile people from the restrictions of the past, were leading to a 'retreat from October'. As he turned his back on reform, mending his fences with Moscow in the process, some of Poland's allies began to step out of line.

By the early 1960s, those most anxious to chart their own course were no longer the 'reformists', but rather, the 'dogmatists' opposed to Khrushchev's renewed campaign for de-Stalinization. In 1961, Albania linked its fortunes with Peking and broke with Moscow, rather than submit to Khrushchev's 'revisionism'.[8] Though no other country went to such extremes, Moscow's summons to de-Stalinize brought resistance from East Berlin and Bucharest.

In East Germany, Ulbricht decided to complete the collectivization of agriculture in 1960, thereby unleashing a chain of events that eventuated in a further tightening of political and economic controls and an added boost to the already massive exodus of young and able-bodied East Germans defecting to the West.[9] It took the erection of the Berlin Wall in August 1961 to stem the flow of refugees and force the country's disaffected populace to come to terms with the GDR's existence. With its people suitably confined, the government sought to increase national well-being by reforming the country's top-heavy economic structure without loosening political control. Under the GDR's New Economic System, its managers became more accountable, its technocratic elite were allowed some flexibility in encouraging initiative and innovation, and its industrial production was rationalized through the use of pricing mechanisms and economies of scale. In effect a by-product of an economic debate inside the Soviet Union, the NES laid the groundwork for the economic 'miracle' that was eventually to transform the country from a despoiled economic backwater to Communism's showcase, attracting shoppers and tourists from all over the Soviet bloc.

In contrast, the Romanian leadership employed more subtle means to strengthen its domestic position. Whilst denying popular participation in political life, it set out to command popular support with an unexpected display of national self-assertion, destroying almost overnight the country's reputation as one of the most pliant 'satellites' in the bloc.[10] If the withdrawal of Soviet troops in 1958 provided the opportunity, Moscow's attempt to persuade Bucharest to abandon plans for rapid industrialization and become an agricultural reserve for COMECON provided the pretext. Romania refused the role of minor partner in a Soviet-sponsored scheme for integrating the economies of eastern Europe, and the project had to be shelved.

But the successful use of the veto over Soviet policy had set a precedent on which the Romanian leader, Gheorghiu-Dej, was anxious to capitalize. It suggested a way of courting popularity without relaxing political or economic control, and its obvious merits encouraged Nicolae Ceauşescu, who inherited the party leadership in 1965, to make a still more ambitious bid for national autonomy. What had begun as a polemic with Moscow and East Berlin over COMECON widened into a rift over the management and political direction of the Warsaw Pact, and soon Bucharest was at odds with both Moscow and Budapest over territorial questions – in particular, those concerning Bessarabia and Transylvania. It became further estranged from its allies by its decision to maintain friendly ties with Peking and Tirana, to recognize Bonn, and to upgrade its embassy in Tel Aviv, rather than close it in conformity with Warsaw Pact policy after the Six Day War of 1967 in the Middle East. Such policies accorded with Romania's determination to diversify its economic and political contacts in order to give added protection to its now much vaunted sovereignty.

Though Romania's southern neighbour, Bulgaria, proved a more reliable Soviet ally, it, too, had periods of disaffection, sometimes bordering on incoherence.[11] In the late 1950s, Sofia had had a brief flirtation with China's 'Great Leap Forward' policy, and though the architects of this policy were demoted when Todor Zhivkov, the chief proponent of de-Stalinization and a Khrushchev protégé, emerged in 1962 as both party leader and premier, there was much factional infighting and, in April 1965, an attempted, possibly pro-Chinese military coup. In the meantime, while continuing with the release of political prisoners and the posthumous rehabilitation of many of the victims of Stalinism, Zhivkov also, somewhat incongruously, reintroduced stringent labour disciplinary measures which had been abandoned in 1957, and in agriculture enlarged the collectivized unit to create 'supercollectives' under stricter government control. In foreign affairs, Bulgaria was slow to effect a policy of 'peaceful coexistence' either with the West or with its neighbour Yugoslavia, with which it was embroiled in a dispute over the status of Macedonia, and was the last country in the bloc to end jamming of Western broadcasts in the mid-'60s. Not until the abortive coup of 1965 did Bulgaria speed the process of economic de-Stalinization – permitting some relaxation in central planning, limited autonomy for industrial enterprises and the use of profit as a guide to production levels, as in the Soviet Union.

Ironically, the country most eager to respond to Khrushchev's renewed call to de-Stalinize was Hungary, which had suffered in 1956 for taking de-Stalinization too far. After four years of repression, the atmosphere of 'terror' suddenly vanished, and soon it was Hungary, rather than Poland, now retreating further into Communist orthodoxy, which led the reformists within the bloc.[12] Most of those jailed in connection with the 1956 events were released, many Soviet 'advisers' to the government in Budapest were returned to Moscow, and merit rather than political reliability became the key to promotion. As in Poland, restrictions on travel to the West and on religious or artistic expression were relaxed, and, in 1967, Kádár introduced the bloc's most far-reaching economic reform to date.

Called the New Economic Mechanism, it was designed to replace the command economy with a much more decentralized structure, responding to the laws of supply and demand. It was to involve cuts in subsidies, rewards for initiative, and freedom for enterprise managers to make their own arrangements, within broad official guidelines, as regards staffing, sales and pricing policy, and even foreign marketing. It was a policy well tailored to a small, relatively homogeneous, and heavily trade-dependent country which had learned from bitter experience what the limits to autonomy were. Wisely, however, Budapest was careful to keep in step with Soviet foreign policy . . . just in case!

The one country that failed to gauge accurately the limits of what the Italian Communist, Palmiro Togliatti, called 'polycentrism' was, paradoxically, the one with the most pro-Soviet and pro-Communist tradition – Czechoslovakia.[13] Here, de-Stalinization had been slow, but, in 1963, a major economic crisis combined with a sudden upsurge of national feeling among Slovak Communist intellectuals led President Novotný to dismiss several leading Stalinists from power and introduce a belated programme of political and cultural reform. It was not, however, enough to satisfy popular aspirations for change, especially when the economy continued to stagnate – its problems compounded by an aid and trade policy determined largely in Moscow. By the end of 1967, after brutal displays of police power against protesting students and workers, discontent reached its climax. The demands proliferated – demands by workers for better living standards; by managers for the power to manage; by intellectuals for an end to repression; by Slovaks for a fairer distribution of power; and by young people for a better tomorrow. Visiting Prague in December, the Soviet leader, Leonid Brezhnev, realized how volatile was the situation and gave the signal for Novotný's removal. In the absence of any obvious successor, the party leader of Slovakia, Alexander Dubček, emerged as a compromise candidate to lead the country in early January 1968.

Though Moscow had exercised no influence in the succession, at the time it cannot have been unhappy with the choice of Dubček. For he was both Soviet-trained and the son of a founder of the Czechoslovakian party. He had, moreover, fought with the Communist underground during the Second World War. Yet within a few weeks of his appointment, he was already causing concern in the Soviet capital by propelling the country into one of the most exhilarating periods in its history, with a seemingly unstoppable series of political and economic reforms. He lifted censorship and restrictions on freedom of assembly, allowed non-Communist pressure groups to operate, and launched what was effectively a nationwide debate on the Communist system.

In April, at the height of what became known as the 'Prague Spring', the party published an action programme 'The Czechoslovakian Road to Socialism', which encapsulated Dubček's hopes of creating a socialist system 'with a human face'. It deplored the 'suppression of democratic rights and freedom of the people' under previous Communist leaders, together with their 'violation of laws, licentiousness, and misuse of power'. It also took to task the central management of the economy, which had produced 'stagnation' in living standards, a housing situation that was 'catastrophic', a transport system that was 'precarious', and goods and public services of 'poor quality'. Even more controversial was its attack on the role of the party hitherto. It rejected the 'monopolistic concentration of power in the hands of Party bodies' and envisaged a Communist organization that would be the servant not the master of the people.[14]

As the Party contemplated its own regeneration, many of the residual Stalinists who had not yet been retired faced the prospect of defeat in the projected elections to the Central Committee – the first to be by secret ballot. Meanwhile, in the economy, steps were being taken towards the decentralization of decision-making along Hungarian lines, and plans were well advanced for large-scale western trade credits. There was also the prospect of constitutional reform, with the Slovaks being promised a fairer distribution of power in a projected federal union of Czechs and Slovaks.

In the face of such upheaval, Dubček's repeated assurances that the one-party system and Czechoslovakia's loyal adherence to the Warsaw Pact would be maintained carried little conviction with its more hard-line allies, who, in any case, had reason to fear that the 'Prague Spring' might prove contagious. In Poland, slogans in support of the Czech reform movement were prominently displayed during the riots sweeping the universities in March. In the USSR, literature printed in Czechoslovakia was felt to be encouraging secessionist feeling in the Ukraine. Certainly, it was being quoted by dissidents in criticism of the current wave of trials of disaffected intellectuals. In East Germany, there was especial anxiety lest Prague's new economic policies give the West Germans a dangerously strong foothold in eastern Europe.

As the Soviet Union and its closest allies grew increasingly alarmed, they decided on a policy of intimidation. In June, they forced Prague to readmit detachments of the Red Army for what was described as 'routine manœuvres'. In July, Warsaw issued what amounted to an ultimatum. The government in Prague had to muzzle the media or suffer the consequences! In early August, following a meeting with Brezhnev at Cierna, near the Soviet border, and with members of the

Warsaw Pact in Bratislava, the Slovak capital, Dubček agreed to amend his reform programme. But, buoyed by the high-profile backing of the Yugoslav, Romanian and western European parties, as well as by the evident enthusiasm of his own people, he decided to continue with the reform. However, on the night of 20–21 August, his country paid the price, as tens of thousands of Polish, East German, Bulgarian, and Hungarian, as well as Soviet troops staged an invasion, arrested most of Czechoslovakia's leaders and took many of them, including Dubček, at gunpoint to Moscow. The reasons for the intervention had already been set out in the 'Warsaw letter' of July, to be elaborated in an article on 'Sovereignty and International Duties' in *Pravda* in September, and confirmed by Brezhnev in a speech in Poland, in November, encapsulating what has come to be known as the 'Brezhnev doctrine'. Whenever Socialism, as interpreted in Moscow, is at risk, the other Socialist countries have a duty to restore it.[15]

The presence of foreign troops in a country free of them since 1945 and by agreement with a government that had originally condemned their presence as a violation of international law, national sovereignty, and 'Socialist internationalism' drastically altered the political face of the country. In less than nine months Dubček and his reform programme were gone and his supporters subjected to one of eastern Europe's most thoroughgoing and vindictive, if bloodless, purges. In the meantime, Prague had completely fallen into line with Moscow on matters of policy, and the populace had been browbeaten into cynicism and apathy.[16]

But the intervention also brought existing rifts in international Communism to a head. Soon after, the major Communist critics of the 'Brezhnev doctrine' of 'limited sovereignty', fearing that it might be used against them, made significant shifts in foreign policy. Albania, which had not attended Warsaw Pact meetings since the early '60s, formally left the organization and began to improve state-to-state relations with Yugoslavia and to cultivate ties with western countries such as Italy, France and Greece.[17] Romania's President Ceauşescu held a series of joint consultations with President Tito, possibly with a view to a secret alliance with Belgrade, and weeded pro-Soviet elements out of the administration and armed forces. In addition, having welcomed President Nixon to Bucharest in August 1969, the Romanian leader seems to have acted as an intermediary to facilitate the first formal contacts between Washington and Peking in 1971.[18] Meanwhile, Yugoslavia intensified its contacts with the nonaligned nations and began to patch up its long standing quarrel with China, which was in process of retreating from socialist extremes and launching a diplomatic offensive to outflank Moscow.[19]

As the Communist opponents of the 'Brezhnev doctrine' strengthened ties with one another, the effects of the intervention on some of the participants was scarcely less dramatic. In Poland, the army's role in helping to suppress the 'Prague Spring' was so widely resented as to increase still further the already yawning gulf between government and governed. For the honeymoon with Gomułka was long over. While most of the country's Communist neighbours had made political and economic advances in the '60s, Poland had stagnated, and, for many, Gomułka's decision to invade Czechoslovakia was the last straw. In December 1970, those smouldering resentments erupted in the bloody riots in the ports of Gdańsk and Szczecin that contributed to Gomułka's fall.[20] In Hungary – a reluctant accomplice, judging by the favourable references to Dubček on Radio Budapest even after the intervention, and the government's evident haste to withdraw its troops – economic reform was, if anything, accelerated in the immediate aftermath of the invasion. Until 1974, when a combination of external and internal pressures forced a temporary retreat, the New Economic Mechanism proceeded apace, encouraged by a government perhaps mindful that the recent turmoil in both Czechoslovakia and Poland had been precipitated by economic failure.[21]

Even the normally cautious and pliable Bulgarian regime, fearing economic slow-down, decided to spur on economic decentralization in the wake of the invasion, allowing a role for private agriculture, which was to account for 27 per cent of total output by 1982. As Sofia moved to reinstate the individual entrepreneur, it also discovered the value of, so to speak, 'wrapping itself in the national flag' and presenting itself as the authentic representative of the Bulgarian national tradition. At one time in evidence only in the dispute with Yugoslavia about Macedonia – the heartland of medieval Bulgaria – national pride began to be reasserted over a much broader front. By 1981, the 1300th anniversary of the foundation of the first Bulgarian empire, Zhivkov and his daughter, Lyudmila, the Politburo member in charge of culture, were encouraging lavish displays of ethnocentricity, including publication of a 14-volume *History of Bulgaria* and a host of artistic creations with patriotic themes.[22] A rather more unsavoury manifestation of national egoism has been the unseemly haste and brutality of the campaign, beginning in 1984, to Bulgarize the country's ethnic Turks, together with what V. Kusin calls 'a rather intimate . . . association of the Bulgarian Secret Services with syndicated crime in the European underworld, especially its drug and arms smuggling branch'.[23]

Of all the participants, it was the GDR on whom the intervention had its most profound, if paradoxical, impact. As in 1962, when Romania stepped out of line, so in 1968, as the Czechoslovak reform programme proceeded apace, the call for sanctions was spearheaded by Walter Ulbricht.[24] As one of eastern Europe's longest surviving Stalinists, he had feared that the 'Prague Spring', if unchecked, would prove contagious. Even more worrying had been Dubček's proposed *rapprochement* with West Germany – a country which had steadfastly refused to recognize the East German regime as legitimate and which had just to Ulbricht's chagrin been given unconditional recognition by his two Communist opponents, presidents Ceauşescu and Tito. Moreover, Ulbricht's cool reception in Prague, as against the warmth of the welcome for the Romanian and Yugoslav leaders in mid-August, had only strengthened his determination to have the 'Prague Spring' suppressed.

Having helped subdue 'the human face' of socialism in Czechoslovakia, Ulbricht seems to have misread the implications. For him, the invasion had effectively drawn a wedge between the two halves of Europe, made imperative the economic integration of eastern Europe along the lines proposed by Khrushchev in 1962 (with a supranational planning authority in which the GDR, as one of the region's most developed countries, would play a dominant role), and made all but the most meagre economic contact with the West unnecessary. Though the Kremlin also wished to encourage greater bloc integration, it was not to be at the expense of economic interchange in the West. For, after the events of 1968, the Kremlin felt that both Communists and non-Communists understood and would respect the Soviet stake in eastern Europe and, faced with an economic slowdown in eastern Europe and the hostility of China, it was anxious to improve its relations with the West in general and to respond positively, if belatedly to the *Ostpolitik* – Bonn's offer of trade, credits and technological know-how to the eastern governments. It was also willing to drop its precondition for better relations with Bonn–West German recognition of the GDR. As a return to East–West détente began to assume a high priority in the Kremlin, the perceived interests of Moscow and East Berlin began seriously to diverge.[25]

For Ulbricht, the political and economic health of the GDR was dependent on the maintenance of East–West tension and restrictions on the West German presence in eastern Europe. The Wall, after all, had made all the difference to the East German economy, and Ulbricht felt that to grant respectability to Bonn, allow the West Germans to compete with the East Germans for Communist markets, and permit

the western powers unimpeded access to West Berlin across East
German territory would reduce the GDR's political and economic
standing and its power to influence the Kremlin.

But, while he stepped up his campaign to resist the encroachments
of what he called the 'revenge seekers' in Bonn, both Moscow and
Warsaw, in their need to encourage dynamism in their flagging economies, were embarking on a dialogue with Bonn that was to result in
the Soviet–West German non-aggression treaty of August 1970, the
Polish–West German treaty of November 1970 and the Four-Power
Berlin agreement of September 1971. Though each of these historic
documents contained significant concessions from Bonn – including its
agreement to recognize the territorial status quo in eastern Europe and,
in principle, the existence of an East German state – they conceded in
return that West Germany was a peaceable country that could have
normal relations with all eastern Europe and guaranteed access routes
across East Germany to West Berlin. For Ulbricht, who does not seem
to have been consulted, the price was too high, and amid his plans for
delaying and hampering implementation of these latest agreements, he
was removed from office with the complicity, if not at the behest, of
the Kremlin, ironically, at the very time his country was about to
receive the status he had long sought for it.

It was left to his successor, Erich Honecker, under pressure from
Moscow, to put an end to the bogey of a hostile and revanchist West
Germany, by concluding with Bonn the Basic Treaty of November
1972, under which the two states recognized each other's separate
existence and exchanged permanent missions. Since then the GDR has
prospered, and its leaders have learned to manipulate the symbols of
nationalism, claiming, with pride, to be the inheritors of a tradition of
nation-builders – from Luther to Frederick the Great; from Scharnhorst
to Goethe; and from Clausewitz to Beethoven. Yet, ironically, the
country is probably less influential today than it was before it ceased
being a pariah in the non-Communist world, since, while the Ulbricht
'tail' had often wagged the Soviet 'dog', his successor was not even free
to visit Bonn before obtaining Moscow's approval, while his hostility
to reform eventually cost him his job.[26]

In view, therefore, of the continuing disparities in the policies, both
internal and external, of the eastern European countries, the initial
fear in some Communist capitals that the 'Brezhnev doctrine' would
mark an end of diversity and a new 'ice age' in relations with the West
turned out to be misplaced. Eastern European 'Communism' continued
throughout the '70s and '80s to encompass a wide spectrum of regimes,
each with its own character and subject to the winds of political and

economic change.[27] Within the bloc, the most reformist countries, like Hungary, which continued with its New Economic Mechanism, despite pressures from its neighbours in the mid-'70s and a serious debt problem in the late '80s, have tended to be among those with the closest ties to Moscow: the most centralized, like Romania, whose leadership became increasingly authoritarian, nepotistic, and megalomanic after the early '70s, to be among the most independent. In eastern Europe as a whole, those with the greatest interest in East–West contacts included countries at both ends of the political spectrum – reformists like Yugoslavia and Hungary, as well as more hard-line countries like Romania in the '70s and the GDR from the mid-'80s, while the Soviet Union itself has tended to shift its ground as its own domestic and international imperatives have changed.[28]

On the other hand, despite their national peculiarities and preoccupations and the kaleidoscopic changes in the international environment, the Communist countries of eastern Europe continued until the late '80s to operate in a political and ideological climate imposing constraints on policy and action. They might differ from one another in their attitude towards Moscow, in their relations with China and the West, and in the degree to which they were prepared to decentralize the economy and experiment with political pluralism. Yet, they had a common political ancestor; were committed, at least in theory, to an ultimately communist world; and remained, despite provisions for power-sharing in Hungary and Poland, essentially one-party states, organized on the basis of 'democratic centralism' and the *nomenklatura* system. In face of dissident demands, backed by the West, for the promotion of western-style 'human rights', following the Helsinki accords concluding the 1975 Conference on Security and Cooperation in Europe, they had tended to close ranks. Moreover, apart from Albania, they were all, to some extent, economically dependent on and militarily vulnerable to the Soviet Union, and, except for Yugoslavia and Albania, were subject to additioned Soviet leverage by virtue of their membership of the Council for Mutual Economic Assistance (CMEA) and the Warsaw Pact.

Of the two organizations, the CMEA made fewer demands of its members.[29] From being a forum for attacking the Marshall Plan and a cover for Moscow's reorganization and exploitation of the economies of eastern Europe (and subsequently condemned as such by the Yugoslavs, Albanians, and Chinese), it had come to respect, under Stalin's successors, the sovereignty principle written into its founding communiqué but probably never intended by Stalin to have much practical significance. In this regard, Romania's success in frustrating a joint

Soviet, East German, and Czechoslovakian initiative to establish a supranational planning authority for the bloc, in 1962, proved decisive. Henceforth, participants would not be bound by CMEA decisions unless they had given their explicit consent, and though this could only further impede attempts at integration in an area still suffering from the Stalinist economic legacy, it meant that membership had something to offer virtually everyone. Despite the clash of interests between richer and poorer socialist countries, the reluctance of member governments to scrap uneconomic plants which had attracted much capital and prestige, the lack of a convertible currency, and the economic disparity between the USSR and all the rest, CMEA was to become a going concern. As its schemes for improving joint investment, specialization and the coordination of national plans inched ahead, particularly after the unveiling of the Comprehensive Programme for CMEA development in 1971, they strengthened an interdependent relationship from which extrication would become increasingly difficult.

For the Soviet Union, the existence of CMEA served to make available from its allies the material and human resources and (from the more advanced) the technology and capital for the kinds of projects which would help alleviate its domestic problems as well as improve its global military and political position. In times of shortage, it would mean, for Moscow, grain and other foodstuffs from any ally with a surplus. In addition, the Kremlin was assured that the burdens of levelling up poorer member countries, such as Cuba and Vietnam, who had both joined in the '70s; of bailing out members in difficulty, such as Poland in 1981; and of funding non-member Third World countries of both Socialist and non-Socialist orientation, would be shared.

Furthermore, by means of CMEA, economic pressure against such Communist recalcitrants as Yugoslavia in 1949, Albania and China in the early '60s, and Cuba, accused in the mid-'60s of squandering CMEA funds, could be coordinated and strengthened. Finally, it served as a framework for a common approach to trade with the West and a shield against the adverse consequences of western tariff barriers, on the one hand, and intrusive economic penetration, on the other. As against this, the terms of trade throughout the '70s and early '80s consistently favoured, much to Moscow's chagrin, its CMEA partners, not least since even the most blatant members tended to unite to oppose any radical change in pricing (one of the 'burdens of empire', according to more cynical western observers).

For the other countries, belonging to CMEA meant participation in a technological community that shared amongst its members some at least of the secrets of its advanced research, and provided credits for costly economic ventures. It also meant a ready market for inferior products not marketable in the West, and a guaranteed source of supply of capital goods and strategic raw materials, such as oil, often at subsidized rates. Jan Vanous of Whareton Economic Forecasting suggests that during the '70s Moscow made available to its allies a hidden subsidy of more than 80 billion dollars as it traded cheap oil for over-priced manufactures, in effect, putting back into eastern Europe at least as much as it extracted in the '40s and early'50s.[30] (Such trading practices also had negative consequences. They did little or nothing to encourage innovation or any appreciable rise in living standards, and engendered serious knock-on effects throughout the region whenever a country, such as Poland, proved unable to meet its export targets of raw materials.) Finally, of course, for the poorer members of CMEA, there was the added advantage of generous financial and technological assistance (though of course, this also imposed a corresponding burden on those having to provide it).

Yet, for all the benefits conferred by membership of CMEA, the legacy of overcentralized, inflexible, and often incompetent planning; the lack of competition; the falsification of statistics and the like, to say nothing of the political squabbles amongst its members, had taken their toll. Until recently, their combined effects limited the organization's ability to provide adequately for the growing economic needs of its members, and their trade with one another decreased in relation to their trade outside the COMECON area. In their search for managerial skills, technology, and foodstuffs they were increasingly drawn to the West for the range and quality on offer and for the credits which the banks, flushed with petrodollars in the '70s and early '80s, were only too eager to furnish.

Only with the world recession, the enlargement and consolidation of the EEC combined with the stem in the flow of Western credits as CMEA debts mounted and the prospects of repayment receded, did members feel obliged to reinvigorate the organization. Clearly, with the world price of fuels dropping as the costs of producing energy within CMEA rose (in part, because of the depletion of the oil wells in the Caucasus and the need to develop new fields in the remote and inhospitable areas of Siberia and the Arctic),[31] the organization was under pressure to remove, so far as was possible in a community of centrally planned economies, obstacles impeding the freer flow of trade, investment, and labour. Yet, the somewhat un-Marxist predominance of political over economic criteria in determining relations among members continues to hamper progress, so that CMEA tends to operate rather like the OEEC (the Organization for European Economic Cooperation), the OECD's forerunner, rather than the more integrated European Economic Community. Ironically, it is the Communist rather than the capitalist world which has found difficulty in working towards a common market,[32] which is perhaps why, as western Europe approaches full economic integration in 1992, President Gorbachev is so keen for his conception of a 'common European house' (including 'Communists' as well as 'capitalists') to achieve western understanding and support.

Like CMEA, the Warsaw Pact has also undergone significant change.[33] When created in 1955, largely as a riposte to West Germany's inclusion in NATO, it merely duplicated the existing complex of bilateral Communist military treaties, enabling Moscow to control eastern Europe's military arrangements from the pact's headquarters located inside the Soviet defence ministry. And, though militarily Moscow has continued to dominate the organization, in that it pays 80 per cent of its running costs; contributes 75 per cent of its manpower; monopolizes the production of sophisticated weapons; determines strategic doctrine; monitors key military appointments; and, exercises leverage through being able to control, and, if necessary, jam eastern European communications, and also through being able to threaten, display, or utilize force in times of crisis, its military pre-eminence is not always translated into political success.[34] It proved insufficient, for example, to intimidate the Polish army, which stood ready to defend Gomułka's leadership against Soviet troops in 1956. Neither was it enough to deter Romania from opting out of joint manœuvres and adopting its own defence strategy in the early '60s or from purging the country's armed forces of pro-Soviet elements in the wake of the intervention against Czechoslovakia. And, of course, no amount of Soviet sabre-rattling could prevent Albania's withdrawal from the pact. But even some of the pact's 'successes' concealed inner weaknesses – witness, for example, the large number of Hungarian troops that turned their weapons against the Red Army in 1956, or the scores of Czech and Slovak forces who, in 1968, used their signals equipment to enable the West to get radio and TV coverage of the occupation of Prague for several days afterwards.

In the meantime, Moscow has proved no more persuasive in getting its partners to accept integration in the Warsaw Pact than in the CMEA. The joint command, which provides an overall strategic structure in time of war, has never served as a supranational body, and, as John Erickson has noted, national units assigned to the WTO remain under national deputy commanders and responsive to national control.[35] Furthermore, Moscow's allies have used the new consultative institutions, such as the Committee of Defence Ministers, the Military Council of National Chiefs of Staff, the Technical Committee of the Joint Armed Forces, and the Committee of Foreign Ministers, created in the wake of the intervention in Czechoslovakia, to exert heavy pressure on the Kremlin.[36] They served, for example, to facilitate eastern European resistance to Moscow's bid to involve them in the Asian theatre during the 1970s, in relation first to China and then Afghanistan, and to Moscow's more recent attempts to secure a fairer distribution of the pact's defence costs (as in NATO, a thorny problem). They are also believed to have been used to persuade Moscow to return to the Geneva talks on arms control after a sudden walk-out in 1983.

Thus, though the Pact was originally little more than an agency for eliciting public displays of regional solidarity in support of Soviet policy and for subordinating eastern Europe's armed forces to the Soviet high command, it, too, has had to come to terms with the divergent national ambitions of its members. At the same time, the WTO offers a multilateral framework for inter- as well as intra-allied diplomacy, while making a useful contribution to the military, political and economic security of all its participants.[37] At the minimum, it denies the region to any great power other than the Soviet Union. Moscow's nuclear 'umbrella', combined with the Pact's formidable array of military might, provides both a credible guarantee against external (though not necessarily internal) attack and a bargaining tool in return for western concessions. Moreover, the WTO's strategic arrangements help contain and constrain the region's traditional antipathies and antagonisms, while giving the regimes involved access to Soviet decision-making on issues of critical importance. In addition, the alliance can offer a repertoire of stratagems, short of military intervention, for assisting the reassertion of control where Socialist regimes are at serious risk.

For example, though it was through the nation's armed forces that Party rule was eventually restored in Poland following months of turmoil during which the independent trade union, Solidarity, with its 10 million members (nearly one in three of the population) articulated the nationwide protest against corrupt, inefficient, and often arbitrary government, their swift and effective action, in December 1981, had been encouraged and facilitated by Poland's alliance partners.[38] In the months leading up to the imposition of martial law, the countries of the strategically vital 'northern tier' of the alliance took measures to try to rein in the anti-Communist opposition and strengthen the hand of the Party leader, Premier and Defence Minister, General Wojciech Jaruzelski. These included public and private denunciations of Solidarity; visits to Warsaw by high-ranking Soviet, Czech, and East

German officials; increasing references to the 'Brezhnev doctrine'; the sealing of frontiers; and joint military manœuvres in and around the country. Their combined effect was to make a WTO military intervention unnecessary, and even though martial law has long since gone, with Solidarity relegalized and in virtual political control, while the Pact remains in being Poland's alliance partners are supposed to ensure that the Communist Party continues to contribute towards the shaping of the country's affairs.

But the Warsaw Pact offers more than the advantages (and disadvantages) of the conventional alliance. Under its aegis, many of its members have been active in the Third World – particularly in what Moscow calls the 'countries of Socialist orientation' in Africa, the Middle East, and Central America – challenging both the Western and Chinese presence. In shipping arms (often manufactured under Soviet licence) and advisers, and offering training facilities to military personnel from developing countries, East Germany, Czechoslovakia, Romania and their allies appear to be acting as Soviet surrogates and proxies, and are sometimes dismissed as such by domestic critics who would rather the national economy took a prior claim on resources.

On the other hand, like Cuba, which is even more active in some of these regions, the smaller WTO countries serve their own interests as well as Moscow's.[39] Their contributions are often commercial in nature – their arms traded for hard currency from such oil-bearing states as Iraq and Libya, their technical services exchanged for much needed raw materials. Moreover, in placing their advisers within the top echelons of the military, security and economic establishments of the more leftward-leaning Third World regimes, the eastern European countries gain significant influence in policy-making and enhance their visibility, which engenders a corresponding rise in international esteem.

Outside the European sphere, the Communist idea had been linked to the concept of national liberation almost from the start. After all, the Bolshevik proclamation of the right of 'self-determination up to secession and the formation of an independent state'[40] seemed as valid for the Communist groups on Russia's periphery as for the non-Russian peoples of the former Russian empire. In addition, by denouncing and renouncing the fruits of empire, giving practical as well as theoretical support to anti-imperialist movements, and encouraging local Communists to follow suit, the Bolsheviks appeared to be giving nationalism their imprimatur. Moreover, in offering to non-Communists as well as Communists the Soviet political and economic system as an appropriate model for the development of a backward society, the Bolsheviks themselves seemed to be blurring somewhat the distinction between Communism and nationalism.

In fact, however, Moscow's endorsement of 'bourgeois' nationalism was largely tactical. Once the Communist party took control – as in Georgia, Armenia, or Azerbaijan within the Soviet Union or Mongolia outside it – it was expected to jettison nationalist slogans whenever Stalin deemed them harmful to the 'interests of the international proletariat', and revive them only in face of regional or ethnic separatism or a foreign adversary. In any case, Stalin was not disposed to permit independent-minded Communist leaders, such as Professor Ch'en Tu-hsiu, the first Secretary General of the Chinese party, to pursue unchecked their own revolutionary strategy, influenced, as they might be, by anarchist, syndicalist, or liberal humanist ideas at variance with Marxism–Leninism as currently interpreted.[41] And as the Bolshevization of the Comintern proceeded apace, non-European Communist leaders were required to follow their European counterparts in submitting themselves and their policies for Moscow's approval and integrating their parties into a supranational political structure controlled from the Soviet capital.

On the other hand, when, in Asia, Communism moved, in Robert Scalapino's words, 'from the salon and the university to the streets, and from the urban centres into the countryside',[42] it became increasingly Asianized. Its leaders now tended to be charismatic figures with military credentials and a rural background who saw the revolutionary route as leading through the village and by means of rural-based guerrilla warfare, rather than through the kind of urban-based action that Moscow had imposed on the Chinese party to its detriment in the 1920s. Above all, in its appeal to the peasant, Asian Communism sought to satisfy a host of local as well as national grievances over such matters as taxation, prices, abuse of authority, corruption, and land control and ownership. Increasingly, the trend in Asia was to diverge from the Soviet model of development and to keep a respectful distance from a Soviet party preoccupied with European affairs and the building of Socialism in one country. In fact, of the Asian Communist countries, only the Mongolian People's Republic – a vast region hewn with Soviet help out of territory claimed by China until the late '40s – has remained broadly subservient to Soviet authority and heavily dependent on Moscow's protection.

Yet, even in Mongolia – the first and reportedly most pliant of Moscow's 'satellites' – the desire for national self-expression had never been extinguished. It was, after all, as an independence struggle against both China and the miscellaneous White forces seeking to incorporate Mongolia into a revived and expanded Russian empire, that the Mongo-

lian People's Republic had its origins in the early '20s.[43] And it was with
a view to achieving and sustaining that independence that Mongolia's
Communists had relied on Moscow for military and economic
assistance.

On the other hand, Tokyo's contest with Peking for the outposts of
the Chinese empire in the '30s and '40s and the rift between Moscow
and Peking, beginning in the '60s, could only increase Mongolia's
dependence on the Soviet Union. As a poor, landlocked country anxious to avoid the political embrace of both Tokyo and Peking, it had
little alternative but to adopt Soviet planning and managerial techniques
throughout the economy, join CMEA, and allow Soviet troops, with an
array of sophisticated missiles, virtually to garrison the Sino-Mongolian
frontier. Yet, the unpalatable facts of political and economic geography
could not obliterate the sense of Mongolian identity, and in the wake
of the recent Sino-Soviet 'thaw' and Gorbachev's call for Moscow's
more burdensome economic clients to try to 'stand on their own feet',
it is beginning to emerge from beneath the Soviet shadow. And, as
Mongolia finds new trading partners in Japan, southeast Asia and
Australasia, Peking's apparent willingness to permit Mongolian exports
transit across China could prove decisive in restoring a sense of national
pride.[44]

As in Mongolia, so in Korea, the Communist movement had emerged
in the course of a struggle for national liberation.[45] The first Korean
Communist organization, created in Khabarovsk in June 1918, consisted
of exiled nationalists seeking Bolshevik assistance against the Japanese,
who had annexed their country in 1910. And though the Korean Communist movement had been fragmented during the '20s and '30s – its
members operating from bases in Siberia, China, Manchuria, and Japan
as well as Korea – it was united in the quest for an independent
homeland. It also wanted Korea unified, and Communists, no less
than nationalists, had protested at the Soviet–American agreement of
August 1945 to occupy and partition their country. If the occupation
merely accelerated the development of separate political systems in
North and South, the rise in the North of the Kim Il Sung Communist
faction seems to have been as much an effect of domestic manœuvring
as of external pressure. In fact, Kim was not Moscow's obvious choice
for the leadership, since in a speech to leading cadres, in August 1945,
he had expressly rejected the Soviet model in favour of an indigenous
type of 'Democratic People's Republic', and, as late as April 1948, at
a conference in Pyongyang, he had agreed with nationalists from both
North and South on the need for unification and the end of foreign
occupation.[46]

Though the Korean War, whose origins probably lie more in the complex politics of the peninsula than in the machinations of the Kremlin, at first brought Pyongyang and Moscow closer together, China's intervention evoked a warmer response. For Kim, Mao's men were repaying in blood the sacrifices Korean Communists had made for the Chinese Communist victory of 1949, and, in the aftermath of the conflict, Kim tilted politically towards Peking, with its virulent anti-imperialism, cult of the leader, and emphasis on agriculture. As Sino-Soviet tensions intensified in the early '60s, North Korean support of Peking became even more pronounced. Like Mao, Kim was exasperated by what he perceived as Moscow's lack of resolve in the face of 'imperialist aggression', and, by the end of the Khrushchev era, there was almost a complete break between the DPRK and the USSR. On the other hand, for North Korea, a diplomatic rupture, such as had occurred between Tirana and Moscow, would have had serious economic and military consequences, and with the onset of Mao's Cultural Revolution, Pyongyang seized the opportunity to patch up some of its differences with Moscow.[47]

However, by the beginning of the '70s, as Chou En-lai took charge of China's foreign policy, North Korea, like North Vietnam and Romania, adopted a policy of neutrality between the two squabbling Communist giants. At the same time, in its commitment to the 'juche' idea, defined as 'self-identity in ideology, independence in politics, self-sustenance in the economy, and self-defence in national defence', it was engaged in a pattern of development largely abandoned by most of the other Communist countries. In practice, the North Koreans had become subject to the most systematic and thoroughgoing ideological indoctrination in the Communist world and to a leadership cult of almost unprecedented fanaticism. Not even Stalin had sought to create a family dynasty, have his son's birthday as well as his own celebrated as national holidays or have his blood relations depicted as the 'revolutionary family'. Nor did he ever acquire a 180-word honorific title, or combine the state presidency and a leading government post with the general secretaryship of the party. As in politics, so in the economy, the 'juche' idea was used to justify rigid central control and all the paraphernalia of the Stalinist command system, with its emphasis on heavy industry, collectivized agriculture, worker discipline and special rewards for political reliability and effort.[48]

If, in its willingness to tap the advanced technology of the West, Pyongyang has diverged somewhat from the Stalinist model, its apparent inability to meet some of its debts tended for a time to reinforce the earlier desire for autarchy – a principle almost wholly at variance with the trend elsewhere in the Communist world. Nonetheless, with its southern neighbour finding increasing export outlets in the Communist world as well as in the West, especially after the successful staging of the Olympics, North Korea is being forced to reassess its political strategy. Certainly, the *rapprochement* between Moscow and Peking and their commitment to economic reform can only diminish Pyongyang's influence in both capitals, and that Kim's most enthusiastic foreign supporter is Romania's President Ceauşescu, himself increasingly a pariah in the Communist world, hardly augurs well for either regime, unless there is a substantial change in policy.

In Vietnam and its Indochinese neighbours, Laos and Cambodia, it was again a national liberation struggle that provided the impetus for the establishment of Communist rule. However, unlike Mongolia and North Korea, the Vietnamese movement had been dominated from the outset by one man – Ho Chi Minh.[49] Converted to Communism in France after World War I, he moved to Moscow to train at the Comintern School, and, from 1925, journeyed from one country to another organizing clandestine groups to rid Indochina of French control. When Indochina found itself under two colonial masters, Vichy France and Japan in 1940–41, Ho returned to the country he had left 30 years earlier to take personal control of the Indochinese Communist Party he had created in 1930 and to merge the Vietnamese component into a broader-based Vietnamese Independence League – the Vietminh – including miscellaneous nationalist groups.

But, having dominated the Vietminh both militarily and politically, the Communists were in a position to take charge after the liberation of Indochina's six northern provinces in the wake of the Japanese defeat. In September 1945, before the French could resume control, Ho proclaimed the Democratic Republic of Vietnam, ironically, in terms redolent with phrases from the American Declaration of Independence and to a text prepared by an American intelligence officer, originally detailed by Roosevelt to assist the Vietminh's quest for national liberation.[50] Hoping to limit Ho's authority to the north, Paris recognized his republic in March 1946, albeit as part of an Indochinese federation linked to France. But the agreement had its critics on both sides, and after nine fraught months it was forcibly ended, as Vietminh troops launched a general offensive against French positions. The evidence suggests that, as in the case of the Greek insurrection two years earlier, the Communist action had stemmed from purely local considerations, and that Ho did not have the support of Moscow, which had little interest in provoking Paris at this juncture.[51]

Lacking Moscow's backing, the regime Ho had established in Hanoi was largely his own creation, though the nationalist component in his thinking tended to become obscured after his forces began receiving aid and sanctuary from China, by which time the first Indochina war had taken on an unmistakably ideological character. With Peking recognizing and giving succour to the Democratic Republic of Vietnam (DRV), the countries of the Soviet bloc followed suit. But to the Americans and their allies, bogged down in the Korean wastelands, France was helping to prevent another Asian 'domino' from falling to Communism, so that when Paris was forced to abandon the struggle, it was not long before Washington decided to pick up the tab.

From 1961 onwards, as the DRV stepped up its aid to the Vietcong – the pro-Communist insurgents in the South – the USA became increasingly involved in support of the anti-Communist regime in Saigon.[52] This led to the extensive bombing, from 1965, of the north and, from 1970, of Cambodia, through which Hanoi supplied the Vietcong. Though Ho died in 1969, before the end of the second Indochina war, the ferocity and indiscriminate nature of the American bombardment probably did more to secure than to undermine the regime he had created, and, in May 1975, following the demoralization and withdrawal of US forces from Indochina, control of South Vietnam passed to Hanoi. Formal reunification occurred the following year, by which time Communist rule had also been established in Phnom Penh and Vientiane.[53] It was at this point that the already tarnished myth of international Communist solidarity received its most shattering blow to date. For, instead of helping one another on a socialist programme of reconstruction, the new Communist regimes were soon at one another's throats, giving vent to nationalist tensions which had long been simmering below the surface.

At the core of the internecine conflict, lay a legacy of Cambodian bitterness after centuries of domination by the Vietnamese. Though Vietnam's expansionism had been checked by French colonial rule, Ho's victory at Dien Bien Phu had raised fresh apprehensions – among Cambodian Communists as well as non-Communists – about Hanoi's intentions. For Cambodian Marxists, already alarmed at the implications of Ho's commitment to an 'Indochinese federation', his apparent abandonment of the Cambodian revolution at the Geneva Conference concluding the first Indochina war in 1954, was hardly reassuring. In fact, the Khmer Communist Party never enjoyed close or easy relations with the Vietminh. As Sheldon Simon noted: 'Its supposed solidarity with Vietnam was more a product of Hanoi's public relations than any real commitment on the part of the Cambodians'.[54] Until the overthrow of Cambodia's neutralist, left-leaning ruler, Prince Sihanouk,

Cambodia's Marxists seemed to prefer his regime to the Vietminh, while whatever assistance Hanoi had to offer seemed to be channelled more to Cambodia's ethnic Vietnamese or to Cambodians domiciled in North Vietnam than to the Khmer Communist Party (KCP). Certainly, Hanoi's aid to the KCP's military wing, the Khmer Rouge, during its five-year struggle against the CIA-backed regime of Lon Nol, who had ousted Sihanouk in 1970, was comparatively meagre, and, by the time Phnom Penh had fallen to the Khmer Rouge in April 1975, a kind of paranoia had gripped its leaders.

Convinced they were surrounded by spies and traitors, the leaders of the Khmer Rouge government drew on theories concerning 'necessary violence', imbibed during their student days in France, to destroy all opposition, actual or potential. Soon they were employing mass liquidations in the service of the most radical prospectus to date for creating a communist society. Renaming the country 'Democratic Kampuchea', they began depopulating the cities, driving tens of thousands of men, women, and children out at gunpoint; destroying all books, papers, and records; incinerating all paper money; impounding all motor vehicles; and cutting off the water supply to and firing rockets at houses showing any signs of movement. Anyone associated with the Vietnamese or of some social standing during the Lon Nol era, including officers, civil servants, businessmen, technicians, teachers and students, could face a firing squad, and life was equally precarious for people at the other end of the social scale – including beggars, prostitutes, the seriously wounded, and the incurably sick. Altogether upwards of a million of the country's seven million inhabitants are believed to have been massacred from the 'Year Zero' when the Khmer Rouge took charge.[55]

Meanwhile, the survivors were organized into rural 'cooperatives', even more radically equalitarian than the PRC's original communes. Money was dispensed with, and the private household exchanged for the communal kitchen and the sexually segregated barracks, while a system of 'collective responsibility' ensured that the regime had at its disposal the most comprehensive and intrusive form of surveillance yet devised.

But, in constructing 'Democratic Kampuchea', Phnom Penh's relations with Hanoi became so inflamed that there were fierce border clashes, and as the conflict escalated, both sides sought outside support. Pol Pot's Khmer Rouge, hostile towards Moscow for maintaining diplomatic ties with Lon Nol throughout Cambodia's civil war, courted Peking, which had been its patron for some considerable time. Hanoi, on the other hand, looked towards Moscow, both because it was better equipped to provide for its military and economic needs and because it was a useful counterweight to Peking, from whom it was now estranged. Their relations, soured during the second Indochina war as the Chinese held up vital Soviet supplies intended for Hanoi's war effort, had deteriorated still further as both countries laid claim to two potentially oil-rich island chains in the South China Sea – the Paracels and the Spratlys. The alleged harassment of Vietnam's one and a half million ethnic Chinese, leading to a mass exodus, and the series of violent eruptions on the Sino-Vietnamese frontier only made things worse, giving Hanoi little alternative but to strengthen ties with Moscow.[56]

In December 1978, having recently joined CMEA and signed a far-reaching 'treaty of friendship and cooperation' with the Soviet Union, Vietnam invaded Kampuchea, thus beginning not only the third Indochina war, but the first full-scale conflict between two 'Communist' countries. In less than two weeks, Phnom Penh had fallen to the Vietnamese, but as Hanoi was consolidating its control of Kampuchea, having already tightened its grip in Laos, another inter-communist conflict escalated into open hostilities.

In February 1979, Chinese troops crossed into Vietnam, and for three weeks there was a bitterly fought border war between the two Communist countries, who less than a decade earlier had been comrades in arms. It was, as Paul Johnson has suggested, 'a gruesome climax to the 'liberation' struggle, which now entered a new phase, with guerrilla movements, supported by China, taking the field against Hanoi, and with Soviet Russia supplying the North Vietnamese imperialists with the helicopter gunships to maintain their paramountcy'.[57] A decade later, despite the 'thaw' between Moscow and Peking and the Soviet-backed phased withdrawal of several thousand Vietnamese troops from Kampuchea, Hanoi, at great cost to its impoverished citizens, was still the ultimate arbiter of government in Phnom Penh, while the Chinese continued to back a Kampuchean guerrilla coalition, including the Khmer Rouge, in a bid to effect a transfer of power.

Uniquely in Asia, Communist rule in Afghanistan was not a product of a national liberation struggle. In fact, the PDPA (People's Democratic Party of Afghanistan) acquired power as a consequence of a coup precipitated by a government clampdown on Communist sympathizers.[58] The charge by some western and Chinese commentators that the coup of April 1978 had been masterminded in Moscow to serve Soviet interests has never been substantiated and is, prima facie, implausible. In the first place, though under a monarchy for much of the twentieth century, Afghanistan had been a close ally of the Soviet Union since the Bolshevik revolution. It had been one of the first countries to conclude a treaty of friendship with Moscow and receive Soviet assistance, and as Soviet technicians had played a crucial role in building the country's military and economic infrastructure, Afghanistan was virtually in the Soviet orbit well before the Communists seized power.

In any case, right from January 1965, when the PDPA was founded in the home of Noor Taraki, who became its Secretary General, the Afghan Communist movement had been riven with factionalism, and though Taraki was to receive a Soviet literary prize, official contact between the PDPA and Moscow had been infrequent. If anything, the Afghan Communists had had closer relations with the Communist Party of India than the CPSU. According to Louis Dupree, very few of Taraki's original cabinet had been Soviet trained. 'Ten . . . had received some advanced education in the United States; two, in Egypt; and one each, in France and West Germany. Four had studied exclusively in Afghanistan. Only the three military men in the cabinet had received training in the USSR, and they considered themselves nationalists rather than pro-Russian'.[59] On the other hand, once Afghanistan had a government that was not merely pro-Soviet, but pro-Marxist as well, the Kremlin felt a special responsibility to assist it.

Unfortunately for Moscow, the new government in Afghanistan was as divided as it was unpopular. An uneasy coalition of two rival Marxist factions – the hard-line Khalq (The Masses) led by Taraki, and the more conciliatory Parcham (The Banner) led by Babrak Karmal – it rapidly degenerated into warring factions, while its socialist and anti-Islamic platform so offended traditional sensitivities as to provoke widespread armed resistance. Amid the ensuing bloody chaos, Taraki demanded ever increasing Soviet support, but, as protector of a hated regime, Moscow's position grew more and more untenable.[60] Hundreds of Soviet advisers were publicly tortured, mutilated and killed by insurgents, and the possibility of further attacks on Soviet personnel only increased as thousands of Soviet-trained Afghan troops went over to the rebels, taking their weapons with them. The palace coup of September 1979, bringing Taraki's former Prime Minister, Hafizullah Amin, to power, only made things worse. Clearly not a Soviet appointee, he further inflamed the situation inside the country by his brutal excesses, and by December he realized that the regime could be saved from the foreign-backed Islamic resistance only by Soviet military intervention under the terms of a friendship treaty with Moscow concluded the previous year.

At the time, the Kremlin seemed to have compelling reasons for responding positively to the call to intervene – a call it may itself have instigated. The USSR, too, had a 'domino theory', with at least as firm an historical base as that of the USA.[61] More particularly, if Afghanistan had gone the way of Iran, bringing a victory for militant Islam, the effect on the 50 million or so Muslims inside the Soviet Union might well have proved destabilizing to the whole of Soviet central Asia. Nor could Moscow have contemplated with equanimity the prospect of three militant Islamic states – Iran, Afghanistan, and Pakistan – on its southern border. In addition, of course, the Afghan mêleé seemed to offer an opportunity for making a major projection of Soviet power in a strategically significant part of the globe. On the other hand, Amin was a liability. He was far too brutal and doctrinaire, which is presumably why, as the Red Army came to the rescue of the beleagured regime, the Soviet authorities had him killed and the more pliable Babrak Karmal installed in his place. But though Moscow then tried to instil in the Kabul regime greater tolerance for the country's Islamic and other traditions, the Democratic Republic of Afghanistan failed to win any substantial popular support.

As the casualties mounted in the war to determine the country's destiny, Mikhail Gorbachev decided to cleanse what he termed 'a bleeding wound', to make further leadership changes and pull the Soviet forces out by February 1989.[62] It was a turning point both for the Communist movement and for Soviet policy. For the first time the Red Army had abandoned to its fate a beleagured Soviet-backed, Marxist–Leninist regime in a country contiguous to the USSR. Though that regime, now led by former Interior Minister, Mohammed Najibullah, has already lasted much longer than most of its critics once thought possible, it remains at risk and has had to jettison much of its Socialist programme. Meanwhile Moscow had learned, to its cost, the folly of jumping too readily to the aid of doctrinaire Marxists who stage coups in Third World countries with little indigenous support. As an ironic footnote, it is worth recalling that, though to many Afghans the PDPA has become the hated symbol of 'Soviet oppression', its fate was largely sealed when it first attempted to revolutionize the country, i.e. in the period before Moscow made its massive military commitment.

As in Asia, so in Latin America, the problem of overpopulation; the glaring contrasts in wealth; the respective conflicts between peasant and landlord, and worker and employer; the pervasiveness of unrepresentative and oppressive governments; widespread corruption; and the general resentment at what is seen as foreign domination should have provided fertile soil for the Communist movement. Yet, until recently, Latin America's Communists (as distinct from their Marxist rivals) lacked a revolutionary tradition. As Ernst Halperin once observed:

'There is probably not a single conservative or liberal party in all of Latin America which has not staged more insurrections, and incited more civil wars, than the Communists. On a continent racked by civil strife, the Communist record has been one of remarkable quiescence'.[63]

Explaining this paradox, Halperin pointed to, amongst other things, the inappositeness of both its organizational principles and its concept of revolution in the Latin American context. 'Democratic centralism' held little attraction for people more used to giving their loyalty to an individual or a family than an organization representing an abstract principle, while the concept of revolution by the organized working class had little relevance among workers not amenable to political organization or particularly interested in contributing to revolutionary change. In any case, many Communists had concluded that any attempt to overthrow the political system would invite a counter-revolutionary strike by the USA, which the Soviet Union, thousands of miles distant and preoccupied with matters much closer to home, would be powerless to prevent. Despairing of the possibility of imminent revolution, many Communist parties had settled for the normal give-and-take of Latin American politics, entering into governments, as in Chile in 1938, in 1946, and again in 1970, but more often degenerating 'into small machines run by professional politicians who hire out their services to dictators and democrats alike in return for petty concessions'.

Significantly, Latin America's first Communist-ruled state, Cuba, emerged from neither a Communist-organized revolution nor any initiative by the country's working class. In fact, the Communists had tended to support the Cuban dictator, Fulgencio Batista, and had opposed Fidel Castro's six-year insurrection until shortly before his victory in January 1959. For, this was essentially a nationalist rebellion of young intellectuals against US influence and enterprise, which they saw as largely responsible for the inequalities, extensive poverty and corruption in Cuba and throughout Latin America and the Caribbean.[64] And it was not so much Marxism as the Latin American populist and anti-colonial tradition, combined with Washington's denial of credit to his new regime, that led Castro to seize and nationalize American assets in Cuba soon after taking power. But, though Washington's economic and military counter-moves drove Castro further to the Communist Left, neither Cuba's Communists nor their Soviet patrons were prepared to accept Castro's Marxist–Leninist credentials when he first produced them in 1961. So far as Moscow was concerned, Castro's Cuba was no more than a 'national democracy' – a stage well short of Socialism, and it dismissed Castro's claim to be worthy of admission to the Communist 'club' when the country's Communists were not even in charge. However, the CIA's abortive Bay of Pigs invasion in April altered perceptions in both Havana and Moscow. Desperate for a long-term commitment from the Kremlin, Castro merged his revolutionary movement with the existing Communist organization, and Moscow obligingly stepped up economic and military assistance.

In little over a year, however, relations between Moscow and Havana were thrown into confusion as a consequence of the Kremlin's handling of the missile crisis, and remained tense for some considerable time.[65] In the first place, their priorities were different. With no guarantee that his republic would fare any better than, say, the Hungarian Soviet of 1919, Castro's priority was to promote revolution throughout Latin America and beyond. He aimed to radicalize the Communist parties, aid non-Communist guerrilla movements, and encourage other governments to follow Cuba's example in rejecting the structural pattern of American dominance and Latin American dependency.

Moscow, on the other hand, was increasingly concerned with the problems of coexistence and of parity of esteem with Washington, whilst seeking simultaneously to outflank the political and ideological pretensions of Peking. It saw Havana's efforts to spread revolution and create revolutionary institutions, such as the Organization for Latin American Solidarity in 1967, as a waste of resources and a threat both to Cuba's economic development and to Moscow's interests in the region.[66] Moreover, they only created fresh divisions in the already fragmented Latin American Left between the more pragmatic Moscow-orientated Communist parties, the more activist Maoist parties and the violence-prone Castroite groups. Worse still, from Moscow's viewpoint, was the fact that, though Havana had had a number of well-publicized rows with Peking, notably over trade, it was in sympathy with the radical egalitarianism and guerrilla style of politics associated with Mao. Like Peking, moreover, Castro was critical of Moscow's ultra-caution regarding the Middle East and Indochina, contemptuous of the test-ban treaty and other examples of superpower accord, and scathing in his condemnation of 'certain Socialist countries' which furnish credits to 'oligarchical governments' in Latin America.[67]

Another major source of contention between Moscow and Havana concerned their different theories of revolution. Castro, his close comrade-in-arms, Ernesto 'Che' Guevara, and the French intellectual, Regis Debray, held that in the developing countries, traditional Marxist notions of class-consciousness and of revolutionary situations were largely irrelevant. In their view, revolutions could be sparked off by a handful of dedicated guerrillas in the countryside (as in the Sierra Maestra mountains to which Castro and 11 fellow revolutionaries had retreated in December 1956), who would secure arms as a result of a few well-planned confrontations with enemy troops, while a campaign of sabotage, terrorism, and strikes in the cities helped to demoralize the government. The key was what Debray called the *foco*[68] – a Red base established at strategic points in countryside, city or even university so as to disrupt the smooth functioning of the political and economic system. Of necessity, the revolution had to be violent – a view increasingly at variance with Moscow and those Communist parties under Kremlin influence.

A further major divisive factor lay in Castro's attitude to party organization. A late convert to the idea of a vanguard party, he continued to see it as a development of the guerrilla *foco*, giving the Cuban Party an idiosyncratic quality, largely dependent on his personality, leadership and machismo. Even after the merger with the Communists, his party, like the political system it was supposed to serve, was not so much '*communista*' as '*Fidelista*'.[69] He made sure that his revolutionary comrades controlled the 'old guard' Communists and not vice versa, having the doctrinaire Communist, Anibal Escalante, exiled to eastern Europe, and, in 1968, jailing some 30 veteran Communists for up to 15 years for 'subversion'. At the same time, by minimizing the number of even nominally elective offices in party or government, and by eventually, combining the posts of head of state, head of government, and commander-in-chief of the revolutionary armed forces, as well as party leader, he has been able to ensure that the party continues to reflect and endorse his views, even if he has had a tendency to change tack after the late '60s.

Amongst other things, Cuba is no longer the revolutionary beacon it once was. At one time more akin to Mao's decentralized economic structure than to the Soviet model, the country is now more centralized, bureaucratized, and regimented than the Soviet Union or, even, China. Moreover, ever since declaring the Soviet-led intervention in Czechoslovakia a 'regrettable necessity' (a standpoint possibly not unconnected with Moscow's recent imposition of limited economic sanctions against Havana), Castro has curbed his revolutionary actions abroad, repudiating many of his earlier ideas as 'superleftist'. In the process, Havana's foreign policy has increasingly resembled the Kremlin's, its spokesmen making the requisite attacks on Moscow's enemies of the day and canvassing support for Soviet policy among the nonaligned, while the Latin American revolutionary parties Castro once supported are left largely to their own devices.[70]

In part, such changes in policy stem from Castro's perception of the situation in which his country finds itself. From being an isolated outpost of Socialism in a hostile continent, Cuba has acquired a host of political and economic links, not only with the Communist countries, but also with the West and in Latin America, despite Washington's continued hostility. As a consequence, therefore, Havana's need to spread the revolutionary idea seems less pressing than before. Moreover, many of Castro's earlier revolutionary conceptions turned out to be misplaced and were no longer sustainable. For example, the guerrilla tactics that had worked in Cuba were not applicable to other Latin American countries,[71] where the security forces were more resolute and formidable, the social inhibitions to change in the rural areas more powerful, and the physical geography uncongenial to the establishment of guerrilla bases – as Guevara discovered in his fatal expedition to Bolivia in 1967. Within Cuba itself, reliance on moral incentives had failed to produce the requisite economic advance, as had the various experiments in forced industrialization, and the government was forced willy-nilly to a degree of 'deradicalization'. But perhaps the most critical factor in Castro's domestic change of course has been his country's desperate economic plight, beset as it is with soaring debts and plunging economic growth rates. To a degree, such unfavourable circumstances were bound to make the country somewhat more receptive to the wishes of its patrons and creditors.

It would, however, be wrong to see Cuba as a mere client of Moscow. For despite Havana's membership of CMEA and reliance on Soviet and eastern European credit, Castro remains his own boss. His success in diversifying Cuba's diplomatic and trade links serves to lessen its dependence on the Soviet bloc, whilst his country's high-profile strategy in Africa on the dissolution of the Portuguese empire, and the establishment of 'Socialist' rule in Ethiopia in the mid-70's has helped boost the country's self-esteem. For, though Moscow encouraged and helped finance many of Cuba's activities on the continent, where it was to have up to 50,000 troops and technicians, Havana needed little prompting.[72] After all, Castro's revolutionary programme had always embraced Africa as well as Latin America. African revolution had been on the agenda at the Tricontinental Conference hosted by Havana in 1966, while the PAIGC guerrillas of Guinea-Bissau and the MPLA of Angola had enjoyed Cuban support well before they took power.

In any case, Spanish-speaking and many of African descent, the Cubans had an especial affinity with Portuguese speakers from countries like Guinea-Bissau and Angola, from which many of their ancestors had been taken as slaves. In fact, Havana's revolutionary nationalism was as well served by success in Africa as in Latin America. In this sense, the Cubans arrived in Africa primarily to fulfill their own mission,

228 The Decline of International Communism

and even if their appearance was at the behest of Moscow, Havana would stand its ground in the event of a conflict over priorities. The same, of course, has held true of the Cuban presence in other countries of Socialist orientation such as South Yemen, Chile during the Allende regime of 1970–3, Nicaragua, and Grenada, prior to the US 'rescue operation' in 1983.[73]

If nationalism affected all 16 countries under Communist rule, it could scarcely have had a lesser effect on the 20 or more Third World countries of Socialist orientation, since most owed their independence to a protracted liberation struggle.[74] For many, however, the problem was one of nation-building rather than the projection of an existing national identity, and the remedy was not always conducive to Soviet interests. Firstly, in a world of competing Communist-ruled states, there was no guarantee that a Socialist orientation would mean a pro-Soviet orientation. In any case, though these countries were pledged to central planning, nationalization, land reform, nonalignment, and rule by a vanguard (even if not proletarian) party, their devotion to the socialist cause was often superficial and opportunistic. In states such as Somalia, Ethiopia, South Yemen, and Angola, a Socialist orientation had been adopted, according to Bogdan Sjaikowski, 'almost overnight in return for military hardware and economic survival kits'. In Benin and the Congo, it was 'rather abruptly embraced by military governments' to legitimize their rule.[75]

But, of course, if a political mantle could be so readily assumed, it could also just as easily be jettisoned, as it was by Somalia in 1978, when Moscow and Havana refused to support its attack on Ethiopia's Ogaden region. Moreover, given the political volatility of such states, they were frequently an embarrassment to Moscow, especially when Marxist–Leninists fought other Marxist–Leninists in the cause of 'national liberation', as in Ethiopia, or in an attempted coup, as in Grenada and South Yemen. Finally, since many of the 'states of Socialist orientation' were among the world's poorest, they were constantly making economic demands their Soviet and eastern European patrons could no longer satisfy, and having to turn to the West in consequence.

The ruling parties' increasing preoccupation with national concerns prompts the question as to how far the 'internationalist' pretensions of the non-ruling parties represent a genuine commitment to the Marxist notion of 'class solidarity' and how far they are but a one-sided bid for aid. In most such parties, there used to be an intellectual core of university-trained radicals whose belief in the revolutionary potential of the world's proletarian masses was perhaps the stronger for their not being themselves of working class origin. Generally fluent in languages and at ease with people of other nationalities with similar political aspirations, some were such passionate 'internationalists' as to be ready to sacrifice liberty and even life in the service of the 'world struggle against imperialism'. From their ranks, moreover, were drawn the core of those international movements primed for sabotage, hostage-taking and the killing of innocents for the sake of the cause.

On the other hand, as Peking and Havana, like Moscow, lost their revolutionary élan and many of the world's Communist parties traded in their radical prospectus for a legal existence, the zealots tended to forsake the Communist movement for more revolutionarily inclined groups – often Trotskyite in inspiration – where their preoccupation with 'internationalism' seemed more relevant. At the other end of the spectrum, there remain those whose 'internationalism' is very much a relic of the past – a linguistic and conceptual residue of a theory and organizational principle to which they once fully subscribed. Between the visionary and the indifferent, are those for whom 'internationalism' has at least a metaphorical significance as part of an ideological package they find more satisfying than any alternative. And, when that 'internationalism' takes the form of practical assistance from a Moscow, Peking, Havana or Hanoi to a Communist organization in an oppressive environment, the concept naturally retains its appeal.

It remains, nonetheless, true that nowadays Communist parties are inclined to recruit support on the basis not of their residual international associations, but of concrete programmes for tackling problems arising out of specific national situations. The effect, of course, is to produce greater variegation and diversity within the movement. For example, though the parties forming the core of what, since 1975, has been known as 'Eurocommunism' have apparently been in accord on broad principles, they have been at odds on matters of practical policy, while their areas of agreement have been largely at Moscow's expense.[76] The Italian party has supported western European integration and NATO membership, the French opposing both in the name of national sovereignty, and the Spanish pro-EEC and anti-NATO. Rhetorically, the 'Eurocommunists' retain their commitment to a socialist world (how could it be otherwise?), but have been as resistant to regional as to centralized Communist organization, and take a gradualist, polycentric approach – socialism on the basis of consensus. To a degree they already practise cooperation with the non-Communist Left, and encourage tendencies to greater pluralism, tolerance and diversity in the Soviet Union and eastern Europe.

Since the 'Eurocommunist' parties have played the democratic 'game' before, as did the eastern European parties prior to Communist rule, and still tend to be organized on the basis of 'democratic centralism', some western commentators remain sceptical of their 'democratic' credentials. They believe these to be mere stratagems for obtaining and holding power. Yet, since in France, Italy, Finland, and elsewhere Communists, in accordance with democratic procedures, have vacated central or local government positions they once held, there would appear to be little warrant for the claim that the Communists aim to seize power. Equally difficult to sustain is the suggestion that they coordinate their strategies with Moscow. After all, until Gorbachev introduced *glasnost* and *perestroika* to the USSR, most were highly critical of the Kremlin's internal and external policies following the invasion of Czechoslovakia in 1968, rejected Moscow's attempts to revitalize the concept of 'proletarian internationalism', with its overtones of Soviet hegemony, and proclaimed themselves in favour of a new concept of 'internationalism', defined by an Italian Central Committee member as 'the need for new relations based on recognition of the autonomy and equality of each party'.[77] In effect, a call for the institutionalization of diversity, the 'new internationalism' would seek to legitimate, in Bernard Morris's words,

> a situation in which the individual party was inviolate and assured of the right to define its own brand of Socialism; to participate in whatever capitalist enterprises it chose; to collaborate with whatever domestic or foreign groups, movements, parties or governments it liked; to criticize other Communists, including the Soviet Union, its internal policies, its policies towards other Socialist countries, as well as its foreign policies generally.[78]

But if this is what the 'Eurocommunists' mean by the 'new internationalism', it is difficult to see what remains of the original Communist commitment to a shared ideology, authority structure and organization. As the demand for a 'new internationalism' is taken up by many parties throughout the Communist world, the party could conceivably be reduced to little more than a repository for articulating a broad spectrum of largely national discontents. And whilst this might increase its attractiveness nationally it would do little to reinvigorate or even sustain the concept of 'international fraternity'.

NOTES

1. *The Marxian Revolutionary Idea* (London, 1970), ch. 6.
2. *Eurocommunism and Socialism* (London, 1978), p. 45.
3. For an analysis of the changing connotations of the term, see M. Light, *The Soviet Theory of International Relations* (New York, 1988), pp. 145–65 and 179–204.

4. See, for example, Roy Medvedev, *On Stalin and Stalinism* (Oxford, 1979).
5. Cited in H. Gordon Skilling, *Communism National and International* (Toronto, 1964), p. 5.
6. See, for example, John C. Campbell, *Tito's Separate Road* (New York, 1967), esp. ch. 8–9.
7. N. Bethell, *Gomułka* (London, 1972), ch. 15.
8. The course of that relationship is traced in Geoffrey Stern, 'Chinese–Albanian Relations: The End of an Affair?' *Millennium: Journal of International Studies*, Vol. 6, No. 3 (Winter 1977–8), pp. 270–4.
9. On East Germany, see J. Steele, *Socialism with a German Face* (London, 1977), esp. ch. 6.
10. On Romania, see J. Hale, *Ceauşescu's Rumania* (London, 1971).
11. On Bulgaria, see J. F. Brown, *Bulgaria under Communist Rule* (London, 1970).
12. See W. F. Robinson, *The Pattern of Reform in Hungary: A Political, Economic, and Cultural Analysis* (New York, 1973).
13. On Czechoslovakia, see P. Tigrid, *Why Dubček Fell* (London, 1971) and R. R. James (ed.), *The Czechoslovak Crisis 1968* (Brighton, 1969). For documents relating to the 'Prague Spring', see *Dubček's Blueprint for Freedom* (London, 1969).
14. An official Czech translation of the Programme is to be found in Paul Ello, *Czechoslovakia's Blueprint for Freedom* (Washington, 1968).
15. Z. Mlynar, *Nightfrost in Prague* (New York, 1980).
16. C. Harman, *Bureaucracy and Revolution in Eastern Europe* (London, 1974), pp. 208–10, 228–33, and 239–41.
17. See P. R. Prifti, 'Albania's expanding Horizons', *Problems of Communism* Vol. 21, No. 1 (January–February 1972), pp. 30–9.
18. See Aurel Brown, *Romanian Foreign Policy since 1965: The Political and Military Limits of Autonomy* (New York, 1978).
19. See Leo Mates, *Nonalignment: Theory and Current Policy* (New York, 1972).
20. See V. Wozniak, *From Crisis to Crisis: Soviet–Polish Relations in the 1970s* (Iowa, 1987), ch. 2.
21. R. Tokes, 'Hungarian Reform Imperatives', *Problems of Communism* Vol. 33, No. 5 (September–October 1984), pp. 1–23.
22. K. Dawisha, *Eastern Europe, Gorbachev and Reform* (Cambridge, 1988), pp. 37–44.
23. 'Gorbachev and Eastern Europe', *Problems of Communism*, Vol. 35, No. 1 (January–February 1986), p. 51.
24. See Peter Marsh, 'Foreign Policy Making in the German Democratic Republic' in H. Adomeit and R. Boardman (eds.), *Foreign Policy Making in Communist Countries* (Farnborough, 1979), pp. 91–3.
25. Ibid., pp. 94–106.
26. See James McAdams, 'The New Logic in Soviet–GDR Relations', *Problems of Communism* Vol. 37, No. 5 (September–October 1988), pp. 47–60.
27. For a useful review of eastern European developments, see N. Ascherson *et al.*, 'A Spectre Haunts the East', *Marxism Today* (February 1988), 22–9.
28. See J. F. Brown *et al.*, 'East–West Relations and Eastern Europe', in *Problems of Communism* Vol. 37, Nos. 3–4 (May–August 1988), pp. 55–70.
29. See Dawisha, pp. 86–99.
30. 'Eastern Europe Economic Slowdown', *Problems of Communism* Vol. 31, No. 4 (July–August 1982), pp. 1–19.
31. See, for example, M. Goldman, 'Is there a Russian Energy Crisis?' *Atlantic Monthly* Vol. 246, No. 3 (September 1980), pp. 55–69.
32. The difficulties of CMEA integration are outlined in Z. M. Fallenbuchl, 'Comecon Integration', *Problems of Communism* Vol. 22, No. 2 (March–April 1973), pp. 25–39.
33. See I. Oldberg (ed.), *Unity and Conflict in the Warsaw Pact* (Stockholm, 1984).
34. Dawisha, pp. 80–6.

35. 'The Soviet Union and the Warsaw Pact' in G. Schopflin (ed.), *The Soviet Union and Eastern Europe* (London, 1986), p. 227.
36. See, for example, D. Herspring, 'The Warsaw Pact at Twenty-five', Vol. 29, No. 5, *Problems of Communism*, (September–October 1980), pp. 1–15.
37. Ibid.
38. Neal Ascherson, *The Polish August* (London, 1981), esp. ch. 6.
39. See E. Gasparini, 'East–South Economic Relations', *NATO Review* Vol. 35, No. 4 (August 1987), pp. 24–32.
40. See Y. Akhapkin (ed.), *First Decrees of Soviet Power* (London, 1970), pp. 31–2.
41. See R. Scalapino, 'Patterns of Asian Communism', *Problems of Communism*, Vol. 20, Nos. 1–2 (January–April 1971), pp. 2–13.
42. Ibid., p. 4.
43. See W. A. Brown and U. Onon, *History of the Mongolian People's Republic* (Cambridge, Mass., 1976).
44. See Margie Lindsey 'Mongolia likely to sign transit deal with Peking', *Financial Times* (1 November 1988).
45. Dae-Sook Suh, *The Korean Communist Movement 1918–48* (Princeton, 1967).
46. I. J. Kim, *Communist Politics in North Korea* (New York, 1975).
47. R. A. Scalapino, 'Current Dynamics of the Korean Peninsula', *Problems of Communism* Vol. 30, No. 6 (November–December 1981), pp. 16–31.
48. Ibid. See also Bruce Cummings, 'Kim's Korean Communism', *Problems of Communism* Vol. 23, No. 2 (March–April 1974), pp. 27–41.
49. See J. Lacouture, *Ho Chi Minh* (London, 1969).
50. Arthur Schlesinger Jr, *The Bitter Heritage* (London, 1967), p. 21.
51. See J. M. Mackintosh, *The Strategy and Tactics of Soviet Foreign Policy* (Oxford, 1962), p. 53.
52. See G. Kahin and J. W. Lewis, *The United States in Vietnam* (New York, 1969).
53. Ellen Hammer, 'Communist but Nonaligned' in *Problems of Communism* Vol. 25, No. 3, (May–June 1976), pp. 1–17.
54. 'New Conflict in Indochina', *Problems of Communism*, Vol. 27, No. 5 (September–October 1978), p. 22.
55. F. Ponchaurd, *Cambodia Year Zero* (London, 1978).
56. D. Tretiak, 'China's Vietnam War and its Consequences', *China Quarterly* Vol. 38, No. 4 (December 1979).
57. *A History of the Modern World* (London, 1983), p. 657.
58. See L. Dupree, 'Afghanistan under the Khalq', *Problems of Communism* Vol. 28, No. 4 (July–August 1979), pp. 34–50.
59. Ibid., p. 40.
60. J. Steele, *The Limits of Soviet Power* (London, 1985), ch. 7.
61. Geoffrey Stern, 'The Soviet Union, Afghanistan and East–West Relations', *Millennium* Vol. 9, No. 2 (Autumn 1980), pp. 135–46.
62. See, for example, Angus Roxburgh *et al.*, 'End Game: Why the Soviets are pulling out of Afghanistan', *The Sunday Times* (10 April 1988).
63. 'Latin America', *Survey* No. 54 (January 1965), p. 154.
64. D. McLellan, *The Marxist Legacy* (London, 1983), p. 143–5.
65. P. Shearman, *The Soviet Union and Cuba* (London, 1987), pp. 11–14.
66. Ibid., pp. 15–20.
67. Cited in Paul Sigmund, 'Marxism in Latin America' in Charles Elliott and Carl Linden (eds.), *Marxism in the Contemporary West* (Boulder, Colorado, 1980), p. 24.
68. See his *Revolution in the Revolution?* (London, 1968).
69. See John Carlin, 'Thirty Years of Fidelity to the Revolution', *Independent* (30 December 1988).
70. See E. Gonzales, 'Cuban Foreign Policy', *Problems of Communism* Vol. 26, No. 6 (November–December 1977), pp. 1–15.
71. See J. Pimlott (ed.), *Guerrilla Warfare* (London, 1985), pp. 104–19.

72. Shearman, pp. 33–56.
73. Ibid., pp. 57–75.
74. See B. Szaijkowski, *The Establishment of Marxist Regimes* (London, 1982), especially ch. 6–7.
75. Ibid., p. 2.
76. See B. Morris, *Communism, Revolution, and American Policy* (Durham, 1987), ch. 5.
77. Cited in ibid., p. 90.
78. Ibid., p. 91.

12.   Communism and Capitalism: the Correlation of Forces

The glaring contradiction between the internationalism of Communist theory and the nationalism of Communist practice has posed serious problems for Moscow. After all, the Soviet regime's very legitimacy had originally rested on the twin claim that the sociopolitical interests of the working class world-wide were virtually identical and that the Soviet Union and the Communist movement, unlike the forces of the Second International, articulated and advanced those interests. Accordingly, the salient contradictions were within the capitalist system and between the defenders of capitalism and the nascent forces of socialism. That the true (i.e. Marxist–Leninist) defenders of the working class might be seriously at odds with one another defied Moscow's basic ideological and political assumptions, while the all too public airing of differences somewhat undermined the Soviet claim, much vaunted in the '70s, that the 'correlation of forces'[1] – the global balance of political, economic, and social, as well as military power – was shifting in the direction of socialism. Moscow's efforts to contain national Communism in such countries as Yugoslavia, Hungary, China and Czechoslovakia have been detailed earlier in the volume. What of the Kremlin's attempts to conceal the extent of 'polycentrism'?

When Khrushchev wound up the Cominform in 1956, largely in deference to Tito who had had such bitter memories of the organization, he hoped to find some alternative means of coordinating Communist action and projecting an image of Communist unity. Two solutions immediately offered themselves – the publication of a theoretical journal to be circulated among the world's Communist parties, in the appropriate languages, along the lines of the Comintern and Cominform journals, and the convening of periodic international conferences of Communist parties. Of the two, the former was easier to achieve than the latter since, with the recent demise of the Cominform journal, there was a ready fund of specialists skilled in conveying the Soviet propaganda line of the day waiting to be tapped. From 1958, indeed, *Problems of Peace and Socialism (World Marxist Review* in its English-language edition) was able to carry on where its predecessor had left off, enthusing about the steady progress to socialism and excoriating those, like the Maoists or Eurocommunists, who, in the Kremlin's view, undermined the process.

Convening international Communist conferences was much more problematic, in that there was no guarantee that the recipients would accept Moscow's invitation, or toe the Soviet line if they did. Moreover, whereas unsold copies of *Problems of Peace and Socialism* would hardly reflect adversely on the world movement, the presence or absence from Communist gatherings of dissident parties would be a much more public gauge of the cohesion of the Communist body politic. In the event, the brief history of the Communist 'congress system' was something of a mixed blessing for the Kremlin.[2]

In fact, the first such conference – in Moscow, in November 1957 – was the least difficult to convene. After all, Communist parties like to celebrate revolutionary anniversaries, and an international gathering to commemorate the 40th anniversary of the Bolshevik Revolution was too good for most of them to miss. In any case, Sino-Soviet differences had not yet become acrimonious, and the Chinese were as interested as the Russians in trying to find a formula for Communist unity after the upheavals of the previous year. In addition, there was a widespread perception that the movement needed an authoritative and generally agreed statement defining, among other things, the status of the CPSU, the principles of inter-Communist relations, and the parameters of political and ideological diversity.

In the event, when the 13 ruling parties, out of the 64 attending the commemorations, went into conclave, they reaffirmed the Soviet Party's leading role, but in terms stressing the historical precedence of the Russian Revolution and the primacy of Soviet power and Socialist achievement, rather than Moscow's right of control. In effect, no party was to enjoy such a right since inter-Communist relations were to be based on the principles of 'Socialist internationalism', defined in the declaration of the 1957 conference as: 'complete equality, respect for territorial integrity and state independence and sovereignty, and non-interference in one another's affairs'. It added: 'Fraternal mutual aid is an integral part of these relations'.[3] On the other hand, in identifying 'revisionism' as the main danger, the signatories had purchased a semblance of unity at the cost of an infusion of 'Maoism' and the renewed exclusion of Tito's Yugoslavia which, alone of the 13 delegations to the conference, refused to endorse the statement.[4]

If the Soviet leaders thought that international Communist cohesion might be secured by such a formula, they will have been sadly disappointed. For the final declaration was a recipe not for an accommodation of differences, but for their exacerbation, as the Yugoslavs felt aggrieved by their second virtual excommunication, and the Soviets began to feel that the price of an accord with China was too dangerously high. In any case, the conference had created no machinery for implementing its recommendations, and soon the signatories of the declaration were bitterly divided as to its implications.

Yet, despite the evident discord between the two Communist giants and the knock-on effects throughout the movement of their widening rift, the aspiration for worldwide unity remained, and there was a record turnout in Moscow for the second (and more comprehensive) international Communist conference, three years after the first. Altogether 81 of the 87 parties in existence in November 1960, turned up for what many took to be Communism's last chance of an agreed platform, and though it succeeded in producing an agreed text, resembling its predecessor save that it was some three times as long, its significance was immediately nullified by the polemical exchanges during and after the deliberations.[5] Once again, conflicting interpretations of a compromise document merely added to the acrimony, and, the conference having rejected a Soviet proposal to establish an international secretariat, there was no authoritative body to resolve the confusion.

For the next few years, no amount of rhetoric could conceal the extent of the decomposition of the Communist movement. For 'Communism' now encompassed several competing currents of thought – Maoism and Castroism to the left of Soviet 'orthodoxy'; Titoism and the 'polycentric' formulations of the Italian Communist Party to Moscow's right. Moreover, each contending school would try to poach members from the others, Peking encouraging young Bulgarians, East Germans, Hungarians and Poles to switch allegiance to Mao; Moscow, trying to persuade officers in the Chinese and Albanian armed forces to maintain their commitment to the CPSU.[6]

Meanwhile, incompatible differences among Communists in Belgium, Italy, Switzerland, India, Australia, Brazil, Mexico, and elsewhere were leading to the existence in those countries of two or more parties, each looking to a different Communist capital for inspiration. And, at least one of these capitals was playing host to Communist dissidents from abroad, and giving them facilities for setting up party organizations of their own. From Tirana, for example, a 'refugee' from Warsaw, K. Mijal, ran a miniscule Polish Communist Party-in-exile with an idiosyncratic programme which would have appealed to Stalin:

> As Marxists, we advocate equal rights for all nationalities. But this does not mean that particular privileges should be given to any national minority.

Even less can we tolerate the appearance in Poland of a Zionist, Trotskyite group of Jewish nationalists who use the concept of equal rights as a cover for their aspirations to establish Jewish domination over 30 million Poles . . . The Poznań riots of 1956 and the October counter-revolution were started and organized by these people, who concluded an alliance with the right-wing nationalist deviationists led by Gomułka.[7]

By early 1964, after the failure of a final, albeit half-hearted effort at reconciliation with his eastern neighbour, Khrushchev, despairing of achieving even a semblance of worldwide Communist unity, was contemplating another conference of the parties – this time to pro-nounce anathema on the CCP. Having recently placated Belgrade, to the evident pleasure of the PCI and the more 'revisionist' parties, he believed he could unite all but a handful of the world's Communist parties on an anti-Chinese platform. In fact, the opposition was greater than he had anticipated, and came not just from China and its allies, but from European parties not normally sympathetic to Peking. In April, the Romanian party stated its objections in no uncertain terms. 'No party has or can have a privileged place, or can impose its line and opinions on other parties. . . . Let all of us unite to bar the road to a split'.[8]

In August, the Italian party leader, Palmiro Togliatti, in what was effectively a valedictory 'memorandum' to the CPSU, warned of the dangers of 'an open schism in the movement, with the formation of an international Chinese centre which would create its "sections" in all countries'. And he went on to commend to the Soviet leader his concept of 'polycentrism'. 'One must caution oneself against forced, exterior uniformity and one must consider that unity ought to be established and maintained in conditions of diversity and full autonomy.'[9] Whether such observations would have dissuaded Khrushchev from proceeding with his proposed conference is unclear since he fell from power before a preparatory meeting he had scheduled for December could convene.

The new Soviet leadership under Leonid Brezhnev refused to drop the idea altogether, but retreated from the campaign to settle scores with China, changing Khrushchev's 'preparatory meeting' into a 'con-sultative meeting' to discuss 'ways for overcoming disagreements and strengthening the solidarity of the world Communist movement'.[10] Despite these less controversial objectives, seven parties out of 26 – the Chinese, Japanese, Korean, Vietnamese, Indonesian, Albanian, and Romanian – refused Moscow's invitation for 'consultations' in March 1965, while an eighth – the American – would send only observers.[11] The disappointing turnout and the less than weighty delib-erations notwithstanding, Moscow evidently thought the effort suf-

ficiently worthwhile to continue to press for yet another world conference. In June 1969, after a critical year for world Communism, which
saw the Soviet-led intervention in Czechoslovakia and the skirmishes
on the Sino-Soviet frontier, the Soviet Union got the conference it had
been trying to arrange for nearly a decade, and though China, North
Vietnam, North Korea, Albania and Yugoslavia stayed away and Cuba
sent only an observer, Moscow gambled on a sizeable attendance and
got it.[12]

On the other hand, though Moscow was able to attract 74 delegations
from abroad, it could no longer count on either overwhelming support
or the silence of its critics. For, the invasion of Czechoslovakia had lost
Moscow the deference of some of its most ardent former supporters,
and they were no longer afraid to speak their minds. While Soviet and
pro-Soviet speakers excoriated both the western 'imperialists' and the
Chinese leadership, others denounced the suppression of the 'Prague
Spring' and the 'Brezhnev doctrine', insisting that their speeches be
reported fairly in the Soviet media.

Moreover, far from healing the principal divisions in the Communist
movement, the conference merely confirmed them, with delegates
expressing widely divergent views on such issues as the nature of Socialist democracy, the national liberation struggle and the prospects of
revolution, the 'correct' attitude to the non-Communist world, the basis
of inter-party relations, and the role of the CPSU. And, though Moscow
was forced to include in the final declaration the clause, 'There is no
leading centre in the international Communist movement', and to omit
almost all reference to Peking or Prague, the terms were still sufficiently
controversial to be rejected, in whole or in part, by 17 of the 75
delegations.[13] Thus, far from effecting the endorsement of policy that
Moscow had been seeking, the conference merely produced an agreement to disagree and what Kevin Devlin has called the 'institutionalization of diversity'[14] in international Communism.

Though Moscow's enthusiasm for world Communist conferences
understandably diminished after 1969, it did not entirely abandon the
conference idea, and in the early '70s began steps to convene a pan-
European Communist conference to try to nip Eurocommunism in the
bud. After much procedural wrangling and delay, the conference finally
met in East Berlin, in June 1976, attended by every European party
save for the Albanian and Icelandic.[15] It was a watershed in Communist
history as the Kremlin's attempt to reimpose a measure of orthodoxy
completely backfired. For, the advocates of polycentrism, many with
an eye on their domestic electorates, were even more vocal than in
1969. Not only did they reject Soviet attempts to revitalize the concept

of 'proletarian internationalism', which implied a Soviet-imposed strategy for all parties, they also openly questioned the legitimacy of Soviet authority, the propriety of its international direction and the adequacy of its socialist model.[16]

It was a challenge, moreover, reflected in the conference's final document, arrived at, for the first time in such a gathering, by consensus after a free exchange of views.[17] Thus, 'proletarian internationalism' was replaced by the notion of 'voluntary cooperation and solidarity' based on the 'principles of sovereign equality and sovereign independence of each party, noninterference in internal affairs, [and] respect for free choice of different roads in the struggle for social change'. And the document insisted on the right of a people to 'choose to develop its political, economic, social, and legal system independently and without outside interference, and to protect . . . its historical and cultural heritage'. And, in a complete break with past practice, it claimed that individual opposition to the policies of particular Communist parties should no longer be construed as necessarily 'anti-Communist' in character. Not surprisingly, the commentators tended to see the conference as a major defeat for Moscow and the final vindication of the PCI's long-held stand that 'an international Communist body does not and cannot exist in any form'.[18]

Yet, though the Kremlin had manifestly failed to contain or conceal the extent of the disarray, it, nonetheless, managed to convince both itself and its enemies that international Communism was still a viable, even dynamic force. For one thing, Marxist–Leninism seemed to be gaining new adherents in the Third World. The withdrawal of British troops from east of Suez; the failure of American policy in Vietnam; the coups in Somalia, Dahomey, and Ethiopia, and the Portuguese decision to quit Africa had created the conditions for establishing new 'countries of Socialist orientation' in the Middle East, Indochina, and Africa. By the end of the '70s, Afghanistan, Grenada, and Nicaragua could be added to the list.

Moreover, if there were splits and divisions within the Communist movement, the Western powers seemed, if anything, in even greater confusion. All were to a greater or lesser degree suffering economic recession in the wake of the quadrupling of the price of oil, and as trade, profit margins, and real wages tumbled, and the number of new bankrupts helped to swell the burgeoning ranks of the unemployed, there were divided counsels as to how to respond. Domestically, as the verbal hostilities between the neo-Keynesians, arguing for greater government spending, and the Friedmanite monetarists, calling for a reduction of state control, intensified, countries such as Portugal, Spain,

France and Italy found themselves facing, in addition, a Communist electoral challenge not seen since the 'hungry thirties'.[19] At the same time, in foreign policy, an increasing chasm was opening up between the USA and its European partners in their divergent reactions to the Middle Eastern war of 1973 and the subsequent use by the Arab states of the oil 'weapon'. Further rifts in the NATO alliance occurred in 1974 as the Turkish intervention in Cyprus, following a Greek-led coup, brought Ankara and Athens to the brink of war; and there followed a succession of mini-'wars' – over agricultural tariffs, fisheries, wine, lamb and British budgetary contributions – sapping the cohesion and vitality of the European Economic Community.

If these factors were not sufficient to clinch the argument that the 'correlation of forces' was moving in the direction of Socialism, a further consideration, arising from more conventional balance of power calculations, appeared more decisive – the phenomenal growth of the Soviet military arm on land, at sea, and in the air. Even allowing for the western tendency to exaggerate the military capability of Moscow and its allies, the erosion or loss of western military superiority during the '70s was undeniable.[20] For example, each of the Soviet Union's four fleets had benefited from a great leap forward in naval construction, so that what had been a mere coastal defence fleet in the early '60s had been transformed, within a decade and a half, into a long-range armada. And, though the western powers were developing Cruise, Pershing, Trident and Minuteman throughout the '70s, the Soviets were deploying missiles both larger and heavier than those of the USA and 'MIRVing' them, i.e. equipping them with multiple warheads, independently targeted. Of especial concern to the western Europeans were the Soviet SS20s – medium-range missiles deployed in western USSR, each possessing three warheads and a speed of over 400 miles a minute, which seemed to put most European capitals within range.

Meanwhile, as the Soviet armoury had become more sophisticated, the Soviet military presence had become far more extended and visible. Its military actions in Czechoslovakia and Afghanistan, and the assistance afforded the Communists in Vietnam, had enabled Moscow to maintain a military presence in all three countries. In Africa, it had several thousand combat troops and advisers to supplement the growing Cuban and/or East German presence in Ethiopia, Angola, Guinea-Bissau, and elsewhere: in the Middle East it was developing the port of Aden in South Yemen, while its military specialists were to be found as far afield as Libya, Syria and Iraq. In Central America and the Caribbean, it had military personnel in Nicaragua as well as in Cuba, while Soviet arms were helping to bolster governments as well as opposition forces throughout the length and breadth of the Third World.

On the other hand, no matter how confident the pronouncements from Moscow, none of the apparent indicators of a shift in the global 'correlation of forces' had any firm foundation. There could be no certainty that generous assistance to a non-Communist Third World country would eventually bring it to Soviet-style Socialism. And, while the burden of supporting impoverished and war-torn countries like Vietnam, Ethiopia, Angola, Mozambique and Afghanistan was going to be colossal, the Kremlin had no guarantee, given the volatility of Third World politics, that lavish grants to such countries would ultimately serve the cause any better than its massive subsidies to such non-Marxist–Leninist states as Indonesia and Egypt. Certainly, it could not assume that the Socialist orientation of a country would prove any more compatible with Soviet policy than had that of, say, China or Albania. And, of course, there was no assurance that the Socialist orientation would itself be maintained.

As it happens, the drain on the Soviet exchequer of assisting so many 'basket cases' in Africa, Asia, and Latin America has proved too great, and Moscow has had to call on them to seek support from the West,[21] even though this tends to weaken their commitment to full-blooded socialism. At the same time, Moscow has had ample cause, since 1969, to question the traditional belief in the irreversibility of Marxist–Leninist rule. After all, in the early '70s, it saw a Marxist–Leninist coalition in Chile overthrown as a result of relentless internal and external pressure; in the late '70s, it witnessed Somalia jettisoning the mantle of Marxism–Leninism as easily as it had assumed it. In the early '80s, it could do nothing to prevent the destruction by foreign troops of a reasonably popular Marxist–Leninist government in Grenada, while in the late '80s its own forces were powerless to prevent a merciless guerrilla onslaught against an unpopular, Communist-led regime in Afghanistan.

As regards the western powers, whilst NATO had been through a series of crises in the '70s, some of which – for example, the threats and counter-threats of protectionism on either side of the Atlantic – survived into the late '80s, its members had for the most part recovered from the traumas of the previous decade. In the process of shrugging off the baleful effects of the energy crisis, most western governments, including the nominally socialist coalitions in France, Portugal, and Greece, had shrugged off the more familiar neo-Keynesian solutions as well. Apparently convinced by recent experience that government expenditure, like antibiotics, needed to be kept under strict control lest it create, in the end, 'antibodies' resistant to treatment, they 'rediscovered' the 'health-inducing' properties of the market.

In its influential Thatcherite guise, the strategy was to reduce the collective bargaining power of labour, cut the money supply and government spending, and raise interest rates in an effort to increase productivity and economic growth. While it was conceded that such a strategy was bound to have unpleasant side-effects in terms of the closure of loss-making enterprises, rising unemployment, and deteriorating public services, it was contended that these were of only short-term duration and that, in the long run, new self-sustaining, innovative and more profitable enterprises would be created which would have a tonic effect throughout the economy. In strictly economic terms, the 'tough medicine' of market forces may be said to have been at least a qualified success. A host of new industries (mainly in the service sector) were under construction, and western growth rates were again surging ahead – in marked contrast to those of the Socialist Commonwealth, which were suffering, amongst other things, the belated impact of the recession of the previous decade. Moreover, unemployment and inflation in the West were again tending to fall, and there had been a general rise in living standards. Though the return to traditional 'capitalist' values had tended to be at the expense of public amenities as well as the poorest and most vulnerable sectors of society, the overall economic benefits were considered sufficiently impressive to encourage many of the countries of eastern as well as western Europe to make a serious study of 'Thatcherism',[22] in the hope of discovering ways of injecting new dynamism into their sluggish economies.

The fact is that by the end of the '80s, it was the Communist rather than the capitalist economies that were in crisis. What had been portrayed as years of advance and achievement in the Socialist economies of Europe and Asia were now being officially decried by Gorbachev as 'years of stagnation' – the consequence of failure to reform an economic system that was overcentralized, too inflexible to reward initiative, innovation or efficiency, too uncompetitive to keep enterprises up to the mark, and inordinately wasteful in the use of resources – human and material. Hence, eastern Europe's experiments with market mechanisms and frequent recourse to the credits, technological know-how, and even grain of the capitalist countries, whose system was supposedly in terminal decay. Hence, too, the anxiety of three of Asia's most impoverished countries – Vietnam, Cambodia and Laos – to break out of their Socialist economic ghetto, reform their economies and fraternize with Japan, ASEAN and the West.

Moreover, it was clear that the 'immune system' that had protected the Communist world from the 'capitalist diseases' of inflation, unemployment, strikes, indebtedness, organized crime, drug addiction, and so forth, had broken down. Ironically, 'Communism' was beginning to overtake 'capitalism' in ways Stalin or Khrushchev could never have imagined. According to *The Economist*, while the annual average inflation rate in the capitalist OECD had fallen below 4 per cent in the latter half of 1988, it was 'officially 18 per cent in Hungary, 19 per cent in China, about 60 per cent in Poland, and 190 per cent in Yugoslavia', and rising. While unemployment had been falling in the West, in the East it was on the increase, 'becoming too big to hide in China, Hungary and Russia', while 'in Yugoslavia the jobless rate [was] already 15 per cent, double the OECD average'.[23]

Moreover, while strikes in the West were both fewer and far less damaging than in the '70s, in the East, where they were generally illegal, they were having considerable political as well as economic effect. In China, where they were combined with mass protest demonstrations in the major cities, they rocked and nearly toppled the Communist system in April 1989. They were instrumental in hastening the downfall of two Polish governments – one in 1970; another a decade later – and played a key role in securing the relegalization of Solidarity and its virtual assumption of political power in 1989. In Yugoslavia, they were not only adding enormously to the country's economic problems, but were also helping to make and unmake governments, both regional and federal, and in the process putting the Serbian authorities on a collision course with the Albanians of the autonomous region of Kosovo. In the Soviet Union, they were, amongst other things, increasing considerably Gorbachev's difficulties in pacifying the inflamed passions of the various ethnic minorities, and, in particular, the Armenians and their neighbours in their dispute over Nagorno-Karabakh, the Armenian enclave in Azerbaijan. Meanwhile, Soviet infant-mortality rates were rising, life expectancy falling, and the country's living standards were to be counted among the lowest in Europe.[24] Small wonder that western wags dubbed the USSR: 'Upper Volta with rockets!'

Politically and militarily, too, the fortunes of both western and Communist alliances had shifted markedly between the early '70s and the late '80s. Whereas confidence in the western governments of the '70s had been severely shaken by such things as the Vietnam débâcle, Watergate, the discovery that the West German Chancellor's chief aide was an East German spy, Britain's 'winter of discontent', and so forth, by the end of the '80s, confidence had been more or less restored.

In many of the Communist-ruled states, however, the process was reversed. In the first place, the manifest and repeated failure to deliver the prosperity, justice and equality predicted by Marx and Lenin was stretching the credibility of Marxism–Leninism almost to breaking point, leading to renewed public displays of anti-Communist feeling in East Germany and Czechoslovakia, as well as in China, the Soviet Union, Poland and Hungary. Secondly, the economic reforms being introduced in many of the Communist countries were proving to be popular with almost nobody. The message that the people were to get used to 'standing on their own feet' and 'taking responsibility for their own actions' was not easily absorbed in societies where the role of the individual had been denied for so long. In any case, in the words of *The Economist*, 'The minority with the nous to exploit new economic freedoms resent the restrictions left in place. The majority, who see their fellows streaking ahead, resent their success'.[25] At the same time, economic mismanagement, corruption and an apparent disregard of environmental factors (so dramatically underlined by Chernobyl) was threatening the party's grip on power.

As people began to turn away from the party and its ideology, they increasingly expressed their frustrations in the kind of nationalism that put them at odds with their neighbours – Armenians versus Azerbaijanis, Georgians versus Abkhaz, Uzbeks against Meskhetians, Balts against Russians, Hungarians against Romanians, Hungarians against Czechs and Serbs versus Albanians. By contrast, the western powers appeared to be settling some of their differences of the previous decade. The customary tensions between the European and Atlantic wings of the NATO alliance were under control, moderated to some extent by Britain, which claimed a 'special relationship' with Washington, while new governments in Turkey, Greece, and Cyprus were helping to reduce the antagonism between Ankara and Athens. More importantly, perhaps, the EEC countries had resolved many of the problems that had bedevilled their relations in the '70s and were progressing steadily towards their goal of a common market by 1992 – in contrast to the countries of CMEA, whose efforts at 'integration' seemed more distinguished by their declarations of intent than by concrete results.

Militarily, too, no matter how formidable the posture of the Soviet Union and its allies, by the end of the '80s, the West had maintained a clear edge in many branches of military-related technology – partly in consequence of America's record defence budgets, which Moscow had difficulty in emulating. In addition, Ronald Reagan's America, possibly in a bid to exorcize the Vietnam 'complex' once and for all, had gone on the offensive against 'soft' allegedly 'Communist' targets, as in Grenada and Nicaragua, and was supporting, to considerable effect, what the President called 'freedom fighters' (i.e. people prepared to use terror tactics in support of a cause he believed 'just') in Central America, Angola, Afghanistan, and elsewhere. In the meantime, Soviet 'peace' campaigns to try to stop the transfer to Europe of American Cruise and Pershing missiles (the latter with characteristics similar to the Soviet SS20s) had clearly failed, and, by the end of the decade, Moscow had decided to negotiate the destruction of several thousand intermediate nuclear forces (INFs) in return for the few hundred already deployed in western Europe.

But, of course, perceptions of threat are based on estimates not only of capability, but also intention. And, by April 1985, when Gorbachev took over as Soviet leader, the world seemed far more threatening than in the early '70s when the exchange of visits between Brezhnev and Nixon appeared to herald the dawn of a new and lasting détente. For one thing, the Kremlin had perceived a weakening in the US commitment to détente well before Reagan's multifaceted, trillion-dollar strategy against what he saw as the 'focus of evil'. For example, in the 'human rights' campaign espoused by President 'Jimmy' Carter on taking office in 1976, Moscow saw not a condemnation of all authoritarian regimes, or, indeed, of all Communist regimes, since the President did not appear unduly concerned about the human rights record of China, Romania, or Yugoslavia, with whom the USA was on friendly terms, and he seemed ready to give Pol Pot's Kampuchean guerrilla coalition the benefit of the doubt in its struggle against the Vietnamese occupation.

To Moscow, therefore, Carter's 'human rights' crusade seemed more like a political weapon to encourage dissidence in the Soviet Union and its allies and destabilize the bloc. And the Kremlin saw, as proof of Washington's half-hearted approach to détente, such things as Carter's playing of the China 'card'; the sudden furore in Washington over the presence of Cuba of a Soviet contingent that had been there for many years; the nonratification of SALT II, linked in part to the Soviet presence in Cuba; and the US tendency to regard the Soviet intervention in Afghanistan (which Moscow had long regarded as being in its sphere) as if it were the most serious crisis since the Second World War – to say nothing of the decision to deploy Cruise and Pershing.

What made Moscow's increasingly troubled relations with Washington all the more worrying was the fact that, whatever their misgivings, most of America's allies had been prepared to endorse the anti-Soviet diatribes of presidents Carter and Reagan, and, to justify their own military expansion, had put the most sinister interpretation on the aims and implications of the Soviet military advance. In fact, Moscow's purposes were probably not significantly different from those of its adversaries. The first was to attain security, which, in the Soviet case, meant protection against several potential enemies, to the west, east, and south. For, whereas NATO had only one major antagonist – the Soviet Union itself – the Kremlin had at least five – the western powers, China, militant Islam (an especial headache in view of the USSR's own rapidly expanding Muslim population), dissident elements in eastern Europe (including, sometimes, their governments) and dissident peoples within the Soviet Union itself – a multinational empire rather than a state. Moreover, at least four of its potential enemies – the USA, Britain, France and China – were nuclear powers. The second was to give reassurance, in the form of support and protection to foreign clients and friends. The third was to barter, i.e. for use as a bargaining counter in return for some military or other concession from an opponent. The fourth was to enhance internal stability – in particular, by conscripting non-Russians into the armed forces and socializing them in the values desired by the (mainly Russian) authorities. The fifth was to increase prestige and lay claim to parity of esteem with the US through the display, threat and occasional use of force.

Unfortunately for Moscow, the Soviet military posture had provoked an ominous response not merely from the West, but from China as well. At one time, Peking seemed to be forging an anti-Soviet alignment of powers east and west of the USSR, including Japan, the USA, much of western Europe and even countries in Moscow's eastern European 'backyard', such as Albania and Yugoslavia. And, as if these foreign threats were not sufficient, Moscow faced serious problems of cohesion and discipline within the Warsaw Pact itself. Poland, the second-largest and most powerful state in the alliance, was frequently in turmoil and the riot squad increasingly used to quell political protest in Prague and East Berlin. Moreover, by the end of the '80's intra-alliance relations had scarcely been worse. President Ceauşescu's nepotism (reportedly, some 40 of his extended family were in top jobs), self-conceit (he did not protest when one journal described him as 'the most intellectual of all intellectuals' and another dubbed him 'a lay god') and grandiloquent philistinism (more than a score of old churches in Bucharest were bulldozed to make way for a new boulevard of the Victory of Socialism, complete with monuments to the 'beloved' leader) had made Romania something of a pariah within the alliance, while his plans for resettling the Hungarians of Transylvania had merely added to the historic animosity between Romania and Hungary. At the same time, however, the rapidly reforming governments in Budapest and Warsaw found themselves increasingly at odds with the more conservative regimes – especially in Prague and East Berlin. In any case, given the troubled history of the WTO, there could be no guarantee that in the event of a serious East–West crisis in the future, Moscow's allies would prove any more reliable than the Hungarian forces who handed their weapons over to the anti-Soviet rebels in 1956 or the Czech soldiers who made their signals equipment over to Dubček's supporters after the invasion of 1968.

In view of the kaleidoscopic changes during the past two decades in the political, economic and military fortunes of the leading powers and the ideologies they profess, it is hardly surprising that Moscow tends nowadays to be somewhat sparing in its references to the 'correlation of forces'. Clearly, the Soviet leadership can no longer have any warrant for the confident prediction of the imminence of world Socialism. On the other hand, political forecasting is a notoriously hazardous enterprise, and it would surely be premature to write world Socialism off altogether as an impossible dream (or nightmare). For, if 'capitalism' has been able to adapt and regenerate, it is difficult to see why Socialism should not do likewise. After all, for all their heretical views, Nagy and Dubček remained Communists, as do the 'pluralists' in the Eurocommunist parties, while the Soviet Union is awash with 'new thinking' about what Communism has been, is, and should be, which cannot but leave a lasting imprint whatever the fate of its progenitor, Mikhail Gorbachev. It would seem, indeed, that until 'capitalism' loses every vestige of the characteristics Marx had found so intolerable, there will always be a place for a Marxist, if not Communist, critique, and, hence, that to pronounce the 'death' of Communism, or of capitalism, would be as foolish as it would be premature.

NOTES

1. The implications of the term are explored in V. Aspaturian, 'Soviet Global Power and the Correlation of Forces', *Problems of Communism*, Vol. 29, No. 3 (May–June 1980), pp. 1–18.
2. Detailed in L. Marcou, *Les Pieds d'argile: Le Communism mondiale au present, 1970–1986* (Paris, 1986).
3. From *Soviet News* (22 November 1957).
4. M. Light, *The Soviet Theory of International Relations* (New York, 1988), p. 176.
5. Ibid., pp. 181–8.
6. See, for example, Geoffrey Stern, *Fifty Years of Communism* (London, 1967), ch. 9.
7. Ibid., pp. 157–8.
8. Quoted in R. H. McNeal, *International Relations Among Communists* (Englewood Cliffs, 1967), pp. 165–6.
9. Ibid., pp. 168–9.
10. Ibid., pp. 169–70.
11. Ibid., p. 118.

12. E. J. Czerwinski and J. Piekalkiewicz (eds.), *The Soviet Invasion of Czechoslovakia: Its Effects on Eastern Europe* (New York, 1972), p. 97.
13. Ibid., p. 97.
14. 'The Interparty Drama', *Problems of Communism* Vol. 24, No. 4 (July–August 1975), pp. 18–24.
15. V. Aspaturian, J. Valenta, and D. Burke (eds.), *Eurocommunism Between East and West* (Bloomington, 1980), p. 74.
16. Ibid., pp. 74–5.
17. Ibid., p. 74.
18. Ibid., p. 75.
19. Ibid., especially ch. 4.
20. The annual reports on 'The Military Balance' issued by the International Institute for Strategic Studies, London, provide convincing evidence to support such a conclusion.
21. See M. Light, *The Soviet Theory of International Relations* (New York, 1988), pp. 300–5.
22. 'As Eastern Europe cuts Free', *The Economist*, (28 January 1989) p. 16. See also Geoffrey Stern, 'Polish Monetarism', *The Spectator*, (10 July 1982), p. 16.
23. 'Marx Turned Upside Down' (24 September 1988), p. 17.
24. See chapter by G. W. Lapidus in R. F. Byrnes (ed.), *After Brezhnev* (Washington, 1983).
25. 'Can Communism Survive' (14 January 1989), p. 16.

13. Has Communism a Future?

At the beginning of this volume, a sharp distinction was drawn between 'communism' and 'Communism' – the former indicating the Marxian classless, stateless world of compatible, self-administered socialist societies, the latter referring to a political movement dedicated to precipitating the Marxist ideal. In any discussion of prospects and possibilities, such a distinction is crucial, since it is by no means certain that the fate of each is dependent on the other. Conceivably, the Communist movement could continue to exist long after people have ceased to consider seriously the notion of a communist world, while a communist order could eventually materialize long after the passing of any effective Communist movement. Since any consideration of 'communism' is bound to be entirely conjectural, it seems appropriate to concentrate the following discussion on the prospects for 'international Communism' – a movement which today encompasses a kaleidoscopic range of principles, practices, and procedures. On issues such as the role of the Party, the virtues of the command economy and collectivization, the place of religion, the antidote to imperialism, the 'correct' response to national liberation movements, and the possibility of eliminating war while capitalism still exists, there is no consensus – not even among the eastern European parties. Nor is Lenin quite as immune from criticism as he once was, and some Communists are inclined to consign the 'sacred cow' of 'democratic centralism' to the political abattoir. Both the Swedish and Spanish parties have dispensed with it altogether, and other western European parties are questioning its continued validity.

Whilst it would be misleading to draw too close a parallel between the condition of 'international Communism' today and the state of Christendom at the end of the Middle Ages, there are some striking similarities. In both, a breakdown of discipline and cohesion followed a crisis of authority as new leaders called in question the conduct of their predecessors. In both, attempts to re-establish the moral and political domination of the former fount of orthodoxy failed to stem the doctrinal and organizational decomposition of the movement, even though a number of 'loyalists' decided to stay in the fold. And, in both, nationalism served to accelerate polycentric tendencies. Here the known resemblances end, though the restoration of Communist unity

in any form other than a very loose and indisciplined fraternal association would be about as improbable as the restoration of Christian
unity along the medieval pattern.

On the other hand, the experience of post-medieval Christendom
does at least suggest that the members of a fraternity can continue to
survive and prosper even if the fraternity's international organization
is repudiated or goes out of existence. In this sense, the nationally
orientated Communist Party, freed from a perhaps embarrassing
relationship with a Moscow-dominated international movement, could
prove as durable as the reformed national Church. Whether it does so
is likely to depend on its continued success in attracting support, in
turn, conditional upon its ability to persuade people that the party can
serve a useful purpose. But does it have that ability?

At present, the fraternity seems to be experiencing something of a
crisis of belief.[1] In many of the countries under Communist rule, a
combination of repressive legislation, economic mismanagement,
careerism and corruption has eroded much of the idealism that once
brought floods of young recruits into the party. Many Communists find
it difficult to feel any sense of 'historical inevitability' when so many of
yesterday's Communist heroes – often people who justified violence in
the name of a lofty ideal – are denounced by their successors, and
established Socialist systems are modified or abandoned to accommodate political and economic practices once derided as anti-Socialist and
'bourgeois'. Nor does it help when Communist countries are at odds,
have to turn to the West for trade credits and technological know-how,
or to align, as have both Yugoslavia and China in their time, with
western countries against their Communist rivals. But the crisis of faith
in the Communist-ruled states has repercussions among the non-ruling
parties. These, after all, have to convince their own members, as well
as a sceptical public, of the benefits of a commitment to 'Communism'
as against some other political force or creed – by no means an easy
task!

On the other hand, people join or vote for a political party for a
variety of reasons, many unconnected with its history or political platform, and, in this sense, a sizeable number of Communist adherents
have been largely unaffected by the crisis of faith. In any case, such
crises can be overcome, especially where there is a new generation, too
young to have shared the illusions and the disillusionment of their
elders. That today so many of the old Communist certainties are under
attack in what was once regarded as the 'homeland of Socialism' could
attract to the Communist movement at least as many as it repels, and
ultimately if Gorbachev succeeds in producing a manifestly better Soviet

society, have a tonic effect on the movement as a whole. After all, the nineteenth-century critics of capitalism, including Marx and Engels, in effect, helped to bring about its regeneration. Possibly Gorbachev's 'new thinking' could do the same for Socialism. Already it has confounded the 'cold warriors' who had hitherto insisted that the USSR was a totalitarian state and, hence, incapable of reform. What, therefore, does Gorbachev's 'revolution without shots' amount to and can it succeed?

As a trained agronomist with a degree in law, a host of acquaintances among the intelligentsia, and some familiarity with the West, having toured France and Italy in a hired car and paid an official visit to Canada as party Secretary in charge of agriculture,[2] Gorbachev had already sensed, before becoming party leader, that the Soviet Union was in the throes of a multifaceted crisis. It was a crisis, moreover, made all the more severe by adverse trends in the world economy – in particular, the fall in the world price of oil – following 18 conservative and complacent years under Brezhnev. The symptoms were all around: absenteeism, alcoholism, drug abuse, worker apathy, and other indicators of alienation; bureaucratism, nepotism, corruption, and abuse of power, as well as the inefficiency and inertia that are the concomitants of a system that tends to stifle initiative and reward mediocrity. And he seems to have concluded that without some drastic overhaul of that system, the vast economic potential of the country – with its rich storehouse of resources – would never be realized, thereby further calling into question the credentials of an ideology whose standing had already suffered grievously as a result of recent developments in such countries as Cambodia, Afghanistan and Poland. However, unlike Khrushchev, whose political programme fell well short of dismantling the array of privileges attached to the bureaucratic caste, and whose economic reforms proved unworkable, largely because of the vested interests of the bureaucracy, Gorbachev has felt it necessary to undertake a root-and-branch restructuring (*perestroika*) of the system – political as well as economic.[3]

From a study of the Khrushchev period and also of such reforming Communist countries as Yugoslavia, Hungary, Poland and China, Gorbachev concluded that there was a need to encourage greater open expression of opinions – *glasnost* – as well as freer access to the kind of information that could assist rational economic decision-making, if *perestroika* was to be successful. Hence his advocacy of political practices hitherto denied the Soviet people, such as the secret ballot, contested elections, a freer press, and a chance to fill in the 'blank spaces' of history, as well as the acceleration – *uskorenie* – of decentralizing tendencies in the economy, including the devolution of decision-making, greater use of incentive schemes, flexible wage and price structures, and a considerably enlarged private and cooperative sector. At the same time, he recognized the need for an equally thoroughgoing review of foreign policy procedures and priorities if Soviet Socialism was to prosper and merit international respect. With an approach derived in part from his domestic concerns, foreign policy had, henceforth, to satisfy the twin criteria of need and cost-effectiveness. 'Is this policy essential?' and 'Is there a more economical way of attaining objectives?' were to become the key questions, the latter involving considerations of personnel as well as policy.[4]

In answer to the first question, he found he could readily dispense with several existing assumptions – in particular, the lingering notion that states were generally to be regarded as hostile unless proven otherwise. In relation to the West, he has begun to shift the emphasis from the inevitability of ideological conflict (implied in the concept of 'peaceful coexistence') to the need to dismantle ideological barriers and establish mechanisms to tackle problems common to humankind. In strategic terms, he has moved away from the idea of parity to that of military sufficiency, making unilateral concessions in the hope of encouraging far-reaching accords on trade and commerce, as well as on disarmament and arms control. Towards the Third World, he has begun to question both the irreversibility of Socialist orientation and the desirability of 'declarative radicalism'. In fact, he seems prepared to grant that the problems of underdevelopment might be better addressed, at least in the short run, by a capitalist rather than a bureaucratic Socialist approach. In addition, he has urged some of his country's Third World clients, as in Afghanistan, Angola, Nicaragua, and the Middle East, to make peace with their ideological opponents, even if it means taking them into government and recognizing the legitimacy of their case.

As regards relations among Socialists, though Gorbachev has continued to press for both closer economic integration and some variant of *perestroika* in each country, he has patched up relations with China and seems willing to jettison the 'Brezhnev doctrine' along with much of the rest of the former Soviet leader's ideological baggage. At the same time, he is in the process of fashioning a new conception – that of a 'Socialist partnership', tolerant of diversity and based on the principle of 'live and let live!' Certainly, he has been as understanding of the trend towards multiparty politics in Hungary and Poland, as of the desire of the Estonians, Latvians, and Lithuanians for greater autonomy, and he appears to be watching with interest the mini-stock exchanges of Budapest and Shanghai.

Perceiving that under Brezhnev, over-reliance on the threat, display, sale or use of the weapons of war had proved counterproductive, merely creating or cementing hostile alignments and discouraging the kinds of relations that might benefit the Soviet economy, Gorbachev and his advisers have devised a high-profile strategy that steps up the Soviet Union's diplomatic presence and utilizes it not to exacerbate tensions, as so often in the past, but to defuse them. It is a strategy with many different dimensions. Firstly, the rhetoric is novel.[5] It tends to be conciliatory rather than confrontational, and it speaks of 'interdependence' and of 'mutual advantage'. It favours multilateral gatherings of interested parties in the quest for agreed rather than imposed solutions to problems. It also embraces what, for Moscow, is a new style of diplomatic bargaining, namely abandoning somewhat intractable and combative negotiating procedures in favour of much greater flexibility, and it also includes the technique, at one time associated with the former US Secretary of State, Henry Kissinger, of the 'pre-emptive concession', i.e. giving something away prior to substantive discussions to sweeten the atmosphere and indicate seriousness of purpose.

A further dimension to the Gorbachev approach is what is sometimes called the 'charm offensive' – a refinement of the old-fashioned 'peace offensive'. At its hub is the tireless Foreign Minister, Eduard Shevardnadze, whose smiling countenance has become almost as familiar as the lugubrious demeanour of his late predecessor, Andrei Gromyko. For, he and his staff journey here, there, and everywhere on well-publicized trips, putting in appearances in countries not normally on the diplomatic circuit, and spreading 'sweetness and light' in countries that generally are. At the same time, some of the USSR's best linguists are usually on hand to give interviews to the foreign media, explaining government policy and enthusing about *glasnost* and *perestroika*. An adjunct of Gorbachev's strategy to 'win friends and influence people' has been the complete restructuring of the bureaucracy of the foreign ministry. He has also revamped the country's overseas representation, replacing those in key positions whose views had seemed almost impervious to change. What was once called the 'Chinese Mafia' – Soviet diplomats who believed in dealing with China only from a position of strength – have gone,[6] as have the more abrasive envoys elsewhere who had made their careers defending hard-line positions under Brezhnev.

In fact, Moscow's new diplomatic strategy, taken in conjunction with Gorbachev's attempts to restructure and democratize the Soviet system, is helping to overcome long-standing animosities to the regime. In fact, the country now has its first leader since the revolution who inspires trust and confidence among those not normally sympathetic to Soviet Socialism. Indeed, nowadays Gorbachev is possibly more popular abroad than at home, where there is resistance to his reforms not merely from the entrenched bureaucracy, who stand to lose their privileges, but also from many ordinary workers reluctant to change the habits of a lifetime in the name of greater efficiency. That the economic benefits of *perestroika* are slow to materialize and that many of the more market-orientated Socialist countries are experiencing problems of serious indebtedness, inflation, and unemployment hardly helps his case with his conservative critics.[7] And that his more relaxed approach only gives heart to national secessionists in the Baltic republics, Transcaucasia and Central Asia alarm all those for whom 'Socialism' is synonymous with order, discipline and central control. Given, therefore, that the Soviet Union is clearly a country on the move, is it proceeding towards or away from 'communism'?

In one sense, this is an unreal question since the fate of 'communism', in its original Marxist sense, cannot depend on what happens in one country alone. If 'communism' is to have a future, it has to be presaged by certain sociopolitical trends worldwide, and very little that has happened in the USSR or, for that matter, China, Cuba, Vietnam, or the other Communist countries and parties suggests that the classless, stateless world of compatible, self-administered socialist societies is even remotely within range. On the other hand, what happens in the Soviet Union is germane to the future of international Communism, even if the movement is increasingly in the hands of disputatious members far from Moscow. For, the USSR is still widely regarded, even in countries like Czechoslovakia, the GDR, and Romania which have been strongly resistant to the 'new thinking', as the most powerful flagship of the movement of which it was for so long the sole exemplar. In this sense, its changing social, political and economic fortunes cannot but affect the image projected by organized Communism and, hence, Communism's potential support.

The first question to ask of the Gorbachev prospectus is not what it should be called, but whether it can succeed in bridging the gap between promise and performance, restoring dynamism to the Soviet economy, and creating among the country's citizens a sense of genuine participation in a collective enterprise to build a better society. As usual, the analysts, both professional and amateur, of Soviet affairs are divided. Many doubt whether Gorbachev can achieve the necessary results in time to prevent a political counter-coup and a return to central direction. Others, on the contrary, see the process of reform, possibly with the active assistance of western enterprise, raising living standards and the quality of life, and leading to the gradual abandonment, as in Hungary and Poland, of the characteristic features of Leninism, i.e. the notion of 'proletarian power', the one-party system, 'democratic centralism', and socialization of industry and banking.

Yet, others see the country's future development largely in terms of the Gorbachev conception of 'Socialist pluralism', in which a multiparty system, as such, becomes unnecessary as the Communist Party submits itself to contested elections, parliament begins to reflect the conflicting interests and views within society, and the Soviets at all levels, local, Republican and Supreme, exercise a brake on corruption, high-handedness and inefficiency in administration. But, since the Soviet Union does not exist in a vacuum, the outcome of the Gorbachev experiment could well depend on whether or not Moscow's former adversaries prove sufficiently accommodating to allow the Soviet leader to order a massive switch of resources from the military to the civilian sector.

On one thing, however, the experts seem generally agreed – that there is no longer any place in the USSR for the kind of Stalinist 'Communism' that proved so costly in terms of lives and material resources, and so damaging to the reputation of Karl Marx, in whose name the Stalinist system was constructed. Moreover, to those on the Left for whom Stalin was an aberration, the Soviet Union now has an opportunity to return to the socialist path from which it strayed in the early '20s.

In the words of Tariq Ali, one of the doyens of the New Left and a veteran of the student activism of 1968, the Gorbachev programme, 'if successful, would represent an enormous gain for Socialists . . . on a world scale'.[8] To those on the Right, however, the Soviet Union could be on the verge of jettisoning socialism altogether and returning to the kind of capitalist democracy that was in prospect after the downfall of the tsar. To quote *Daily Telegraph* columnist Ferdinand Mount: 'Socialism is a busted flush. . . . Mr Gorbachev's claim to our attention is his willingness to accept that the socialist project has been a disaster, and that he can hope to succeed only by dropping it bit by bit, and moving towards a society based on individual liberty, private property and the free market.'[9] If, as seems likely, both Ali and Mount are predicting much the same future for the USSR, but using different terms to describe it, it is a reminder of how elastic and imprecise is the vocabulary of politics. Yet, ultimately, what matters, surely, is how responsive a system is to the needs of the individuals it is designed to serve, rather than what people choose to call it.

So, has 'communism' a future? If it has, the Communist movement so far has done little to promote it. For, Marxism–Leninism has proved infinitely malleable, serving often incompatible purposes, many far removed from the original prospectus. From an instrument for hastening the revolutionary transformation of a world in the throes of one of history's bloodiest and most senseless wars, it has since been pressed into service by conservative-minded politicians and bureaucrats to resist radical change. It has been used both to promote and prevent trends towards authoritarianism, and to justify economic decentralization, as well as the planned economy; consumerism, as well as economic austerity; conservation, as well as rapid industrialization; and peasant ownership, as well as collectivized agriculture. Moreover, once a vehicle for class solidarity, Marxism–Leninism has been employed to promote both national liberation and territorial expansion, as well as anticolonialism; to endorse anti-Semitism, as well as antiracism; homophobia, as well as sexual equality.

Clearly, therefore, many governments, as well as their critics, have found Marxism–Leninism, in one or other of its many guises, an indispensable instrument. As such, its serviceability would probably remain even were its adherents finally to write off 'communism' as an impracticable goal; 'international Communism' as a political corpse and the antithesis between 'capitalism' and 'Communism' as an irrelevant anachronism. More importantly, wherever there is perceived injustice, oppression, exploitation and abuse of power, there will still be a need for an organization of political protest armed with an emotionally reassuring set of action-based theories, and, in this sense, the future of many a Communist party is probably assured, even if 'communism' and 'international Communism' are not.

NOTES

1. See, for example, the reflections by Communists from various parts of the world in 'Communism Now' – a three-part series in the *International Herald Tribune* (23, 24, and 25 January 1989).
2. His Canadian trip appears to have played a crucial role in fashioning Gorbachev's views on agriculture. According to one British diplomat, Canada's climatological and topographical resemblance to the USSR, and the prosperity of Canadian farmers of Russian or Ukrainian origin, finally convinced him that the problems of Soviet agriculture were systemic and could not be blamed on the weather or the soil.
3. For an analysis of the conditions to which Gorbachev's 'new thinking' was largely a reaction, see for example, M. Lewin, *The Gorbachev Phenomenon: A Historical Reinterpretation* (Berkeley, 1988).
4. Gorbachev's 'new thinking' on foreign policy is elaborated in M. Light, *The Soviet Theory of International Relations* (New York, 1988), pp. 294–315.
5. Just how novel can be ascertained from Gorbachev's own volume, *Perestroika: New Thinking for our Country and our World* (London, 1987).

6. See, for example, 'China "mafia" doomed as ties with Peking improve', *Far Eastern Economic Review*, (14 August 1986), p. 36.
7. See 'Marx Turned Upside Down', *The Economist*, (24 September 1988), p. 17.
8. *Revolution From Above* (London, 1988).
9. 'Reflections on Labour's Counter-Revolution', *Daily Telegraph* (24 March 1989).

Name Index

Alexander II, Tsar 25
Ali, Tariq 255
Althusser, Louis 137
Amin, Hafizullah 222–3
Atatürk, Mustafa Kemal 64
Attlee, Clement 114
Axelrod, Paul 26, 28

Babeuf, François-Noel 'Gracchus' 7–8
Balabanov, Angelica 51, 57
Ball, John 5
Barbusse, Henri 75–6
Barthou, Louis 76
Batista, Fulgencio 224
Bebel, August 23
Bebler, Alex 114
Beethoven, Ludwig Van 208
Beneš, Eduard 101, 161
Beria, Lavrenti 147, 149–50, 157–8, 160, 164
Bernal, Prof. J. S. 140
Bernstein, Eduard 22–3, 26
Blanc, Louis 8
Blanqui, Louis Auguste 8
Blum, Léon 78
Bonaparte, Napoleon 68
Brandler, Heinrich 74
Brezhnev, Leonid 187, 192, 203–204, 207, 245, 251, 253
Bronstein, Lev Davidovich see Trotsky
Brzezinski, Zbigniew 142
Bukharin, Nikolai 33, 56, 69, 71–2, 74, 86, 145
Bulganin, Marshal N. 163, 168
Byrnes, James 126

Carr, E. H. 56, 66
Carter, President 'Jimmy' 190, 245
Castro, Fidel 186, 224–7

Ceauşescu, Nicolae 201, 205, 207, 218, 246
Ch'en Tu-hsiu, Professor 215
Chiang Kai-shek 70, 81–3, 121, 125–6, 130, 131
Chicherin, Grigori Vasilevich 74
Chou En-lai 81, 131, 175, 189, 217
Churchill, Winston 96, 104, 110, 111, 145
Claudin, F. 155, 196
Clausewitz K. von 208
Clementis, Vladimir 102
Cromwell, Oliver 6

Daladier, Edouard 76, 78
Darwin, Charles 21
Debray, Regis 225
Devlin, Kevin 238
Diaz, José 80
Dimitrov, Georgi 73, 77, 94, 100, 114–15
Djilas, Milovan 108, 166, 199
Donskoi, Dimitri 93
Doriot, Jacques 76
Drachkovitch, Milorad 58
Dubček, Alexander 189, 203–205, 207, 247
Duns Scotus 5
Dupree, Louis 222
Dzerzhinsky, Felix 146

Eberlein, Hugo 56
Ehrenburg, Ilya 150, 158
Eisenhower, President Dwight 179
Eisenstein, Sergei 36
Engels, Friedrich 3–5, 8, 13, 15, 18, 21–2, 29, 118, 121, 140, 197, 251
Erickson, John 212
Escalante, Anibal 226
Everard, William 6

Fischer, Ruth 65, 74

259

Subject Index

and Albania 97, 101, 112, 205,
209–10, 212, 238
and China 64, 73, 80–83, 93–4, 121,
125–7, 130, 173–94, 221,
235–8
and Cuba 186–7, 210, 214, 224–8,
238, 240
and Czechoslovakia 84, 103, 113,
115, 161, 163, 178–9, 203–205,
240, 247
and German Democratic Republic
103, 159, 161, 207–209
see also Germany
and Hungary 54, 104, 115, 162–3,
169–71, 204–206, 212, 252
and North Korea (Democratic
People's Republic of Korea)
128–31, 159, 182, 216–18, 238
and Poland 57, 67, 85, 96, 98–9,
104, 108, 113, 115, 126, 141,
148, 167–9, 170, 175, 205,
213–14, 252
and United States 37, 76, 96, 101,
102, 128, 186, 193, 224, 240,
244, 246
and Vietnam 188, 190–92, 210,
217–21, 240–42
see also Indochina
and Yugoslavia 95–6, 97, 101, 104,
106–18, 135–6, 163–6, 170,
176, 177, 185, 199, 205, 210,
234–8, 246
post-Stalin interregnum 156–60
under Brezhnev 187–93, 203–13,
237
under Gorbachev 242–3, 245, 247,
250–55
under Khrushchev 157–71, 173–87,
200–202, 234–7

under Stalin 67–74, 84–7, 93–9,
101–104, 108–18, 120–21,
125–8, 134–50, 197
see also Russia
Utopia 5
'Utopian Socialism' 8–9

Versailles, Peace Conference 106
Vietnam 46, 132, 182, 188, 189, 190,
191, 192, 193, 210, 217–21, 238,
239, 240–42, 243
see also Indochina

Warsaw Pact (WTO) 169, 177, 200,
201, 204, 205, 209, 212–14, 246
Workers 18, 22, 23–4, 26, 27, 28, 31,
37, 38, 52, 54, 64, 68, 69, 72, 85,
95, 124, 127, 158, 161, 203, 223,
224, 228, 234
exploitation of 13–17
Lenin on 28, 33, 35, 36, 48
World War
First 23, 33, 45, 48, 52, 183, 196
Second 37, 79, 95, 183, 189, 198,
199, 203
World Congress against War (League
against War and Fascism) 75

Yugoslavia 46, 54, 86, 93, 95–6, 97,
98, 101, 106–18, 125–6, 135, 136,
138, 148, 150, 163–4, 166, 174,
185, 199, 202, 205, 206, 209, 210,
234, 235–6, 238, 243, 245, 246,
250, 251
friction with Soviet Union 104–19,
170, 176, 177

Zaire 191
'Zimmerwald Left' 48